Uruguay, 1968

VIOLENCE IN LATIN AMERICAN
HISTORY

Edited by Pablo Piccato, Federico
Finchelstein, and Paul Gillingham

Uruguay, 1968

*Student Activism from Global Counterculture
to Molotov Cocktails*

VANIA MARKARIAN

Translated by Laura Pérez Carrara
Foreword by Eric Zolov

UNIVERSITY OF CALIFORNIA PRESS

University of California Press, one of the most distinguished university presses in the United States, enriches lives around the world by advancing scholarship in the humanities, social sciences, and natural sciences. Its activities are supported by the UC Press Foundation and by philanthropic contributions from individuals and institutions. For more information, visit www.ucpress.edu.

University of California Press
Oakland, California

Originally published as *El 68 uruguayo: El movimiento estudiantil entre molotovs y música beat* (Buenos Aires: Editorial de la Universidad Nacional de Quilmes, 2012). Copyright © Vania Markarian 2015.

Library of Congress Cataloging-in-Publication Data

Names: Markarian, Vania, 1971– author. | Pérez Carrara, Laura, translator. | Zolov, Eric, writer of foreword.
Title: Uruguay, 1968 : student activism from global counterculture to Molotov cocktails / Vania Markarian; translated by Laura Pérez Carrara; foreword by Eric Zolov.
Description: Oakland, California : University of California Press, [2017] | "Originally published as El 68 uruguayo: El movimiento estudiantil entre molotovs y música beat (Buenos Aires: Editorial de la Universidad Nacional de Quilmes, 2012). Copyright " Vania Markarian 2015." | Includes bibliographical references and index.
Identifiers: LCCN 2016037110 (print) | LCCN 2016039881 (ebook) | ISBN 9780520290006 (cloth : alk. paper) | ISBN 9780520290013 (pbk. : alk. paper) | ISBN 9780520964358 (epub)
Subjects: LCSH: Student movements—Uruguay—History—20th century. | College students—Political activity—Uruguay—History—20th century. | Youth—Uruguay—History—20th century—Attitudes. | Nineteen sixty-eight, A.D.
Classification: LCC LA603.7 .M3713 2017 (print) | LCC LA603.7 (ebook) | DDC 371.8/109895—dc23
LC record available at http://lccn.loc.gov/2016037110

Contents

Foreword

Over the past fifteen years, scholars of European and U.S. history have begun to periodize the late 1950s through early 1970s as constituting a "long 1960s" and, more recently, a "Global Sixties." In doing so, historians are demonstrating how local and regional particularities are best understood within a wider global circulation of people, ideas, imagery, fashion, discourse, and music—what Jeremy Suri aptly captured as a "language of dissent." Vania Markarian's *Uruguay, 1968* represents the best of Latin American scholarly engagement with this broader historiographical transformation.

For Latin Americans, the stakes in this recovery of historical memory are especially high. For one, Latin America was wracked by extraordinary levels of social and political violence. This violence tore apart the fabric of the body politic and nearly everywhere culminated in prolonged military rule. Uruguay, once known as the region's most successful democracy ("the Switzerland of Latin America"), succumbed to this common trajectory in 1973. It would be almost two decades after the transition to democratic rule in 1985 before state archives became accessible to researchers. Even so, countless of the tortured and disappeared simply do not appear anywhere in the official record. For many participants and family members of those affected by the violence, the era remains a tender wound.

There is a second, equally fundamental obstacle to this recuperation of memory. Until quite recently, a certain metanarrative—that is, a *way* of thinking about the past—has prevailed in historical analysis of Latin America in this period. This approach to understanding the past was shaped largely by an earlier generation of historians and activists, often former participants in the era's struggles whose interpretations have tended to remain circumscribed by a focus on the dynamics of "heroic" and "antiheroic" struggle. This somewhat narrow focus on the "politics of struggle" generally ignored or relegated to the background any serious discussion of culture as a dimension of struggle itself. What has been missing is not only an understanding of the *productive* aspects of consumptive practices—for instance, understanding the relationship between clothing styles and challenges to patriarchal authority—but the subjectivity of youth experience more generally. Vania Markarian refers to this displacement of cultural practices as constituting the "fractured memory" of 1968. In a fundamental sense, her efforts to transcend the influence of this metanarrative constitute the revisionist core of Markarian's scholarship, both here and in her other writings.

Some readers may scratch their heads when considering Uruguay as a focal point for studying the 1960s in Latin America. Squeezed between mighty Brazil and Argentina, Uruguay has historically served as a geopolitical buffer zone, a nub of a nation whose political and cultural identity has been overshadowed by the doings of its powerful neighbors. The English-language literature, especially, has tended to foreground the significance of student rebellion in Mexico, Brazil, and, more recently, Argentina. Yet during the 1960s this small country—a periphery within the periphery that is Latin America—became a vital nodal point for political and intellectual debate. The tendency to overlook the importance of Uruguay in Latin America's Global Sixties similarly constitutes part of a "fractured memory" that historians need to confront.

In political terms, by the mid-1960s Montevideo had become one of the last remaining refuges for dissidents from countries that had succumbed to military rule. Those dissidents encountered not only political solace, but a vibrant democratic culture spanning the ideological spectrum. It is no coincidence that one of the most influential left-wing periodicals in all of Latin America during this period, *Marcha,* was published in Uruguay.

Among the central questions debated across the pages of *Marcha* and in the pulsating café culture of Montevideo was whether or not the "Cuban way" of leading a peasant-based revolution from the countryside was the *only* way to achieve a revolutionary victory. What about a country such as Uruguay (or Argentina), which lacked a peasant-based population? When the urban-based guerrilla organization, the Tupamaros, emerged on the scene around 1966, these debates shifted from the theoretical to the concrete. Although in a certain sense, the Tuparamos' combination of pranksterism and military discipline marked them as unique among Latin American guerrilla organizations, at the same time their revolutionary success made them paradigmatic. Historians are now beginning to recognize the importance of the Tupamaros and the intense intellectual and political debates that transpired in Uruguay during this period as establishing a foundational template for the subsequent emergence of urban guerrilla warfare elsewhere in the region during the 1970s. Yet Uruguay's significance was not only political; it was countercultural as well. There is now an ample and growing literature in English on the importance of the countercultural rock movements that characterized Mexico, Brazil, and Argentina and the intellectual debates in those countries concerning the relationship between rock (both foreign and local), folk protest song, and political commitment. Uruguay's vibrant rock and countercultural scenes, however, have been almost wholly overlooked, at least in the English-language historiography.

One of the most notable of Uruguay's groups was El Kinto, which formed in the context of the shifts in political discourse and praxis that Markarian charts here. In the late 1960s, this unconventional rock quintet looked inward for musical inspiration, incorporating the *candombe* and other rhythms associated with the country's once sizable slave population while staying engaged with vanguard experimentations in rock happening elsewhere. By channeling an emergent countercultural ethos, El Kinto hurtled the country's youth toward new frontiers of cultural experimentation. Paradoxically, a key interlocutor on the countercultural scene was Horacio Buscaglia, who promoted El Kinto (and played with them at times) while also editing the Communist Party's cultural magazine, *La Morsa*. It was a highly unusual connection that helped legitimize El Kinto among the country's left-wing intelligentsia and reveals the porous boundaries that existed between "countercultural protest" and "political engagement" in Uruguay.

The manifestations of violence in Uruguay and elsewhere in the Americas during this period were many and nuanced. Violence was most profound in the widespread use of state-sponsored terrorism—kidnappings, bombing, torture, and disappearance—as well as the deployment of the military to repress and police legitimate political protest. There was also the multifaceted violence directed at leftist youth by right-wing individuals and groups nominally (and often covertly) affiliated with the state. Ironically, much of this paramilitary violence was soldiered by young people who were diametrically opposed to the pro-Cuban revolutionary sentiment that historians have too often presumed define the whole of student rebellion during this period. Finally, and in some ways least examined, is the violence that emanated from the political Left. There was the quotidian street-level violence—the "hijacking" of public buses, the smashing of storefront windows, and the hurling of projectiles at the police. But more fundamentally, there was the decision by certain youth to embrace an epistemology of violence as a strategically valid and ethically legitimate response to the "structural violence" of capitalism. This was by no means a universal position, and across Latin America the political Left was riven by competing factions that argued over the utility of violence versus the importance of political engagement. Uruguay, which boasted one of the most formidable and politically relevant Communist Parties in the entire hemisphere, became a microcosm for these debates. At the same time, the deeply intermeshed relationship between youth from different partisan positions, whose lives were often bridged through countercultural practices, reveals the problematic of establishing a rigid dichotomy between a "New Left" ideologically committed to violence and an "Old Left" committed to the strategy of mass organization.

With *Uruguay, 1968* Vania Markarian has not only amplified the English-language conversation about the 1960s in Latin America, she has widened the historiographical field for scholars of the 1960s in the Americas and beyond. The significance of her text lies not only in the fact that it is a case study of 1968 student protest politics in a country that has thus far been overshadowed by other, more well-known examples. It is an opportunity for students to explore and ponder the forces that produced the simultaneity of "like" responses across disparate geographic contexts, a condition perhaps distinctive to the period 1958–73 that forms the core of interpretive investigations into the significance of an era increasingly referred to as the Global Sixties.

Eric Zolov

Stony Brook University

Acknowledgments

This project has been a part of my life since 2004, when a grant from Fondo Clemente Estable, at the time operated under the Consejo Nacional de Investigaciones Científicas y Técnicas (CONICYT), allowed me to return to Uruguay and pursue my work here after completing my PhD studies in the United States. As I did all those years ago, I would like to thank José Pedro Barrán for his continuous support throughout my academic development.

Some time later, that initial interest in the relations between youth, the Left, and the counterculture found an unexpected space in a joint project ("Violencia Política en Uruguay, 1959–1973") that I embarked on with Jaime Yaffé, Aldo Marchesi, Gabriel Bucheli, and Felipe Monestier, with the support once again of Fondo Clemente Estable, now under the Agencia Nacional de Investigación e Innovación (ANII). The insightful feedback from my colleagues on the team (in particular the long discussions with my friends Aldo and Jaime and their critical readings of my writings), as well as the contributions by José

Rilla and Gerardo Caetano, were vital at that stage, which resulted in the first draft of what was to become this book.

Parts of my manuscript were enhanced by careful readings by Magdalena Broquetas, Hugo Achugar, and Eric Zolov, during the conferences "Segundas jornadas de historia política," organized by the Instituto de Ciencia Política, Facultad de Ciencias Sociales, and held in Montevideo in 2008; "Jornadas de reflexión académica a propósito del 35° aniversario del golpe de Estado en Uruguay," also held in Montevideo in 2008; and LASA2010, held in Toronto.

Other important events allowed me to discuss advanced versions of my research with colleagues and benefit from their invaluable comments, including the Tuesday Luncheon Seminar Series organized by the Program in Latin American Studies, Princeton University, where I spent a productive semester in 2008 as visiting professor; a meeting of Núcleo Memoria of the IDES (Buenos Aires) in October 2008; the conference "Terceras jornadas sobre partidos armados en la Argentina de los sesenta," at the Universidad Nacional de San Martín (Buenos Aires) in early 2009; the "Recordar para pensar" workshop organized by the Universidad de Chile and the Heinrich Böll Foundation (Santiago de Chile) in April of that year; and the Tercer Congreso Uruguayo de Ciencia Política, Montevideo, in October 2010.

Some of those texts were published in the *EIAL* and *Secuencia* magazines, in 2010 and 2011, and received constructive comments from anonymous readers.

I would also like to thank Jeremy Adelman, Laura Ehrlich, Gabriel Lagos, Gerardo Leibner, and Adriana Petra for reading different parts of the manuscript at various stages of my research and offering their views. My friend Isabella Cosse read the final version in its entirety and contributed with her always insightful comments.

Luis Alberto Romero was the first to suggest that the book could find an audience in Buenos Aires.

The original Spanish version of this book was made possible by the interest and kindness shown by Jorge Myers and the publishing team at Editorial Universidad Nacional de Quilmes, in particular Rafael Centeno.

In Montevideo, the staff at Biblioteca Nacional, the library of Facultad de Derecho (Universidad de la República—UDELAR), the Centro de Estudios Interdisciplinarios of Facultad de Humanidades y Ciencias de la Educación (UDELAR), and the Centro de Fotografía de Montevideo were all very helpful in my search for sources. The difficulties I faced accessing the files held by the Dirección Nacional de Información e Inteligencia (DNII) of the Interior Ministry of Uruguay merit special mention, and I highlight them here in the hope that in the not so distant future these files may be available to the general public under clear-cut and secure conditions.

Joshua Frens-String brought to my attention several documents discovered by him in the course of his research at the National Archives and Records Administration (NARA), College Park, Maryland.

A number of interviews and personal communications were a source of valuable information and firsthand accounts. I would like to thank Clara Aldrighi, Rodrigo Arocena, Horacio Buscaglia, Roberto Markarian, and Clemente Padín for generously giving their time to help in my research. In addition to sharing memories and detailed knowledge of events, Gonzalo Varela Petito kindly read the final version of the manuscript and helped me improve it.

In my acknowledgments for this English edition, I would like to add my appreciation to Laura Pérez Carrara for her translation, to Kate Marshall and Zuha Khan at the University of California Press, the readers for the press, and the series editors, Pablo Piccato, Federico Finchelstein, and Paul Gillingham. Special thanks to my friends Eduardo Elena and Eric Zolov.

Last on the list are those nearest to me. I would like to express my thanks again to my father, Roberto Markarian, for his constant support and encouragement. Thank you also to my mother, Leny Durán, who is always there for me. And I close this brief run-through of the many to whom I am indebted with my daughter, Juana Delgado, for being so unabashedly rebellious.

Abbreviations

ADNII	Archives of the Dirección Nacional de Información e Inteligencia (National Information and Intelligence Agency)
AEBA	Asociación de Estudiantes de Bellas Artes (Association of School of Fine Arts Students)
AEMM	Asociación de Estudiantes de Magisterio de Montevideo (Montevideo Association of Normal School Students)
AFP	Alliance for Progress
AGE	Acción Gremial Estudiantil (Student Union Action)
AREA 3	Asociación Revolucionaria Estudiantil de Arquitectura 3 (Revolutionary Association of Architecture Students 3)
CDC	Consejo Directivo Central, Universidad de la República (Central Governing Board of the University of the Republic)

CELAM	Consejo Episcopal Latinoamericano (Latin American Episcopal Council)
CESU	Coordinadora de Estudiantes de Secundaria del Uruguay (Coordinating Unit of High School Students of Uruguay)
CEUTU	Coordinadora de Estudiantes de UTU (Coordinator of UTU Students)
CIDE	Comisión de Inversiones y Desarrollo Económico (Economic Development and Investment Commission)
CNT	Convención Nacional de Trabajadores (National Workers' Convention)
DNII	Dirección Nacional de Información e Inteligencia (National Information and Intelligence Agency)
FAI	Frente de Acción Independiente (Independent Action Front)
FAU	Federación Anarquista Uruguaya (Uruguayan Anarchist Federation)
FER	Frente Estudiantil Revolucionario (Revolutionary Student Front)
FEUU	Federación de Estudiantes Universitarios del Uruguay (Federation of University Students of Uruguay)
FIDEL	Frente Izquierda de Liberación (Liberation Leftist Front)
GAU	Grupos de Acción Unificadora (Unifying Action Groups)
HDP	*Los Huevos del Plata*
IAVA	Instituto Alfredo Vázquez Acevedo (Alfredo Vázquez Acevedo Institute)

IMF	International Monetary Fund
IPA	Instituto de Profesores Artigas (Artigas Teachers' College)
MAPU	Movimiento de Acción Popular Unitaria (United Popular Action Movement)
MIR	Movimiento de Izquierda Revolucionaria (Revolutionary Leftist Movement)
MLN-T	Movimiento de Liberación Nacional–Tupamaros (National Liberation Movement–Tupamaros)
MNDLP	Movimiento Nacional de Defensa de las Libertades Públicas (National Movement for the Defense of Public Liberties)
MRO	Movimiento Revolucionario Oriental (Eastern Revolutionary Movement)
MUSP	Movimiento de Unificación Socialista Proletaria (Proletarian Socialist Unification Movement)
OAS	Organization of American States
OCLAE	Organización Continental Latinoamericana de Estudiantes (Latin American Continental Organization of Students)
OLAS	Organización Latinoamericana de Solidaridad (Latin American Organization for Solidarity)
PCU	Partido Comunista Uruguayo (Uruguayan Communist Party)
PDC	Partido Demócrata Cristiano (Christian Democratic Party)
PRI	Partido Revolucionario Institucional (Institutional Revolutionary Party, Mexico)
PS	Partido Socialista (Socialist Party)

PSP	Public Security Program
ROE	Resistencia Obrero-Estudiantil (Worker-Student Resistance)
UJC	Unión de Juventudes Comunistas (Union of Communist Youths)
UP	Unión Popular (Popular Union)
UTAA	Unión de Trabajadores Azucareros de Artigas (Union of Sugarcane Cutters of Artigas)
UTU	Universidad del Trabajo del Uruguay (Vocational High Schools)

Introduction

In the 1960s, a generation of young Latin Americans threw themselves into politics by embracing a heroic view of activism that coexisted—often in conflict—with new cultural patterns originating among their peers in Europe and the United States. Rock music, new clothes, and provocative hairstyles together with fresh ideas about sexuality and a previously unknown passion for certain iconoclastic cultural figures captured the imagination and changed the lives of young people around the globe. This book is prompted by an interest in determining how those globally circulating ideas and practices regarding what it meant to "be young" contributed to shaping political identities locally. In the specific case of Uruguay, I focus on the links created between certain representations of youth and the positions of the various sectors of the Left in relation to the demands of revolutionary struggle. The association between left-wing activism and political violence was clearly not something new in the 1960s, nor was political violence limited to youth activists. However, during this decade, conversations about the "paths to revolution" flourished everywhere, with many activists throughout the world emphasizing a need for armed struggle and discussing the role of younger generations in these political processes. The pages that follow address these issues by looking closely at the Uruguayan student movement in 1968, a year in which young people took center stage, erupting into the streets of Montevideo and feeding the explosive growth of various left-wing groups. I offer a layered analysis: first, a chronological narration of the six months of protests staged by students; second, a look at the material and symbolic expressions of student violence deployed during those days of protest, in dialogue with the unprecedented repressive escalation unleashed by the government; third, an exploration of the impact that such forms of violence had on the ways students organized; fourth, a mapping of the differences generated in the political Left by the series of changes that occurred in such a short time; fifth, an attempt to show the impact of youth culture on the radicalization of Uruguayan students while also considering their perceived identities in terms of class and gender; and sixth, an appraisal of their experience vis-à-vis other national cases in order to contribute new insight into the authoritarian turn that took the Southern Cone of Latin America by storm during those years.

Heuristically, the unique contribution of this study is that it is the first analysis that draws on files from the National Information and Intelligence Agency (Dirección Nacional de Información e Inteligencia, or DNII) of the Uruguayan police, which had been closed to the public until very recently. The access provided was limited, however, and no documentation was made available on several important subjects and issues. Thus most of the information in this book is gleaned from sources already known in historical studies of the student movement, including national periodicals and the minutes of the Central Governing Board (Consejo Directivo Central, or CDC) of the University of the Republic. The views gathered from these documents were contrasted to others that may not seem as relevant but that contribute original and enriching perspectives, such as the case of the counterculture magazine *Los Huevos del Plata* and the traces of the artistic life of Ibero Gutiérrez, a young student murdered by a paramilitary group in 1972.

The main goal of this heuristic and narrative strategy is to present from different angles the specific context of the positions adopted by the groups and sectors of the Uruguayan Left during this period. The intention is to go against the grain of other studies on similar issues that privilege the examination of ideological cleavages to explain attitudes and controversies on specific aspects. This approach also attempts to integrate the multiplicity of levels in which these clashes were deployed, across a territory in which borders between politics and culture were blurred. Only at the end, after exploring these courses, do I try to reposition the 1968 student movement—and its political meanings—in a longer-term history connecting it both to the paths taken by left-wing groups afterward and to the region's advancing authoritarianism up to the June 1973 coup d'état in Uruguay. Through these historical and conceptual linkages I seek to reexamine certain categories that have been used to analyze the long decade of the 1960s in Latin America, especially the notions "New Left" and "Revolutionary Left." With the aim of paving the way, this introduction begins with a brief description of the social and political climate that preceded the 1968 protest movement, in which students played a leading part.[1]

The wave of discontent that spread across Uruguay in 1968 challenged several decades of relative stability in the region.[2] In the first quarter of the twentieth century, during what is known as the "Batllista" period,[3] Uruguay had built a democratic regime based on the negotiated resolution of conflicts, thus limiting political polarization and toning down the differences between the two "traditional" parties (the Colorado Party and the National, or Blanco, Party). This inclusive arrangement was underpinned by the primacy of civilian rule and the secular values of citizenship and consensus. This institutional structure was supported by an agro-export economy with open financial markets, which supplied the resources necessary for the development of a state bureaucracy, a social welfare system, and even an attempt at import substitution industrialization. By the mid-twentieth century, with a population of two and a half million, the country compared well with the rest of the continent, boasting not only high levels of urbanization and education but also a low infant mortality rate and longer life expectancy.

This explains why several scholars of this period have stressed that Uruguay was a spectator stunned by its own crisis. In effect, some unique features of its national experience in the context of the region—such as the preeminence of civilian rule, the regularity of democratic procedures, and the strength of wage-earning middle sectors—had fed a complacent self-image that minimized defects and overshadowed possible critical views. The representation of the country as the "Switzerland of America" was a widely held perception among Uruguayans, who felt fortunate to live in a "happy country" where social equality, consensual conflict resolution, political democracy, and public education defined a distinct national identity that was in contrast to the "backwardness" of Latin America at large.[4] Toward the 1960s, however, very few people could ignore the country's deteriorating economic indicators and the climate of growing social and political polarization. At the same time, a crisis in the government and the traditional two-party system became increasingly evident and the armed forces made their first, unprecedented forays into politics. These changes led all the actors involved to rethink their positions and assess their responsibilities. In the case of left-wing groups, the focus of this analysis, this situation prompted the formulation of new projects and a more forceful argument that revolutionary transformation was a logical outcome of historical forces and a desired goal for the country. International events, especially the Cuban Revolution, also had a profound influence on their political discourse and conduct.

One of the first signs of decay in the decade leading up to 1968 was economic stagnation. This affected the standard of living and the expectations of upward social mobility of broad sectors of Uruguayan society that had from 1945 to 1955 benefited from the 8 percent annual growth rate. Such growth, sustained by an industrialization program based on national goods, relied on capital generated by the agro-export sector and faltered as agricultural productivity fell and international prices dropped. The decline in productivity and an unprecedented rate of inflation spurred financial activities and speculative investment.[5] Faced with this situation, the country's large agricultural producers launched a campaign to defend their interests. This met with resistance from industrial sectors, which had until then been protected and now responded by blocking redistributive measures in favor of workers. Workers, in turn, staged strikes and work stoppages to protest their loss of purchasing power. In the months prior to the 1958 national elections, the labor movement backed students who demanded greater participation and other reforms in the governing system of the University of the Republic—at the time the only institution of higher education in the country—and both sectors joined together in demonstrations to protest the economic crisis. The Colorado government wavered and failed to fully satisfy any of these pressure groups. The political system seemed increasingly incapable generally of dealing with all the social demands triggered by the crisis. In that context (and for the first time in the twentieth century) an influential leader emerged outside the traditional parties and managed to present a joint ballot under the Blanco Party ticket.[6] This explains why in 1958, for the first time in ninety-three years, the Colorado Party lost a national election. Besides the Blanco Party, left-wing groups also improved their performance at the polls that year, cashing in on the popular discontent with the Colorado government. But with 3 percent of the vote for the Communist Party (Partido Comunista del Uruguay, or PCU) and 4 percent for the Socialist Party (Partido Socialista, or PS), they were still far from any real electoral importance. The 1958 elections marked a turning point in the history of Uruguay, but they also represented continuities. Foremost, it was clear that citizens as well as most social and political actors still believed that electoral politics held the key to solving the country's problems. Therefore, the change in governing party was seen as a way out of the crisis. Over the following years, as the economy continued to deteriorate, social conflict increased, and the political system failed again and again to provide an adequate response, this belief was repeatedly put to the test.

In any case, the new Blanco government attempted a change of direction. Its economic agenda went against the interventionist and redistributive policies of the preceding period. In mid-1959, an International Monetary Fund (IMF) mission dictated guidelines to reverse the country's protectionist and industrializing tendencies, and soon after the government established a free financial market, liberalized trade, and eliminated industry subsidies. Although these adjustments secured the Blanco government a large loan to cover increasing trade deficits, they did very little to reverse the economic downturn. This first agreement with the IMF left the country deeper in debt without solving its crisis.[7]

In the 1960s, international events affected the domestic scene in Uruguay and in other Latin American countries with even greater force than in previous periods. After the Cuban Revolution in 1959, the United States stepped up its imperial presence in the region, expanding the role of U.S. capital and demanding standardized responses to the specific problems of each nation. In line with its own economic needs, the U.S. government supported the IMF's policies and pushed for liberalization in the subcontinent to further its business interests and investments. It also tried to implement new programs to prevent the emergence of revolutionary movements through economic growth and the strengthening of political institutions. The Alliance for Progress (AFP), established in 1961, expressed a new view of state intervention aimed at promoting development and preventing social insurrection. After Fidel Castro declared Cuba's alignment with the Communist world and the "missile crisis" brought the Cold War to the Caribbean, the United States redoubled its efforts. Its dominance in the hemisphere peaked in 1962 with the suspension of Cuba from the Organization of American States (OAS).[8] At the same time, the Cuban Revolution was becoming a source of inspiration for many in Latin America, and it provided a viable model for all those who were discontent with the prevailing state of affairs and, in particular, with the role played by the United States in the region.

In Uruguay, these international factors affected an internal state of affairs that was already complicated. The 1962 national elections revealed two major changes: the traditional parties were increasingly fragmented; and the Left was beginning to form successful, although still modest, coalitions. The Blanco Party retained its dominant position. At the same time, two Blanco leaders, Enrique Erro and Ariel Collazo, broke away from the party to join leftist coalitions. The Popular Union (Unión Popular, or UP), formed by Erro, and the Socialist Party embodied the ideas of a group of young people who opposed the liberal inclinations of the PS senior leader Emilio Frugoni and called for a firmer defense of the working class and a greater nationalist and Latin Americanist emphasis. The coalition had a very poor performance in the elections (with only 2 percent of the vote, when the Socialist Party alone had secured 4 percent in 1958). Meanwhile, the Communist Party of Uruguay was going through a phase of redefinition under the leadership of Rodney Arismendi and formed a coalition, the Liberation Leftist Front (Frente Izquierda de Liberación, or FIDEL), with small splinter groups from the traditional parties, including the Eastern Revolutionary Movement (Movimiento Revolucionario Oriental, or MRO) headed by Collazo. FIDEL was more successful than the UP, with 4 percent of the vote compared to the 3 percent previously obtained by the Communists alone. Another new development of the 1962 elections was the Christian Democratic Party (Partido Demócrata Cristiano, or PDC), which ran for the first time and received 3 percent of the total vote. This new party gathered activists from the country's Catholic party, the Civic Union (Unión Cívica, or UC), who had reformulated their ideas inspired by the guidelines of the Second Vatican Council and encouraged by the prestige of European Christian Democrats and the growth of Chile's Christian Democratic Party.[9]

These electoral results were somewhat timid responses to what was perceived as the political system's inability to address changing social conditions. The new Blanco government, too, proved incapable of making quick decisions in turbulent times. Initially, it tried to move away from the orthodox dictates of the IMF and welcomed the advice of the Economic Development and Investment Commission (Comisión de Inversiones y Desarrollo Económico, or CIDE), a planning agency set up to receive U.S. aid channeled through the AFP. This commission proposed a series of developmentalist-inspired recommendations but failed to garner the political consensus necessary for their effective implementation in the short term.[10] While the agricultural and industrial sectors remained stagnant, speculation increased dramatically. This combination of stagnation in production and financial speculation distinguished Uruguay from the rest of Latin America. In 1965, the banking system collapsed, and there was a new move to implement IMF guidelines.[11] Social indicators evidenced the sustained deterioration of the standard of living of the working and middle classes, including a drop in real wages and social benefits, growing unemployment, increasing poverty, and the beginning of mass emigration.[12]

In this climate, the education system was often perceived as both an obstacle and a potential solution to the crisis. This association between public education and the general welfare of any given society, which was prevalent at the time in modernization and developmentalist theories all over the world, resonated deeply in a country enormously proud of its early achievements in the field, including high literacy and primary school enrollment rates, as well as a recent surge in the number of students in secondary school and the availability of free tertiary education. Therefore, the perceived lag in meeting the challenges of scientific and technical standards in research and teaching was often quoted in the media and other forums as an explanation for the economic stalemate and ensuing social decay. In addressing this situation, education authorities, teachers, students, and the successive national governments often clashed with each other over resources, management, and the very orientation of proposed transformations. The lack of support for consensual reform paved the way for authoritarian solutions, such as increasing central control over the different branches of the education system and depriving organized students (at the university) and teachers (at both the university and the secondary schools) of their traditional representation in governing bodies.[13]

These shortcomings in addressing the predicaments of public education echoed similar failures to achieve political consensus for any solution proposed for the country's problems. The traditional parties repeatedly laid the blame on institutional arrangements such as the collegiate structure of the executive branch. Negotiations thus were undertaken to reform the national constitution and restore power to the president. The fact that both the diagnosis and the solution were old and had been implemented before revealed once again the quandary in which the political system found itself. In the preceding thirty years the country had gone to the polls seven times to elect a national government and considered eleven proposals to amend the constitution, all of which focused on modifying the executive branch. In addition, after a decade of Blanco Party governments, the rotation of the two parties in power had proved incapable of solving the crisis. However, the outcome of the 1966 elections was both a new constitution that gave more power to the president and the election of a Colorado candidate, Óscar Gestido, to lead the government with the newly heightened powers.[14] The sectors that supported the strengthening of presidential authority were, nonetheless, driven by a new motive: the need for efficiency and celerity to maintain "social peace" and stifle popular discontent. Although this was not immediately evident during Gestido's administration, it laid the groundwork for the escalation of authoritarianism that was to come.

The president initially used his new powers to dismantle the economic and social policies applied since 1959 by the Blanco administrations in line with IMF guidelines. But in late 1967, amid great internal differences and intense social conflict, Gestido once again changed the course of the government. He resorted to instituting Prompt Security Measures (a limited form of state of siege stipulated under the constitution that allowed the president to suspend the rights to strike, freedom of assembly, and freedom of speech) and implemented the recommendations of the international financial body. That year, inflation peaked at more than 100 percent, the highest ever in the history of the country.[15]

By then, most social and political actors were already fully aware of the seriousness of the country's situation. While the traditional political system tried to react, a host of new and old actors was organizing to respond: trade unions successfully concluded a long process of unification to form a sole confederation; the student movement became increasingly radicalized and joined workers in their demands and actions; and the old parties of the Left reviewed their positions, with new groups emerging to address the crisis and promote change through different means. Until that moment, the political Left—represented primarily by the PS and the PCU—had been unsuccessful in its attempts to take advantage of the failures of the traditional parties and improve their electoral performance. Their first coalition-building experiences were not very successful. Of the senators and congresspersons elected in 1966, the only representatives of the Left were members of FIDEL, the coalition formed in 1962 by Communists and some small breakaway groups from the traditional parties, which received 5.7 percent of the vote. Since its founding in 1921, the PCU had embraced electoral politics and gained the support of unionized workers. Neither its renewed assessment of Uruguayan society and history in the late 1950s nor the recent impact of the Cuban Revolution seemed to shake the party's faith in elections and the forging of political alliances. The PDC, which leaned closer to the Left after incorporating the changes in the global Christian movement, also secured a small representation in parliament.[16] Other left-wing organizations that ran in the 1966 elections, such as the PS and the group headed by the former Blanco senator Enrique Erro, could not settle on joint candidates and suffered the consequences of their disagreements.[17]

While they continued to pursue possible electoral paths as a means to tackle the country's crises, all of these groups took part in the ideological and political debates under way at the regional level. In 1967, the Latin American Organization for Solidarity (Organización Latinoamericana de Solidaridad, or OLAS) gathered representatives of the Left from across Latin America at a conference convened in Havana to discuss the main concerns of their peers from the rest of the world. The opposition between the Soviet Union and China, the new challenges faced by the Cuban Revolution, and other controversies in socialist countries divided participants into different bands. The meeting was preceded by a message from Ernesto "Che" Guevara—who many of the participants did not know was in Bolivia—that extolled violence and criticized the Soviet Union, two attitudes that would characterize a large part of the region's Left in the following years.[18] While these issues were already contentious topics within the Left, the debates in the OLAS sparked greater controversy across the continent.[19] The Uruguayan Left, then, also had to deal with the ideological dilemmas of their comrades around the world and clearer stances with respect to the singularities of the revolution in Latin America. Many of the issues examined in the following chapters are marked by these debates.

The Uruguayan delegation that attended the OLAS meeting was composed of members of the PS and FIDEL. There were no official representatives of the various other radical groups that existed then, or of the National Liberation Movement–Tupamaros (Movimiento de Liberación Nacional–Tupamaros, or MLN-T), which would soon become Uruguay's leading guerrilla movement.[20] Although they had begun organizing in the early 1960s, the Tupamaros only came to public attention in 1968 with their first bank heists and the kidnapping of the head of the state power company. While the Havana meeting backed their strategy in general, the Tupamaros professed to avoid the kind of explicit ideological controversy expressed there.[21] The meeting clearly had an impact on the rest of the Uruguayan Left as well. The PCU questioned the core definitions adopted at the meeting with respect to the role of armed struggle in Latin America's revolutionary experience, but most of the other groups openly embraced that creed.

In December 1967, President Gestido died and was succeeded by Vice President Jorge Pacheco Areco, also of the Colorado Party but until then virtually unknown. A week after taking office, Pacheco passed a decree banning the Socialist Party and other groups that had publicly supported the OLAS platform. As will be seen in greater detail below, these measures had major consequences for the future of the Uruguayan Left. Some activists were accused of advocating armed struggle and thrown in jail. Two newspapers were shut down. Among the banned groups were long-standing direct action organizations such as the Uruguayan Anarchist Federation (Federación Anarquista Uruguaya, or FAU), which continued operating through the Worker-Student Resistance group (Resistencia Obrero-Estudiantil, or ROE). More recently formed groups inspired by the Chinese or the Cuban Revolution were also declared illegal, including the United Popular Action Movement (Movimiento de Acción Popular Unitaria, or MAPU), the former Communists of the Revolutionary Leftist Movement (Movimiento de Izquierda Revolucionaria, or MIR), and the MRO, which had distanced itself from FIDEL.[22]

While the pro-OLAS stance of these groups is not very surprising, the position of the long-standing Socialist Party merits a brief explanation. At the time, the PS was going through a complex process of ideological renovation, in many ways similar to the PCU's. In contrast to the Communists, many Socialists, seeing the Cuban experience, abandoned electoral politics as the leading path to social change in Uruguay. Moreover, the efforts to trace their roots to rural insurrections of the nineteenth century and the new nationalist and anti-imperialist emphasis prompted the party—under the guidance of Vivian Trías—to move away from its former political liberalism, represented by the traditional leader Emilio Frugoni.[23] Like others who applauded the definitions adopted at the OLAS, a number of Socialist activists embarked on armed struggle projects. The party as such did not go down that path, however. Raúl Sendic, leader of the Tupamaros, began his political shift to revolutionary violence while he was still heading the PS's efforts to unionize rural workers. He soon left the party to take the helm of the MLN-T.[24]

Although the OLAS platform was not formally discussed by trade unions, the debates on revolutionary strategy were part of the labor movement's long process of unification. With the founding of the National Workers' Convention (Convención Nacional de Trabajadores, or CNT) in October 1966, Uruguay's trade unions finally coalesced into a single federation. The CNT drew up an agenda with specific labor demands regarding wages and benefits, as well as a number of proposed structural responses to the crisis, including agrarian reform; the nationalization of certain industries, banks, and foreign commerce; state-led industrialization policies; and a tax system reform.[25] The various left-wing groups were involved in the process of creating the CNT and supported its agenda in general terms. However, there was a clear-cut division between those who were in favor of gradually stepping up actions for concrete demands and those who pushed for a more confrontational strategy that would force greater radicalization and immediate responses. The former highlighted the importance of participating in elections and the role of political organizations in determining the course of revolutionary action; the latter emphasized the independent role of unions in these processes. Something similar occurred in the combative student movement, which was closely tied to the labor movement and was more inclined to adopt confrontational tactics. In general, these debates of the late 1960s among unionized workers and students mirrored the rift in the Uruguayan Left with respect to the OLAS, with the PCU and its allies on one side and the sectors that would later converge in the "tendency" on the other.[26]

This brief description of the shaping of different ideological camps within the Uruguayan Left provides a general understanding of the conditions under which these groups confronted the Pacheco government in 1968. There is, thus, no need to elaborate further on the historical context in which the protest movement erupted or its developments and outcomes over the next five years leading up to the 1973 coup d'état staged under the authoritarian wave that swept over Latin America and that will be considered in the conclusion. By pausing here, I aim to restore contingency to the events of 1968, which scholars and protagonists alike have frequently described solely as the opening scene of this authoritarian upsurge. In contrast, my approach seeks to highlight the tension that existed between the growing discontent, struggles, and expectations, which can be traced back almost a decade, and the specific events of 1968, which involved unique forms of expression and consequences. These events were especially novel in their capacity to lead thousands of people to shift course and change their aspirations with respect to society and politics.[27] Although the chapters that follow emphasize this last aspect, focusing on the multiple dimensions of the student movement and the leading role played by young people, I refer to this previous stage as a counterpoint to underline the continuities and ruptures that became evident then. In other words, before moving on to the focus of this study, I would like to posit that while 1968 struck Uruguay with the force of a thunderbolt, it was not the first time in the country's history that such a disruption occurred; it did, however, illuminate the dark clouds that had been gathering in the shadows.

I would like to offer some additional remarks, of a more conceptual nature, to help navigate the rest of this book. In particular, I would like to look at the relations between the Left and young people, which I believe are key to understanding the events of 1968. This entails examining first the emergence of young people as political actors within the Left and then how the various groups reacted to the circulation of typically young cultural trends originating in Europe and the United States. My analysis is not based on any given theoretical framework, nor does it rest on excessively rigid definitions; rather it tries to pay attention to the meanings attributed to these issues by the actors of that time. Nonetheless, an overview of these relations in the Uruguay of the 1960s is necessary, as is elucidating some of its analytical implications for addressing the development of the 1968 student movement.

To begin with, while some left-wing parties, such as the PCU and the PS, had youth chapters even before this period, it was during the 1960s that they gained strength, attracted more activists, and achieved greater visibility. The more radical groups, associated with direct action and armed struggle, also grew among young people at this stage. These processes are not only observed in the Left, but also in political organizations across the ideological spectrum, including the Right. Student activism, for its part, can be traced to the beginning of the century, most notably in the previously mentioned struggles of the 1950s over how the university should be governed and run but also in more general issues in coordination with labor unions. Toward the end of the 1960s, organized students had an even broader agenda that included both global issues from an anti-imperialistic perspective and the search for solutions to the national crisis.[28]

To what extent was a political awakening among the younger generations connected with the new wave of cultural trends that shaped the emergence of a new youth identity around the world? It would appear that at least until the early 1960s young activists in Uruguay were not very innovative in their actions and practices. Studies on the 1958 protests calling for student participation in university government, for example, highlight the capacity of student organizations to articulate demands, as well as their tenacity and reach, but they mention almost no typically youthful features in their forms of struggle or in the ways in which their members socialized (beyond certain playful expressions that can be traced to traditions passed down from European universities).[29] The low visibility of distinctive generational cultural trends may be explained by the eruption that occurred in the second half of the 1960s, which made any innovations and conflicts of the immediately previous period pale in comparison. As I discuss in later chapters, the students mobilizing in 1968 were more outspoken in their disagreement over the curriculum of the education system and how it was run, and at the same time they objected to certain forms of struggle of their predecessors and criticized the positions of the traditional Left. Many contemporaries also noted that these experiences with youth mobilization created a new cultural universe, one that had nothing to do with the modes of protest common to earlier generations.[30]

Until very recently, the literature on other historical cases, including countries from the region, tended to separate the political involvement of young people from youth culture while also examining their points of agreement and disagreement.[31] Although in Uruguay it would seem that the rise of young people as political actors was more evident than the expansion of youth "counterculture," this book joins new scholarship on the "Global Sixties" that seeks to show how certain modes of cultural rebellion had a great impact on large contingents of young people and were perceived by various actors as signs of change and defiance of traditional values, thus acquiring unmistakably political meaning.[32] In this sense, my study is concerned with finding—always with respect to the 1968 student movement—the points of convergence and divergence between those who placed themselves in the front lines of the struggle against the status quo and the new patterns of generational behavior.

The analysis poses several theoretical and practical challenges. One such challenge has to do with the usefulness of the category "generation" for understanding historical processes, in this case the processes that took place in the late 1960s. Some authors see it merely as the corroboration of the tendency of groups to think of the past in terms of the rhythm of the human life cycle. In Pierre Nora's words, "A generation is the product of memory, the result of a conscious attempt to remember. It does not know itself but through difference and opposition."[33] This has not prevented historians and other social scientists from taking up the idea and turning "youth" into an object of study. Some, such as the sociologist Norbert Elias, view generational conflict as a key element for understanding certain political and social phenomena.[34] It was not until well into the twentieth century that these issues began to be explored, in connection with the also relatively recent delimitation of adolescence and youth as specific stages between childhood and adulthood that can be traced to the 1950s.[35] Already in the 1960s, the concept of generations and the idea of conflict between groups defined by age were generally considered key to understanding social life and its transformations. This study takes into account the importance assigned to these categories by contemporaries and seeks to put them in historical perspective by looking at debates over their use in the 1960s.[36]

Another challenge of this research has to do with the dissemination of trends from a European- and U.S.-grown youth culture to countries in the periphery such as Uruguay in the early years of the second half of the twentieth century. These new cultural modes were not rapidly adopted locally, and they took on creative forms and multiple meanings. Focusing on left-wing activism also requires addressing the relationship between the political and cultural spheres. An initial step is to recognize, along with Raymond Williams, the range of often overlapping meanings assigned to the word *culture,* to then focus on the signifying or symbolic systems that give meaning to human activities and, more specifically, on intellectual and artistic practices and products.[37] This methodology is prevalent in the fields of intellectual history and cultural studies, disciplines that are considered in this research.

This delimitation in my approach is the basis for analyzing the relations between certain political and ideological agendas—in this case, the agendas of certain sectors of the Uruguayan Left—and a number of demands and concerns articulated in the field of culture. The notion of "field" is drawn from Pierre Bourdieu, in the sense of a configuration of social relations, or, in his words, "a state of power relations between the agents or institutions involved in the struggle."[38] It is thus clear that the cultural field is formed as a social space that is relatively autonomous but pierced by power relations that transcend it. In the period considered in this book, it was conceived simultaneously as an arena of struggle, an instrument of change, and a space where young people with a newly awakened political commitment could experiment as they sought to bring about the social transformations they believed were within reach. The challenge, then, is to discern the multiple tensions between the innovative proposals that were emerging and some of the projects of change that characterized this stage of Latin American history, marked both by the awareness of living in a revolutionary era and by "the shared perception of the inevitable and desired transformation of the universe of institutions, subjectivity, art, and culture," in the words of Claudia Gilman.[39]

It is in this general context of change and desire to break with the prevailing order that the profound transformations in the behavior and practices of large youth sectors occurred globally, often in open defiance of dominant values—in other words, the development of what has been termed "counterculture." The classic reference is the 1969 study by Theodore Roszak, *The Making of a Counterculture,* which addressed the emergence of a youth protest movement against the dominant values of the 1960s in the most highly developed societies of the capitalist world. For Roszak, "counterculture" included a wide range of practices and discourses connected with sexuality, drug use, religiosity, work, and leisure, always under the sign of resistance against mainstream social mores.[40] Since his study, the adjective *countercultural* has been used to refer rather loosely to any behaviors, styles, and opinions that certain youth sectors, always relatively small in numbers, have adopted to rebel against the world of their elders and mark a generational identity.

Several scholars who have studied these issues emphasize the correlation between the adoption of such an identity and the creation of a youth market and consumer public for certain more or less mass culture products.[41] In this way, the "counterculture" that originated in the 1960s helped spread the image of young people as a cult object and an ideal of personal fulfillment that had been developing in the previous decade. In this sense, the term can be defined as a set of cultural patterns that are initially produced and consumed, in the context of mass society, by a limited group and are later mainstreamed through cultural industries and other market mechanisms. One of the questions that this study raises (without fully providing an answer) has to do with the role of the Uruguayan Left in the shaping of these contradictory relations between cultural resistance and the logic of capitalist consumption that came to the fore in the country in 1968 with the rise of young people as political actors.[42] Assuming, then, the risks involved in using the category "generation," the challenges of analyzing the tensions between culture and politics, and the difficulty of defining *counterculture*, this study combines a focus on the leading role of young people and their cultural expressions in the late 1960s with an interest in the history of the political Left in Uruguay. It draws on a number of research studies of the same period in other parts of the world. In the case of the United States, as I discuss in the conclusion, there is an abundant literature that skillfully connects the changes in the behaviors and forms of socializing of young people born after World War II—amid profound transformations in family structure and values—with the eruption of protest movements around political demands and the mainstreaming of certain forms of countercultural resistance. The works on student activism of the late 1960s are perhaps the best example of this literature, but the same could be said of several of the analyses of the struggles for civil rights in the previous years.[43] These studies show the advantages of intersecting research on the social, political, and economic context in which these movements arose with issues such as gender, race, art, and cultural industries in order to gain greater insight into the 1960s "cultural revolution," to use the expression of the British historian Eric Hobsbawm.[44]

There are also several interesting analyses of Latin America. A good example is the study by the U.S. historian Eric Zolov, which questions the idea that the diffusion of a number of pop culture expressions from the United States in the 1950s merely permeated Mexican politics with their commercial consumerist values, thwarting progressive forms of resistance and struggle.[45] Zolov thus challenges reductionist approaches that simplify the idea of "cultural imperialism" and ignore the liberating impact that new cultural forms can have even when they originate in the global centers of power.[46] In his analysis of the relationship between the musical style known as *La Onda* (The Wave) and student mobilizations in the 1960s, Zolov underscores the ability of both movements to subvert the ideal stabilizing model of the "revolutionary family" promoted by the government of the Institutional Revolutionary Party (Partido Revolucionario Institucional, or PRI). His reflections also provide insight into the extent to which the combined efforts of co-optation and repression of youth cultural expressions by the state apparatus, on the one hand, and the exaltation of the sacrifice of the political Left, on the other, robbed the 1960s generation of its festive and celebratory component, inscribing the repressive episode known as the "Tlatelolco massacre" as the essential myth of the decade in the memory of the Mexican people.[47] The analysis of the public debates over that country's student movement shows that those who identified themselves as the "inheritors of '68" did not initially highlight the deep connections, aptly described by Zolov, between youth rebellion in the cultural field and proposals for social and political change, opting instead to underscore the heroic contribution of their generation to the opposition movement against PRI rule.[48] In a more recent study, Jaime Pensado shifts the focus by recognizing certain "festive attitudes of *desmadre*" (a more aggressive culture of youth defiance) or *relajo* (playful disorder) as features of student activism in 1960s Mexico and emphasizing their intricate connection with the authoritarian tradition that cut short the revolutionary thrust of that wave of protest and strengthened the mechanism of state control in the next decade.[49]

The nuances that emerge from this very brief overview of events in Mexico suggest similar lines of research for other countries where both government repression and the exaltation of leftwing resistance could have had analogous effects on the relationship between political protest, cultural rebellion, and authoritarian tendencies. The Southern Cone of Latin America offers paradigmatic examples. In Brazil, authors such as Marcelo Ridenti, Christopher Dunn, and Victoria Langland—the latter in particular with respect to the student movement—have clearly identified the links that existed between various cultural expressions and the changing forms of protest against the authoritarian government that took power in 1964.[50] The very existence of these approaches is explained, moreover, because in that country, as these and other analysts acknowledge, the expansion of cultural industries and the media in the 1970s and 1980s (combined with the selective repressive policies deployed by the government) opened up spaces for the dissemination and continuation of some of the youth expressions of the previous decade, thus allowing them to reemerge in the democratic transition struggles.[51]

If we move farther south, to the Río de la Plata, we find instead that until very recently most literature emphasized the period's committed activism, social polarization, and political violence, without connecting them systematically to changes in behavior and other processes of cultural transformation. This may be due to a possible fracture in the collective memory, which prevented the bridging of the spaces of expression of a vibrant youth culture that emerged in the 1980s with similar forms in the 1970s. These had remained concealed under the repeated images of revolutionary passion and political activity that dominated how the decade was remembered, often mentioned only as the prelude to the authoritarian and repressive wave that came after it. The break was clearly much more drastic in Uruguay than in Argentina, where the continuity between the two moments is evident in the careers of certain musicians and in the many commercial products associated with rock music and other typically youthful cultural forms. That continuity in Argentina can also be seen, much like in the case of Brazil, in some more or less academic works that are important antecedents to this study. For example, there have been several analyses of the convergences and divergences between the "aesthetic vanguard" and the "political vanguard" in the 1960s and 1970s, as well as analyses of the relationship between university intellectuals, the leading role played by the younger generations, and youth trends of the time.[52] In addition, numerous studies on the social and political aspects of those years generally openly acknowledge the leading role of the younger generations as a distinguishing feature of the period.[53] Despite their limitations, often determined by their essayist or testimonial tone, aimed at reaching a broad readership, all of these works have an interest in problematizing the relations between culture and politics in order to understand the protest movements that emerged after the Cuban Revolution and that were in many cases brutally repressed by the authoritarian governments that followed. More recently, historians like Valeria Manzano and Isabella Cosse have highlighted the profound linkages between the various expressions of cultural change of the 1960s, with an emphasis on young people, and the explosion of protest until the authoritarian onslaught and the ensuing shattered expectations of more or less radical social change of large sectors of Argentine society.[54] In closing this overview, it should be noted that something similar occurs with the proliferation of studies on the middle classes and the processes of modernization during those years.[55]

These examples stand in contrast to the Uruguayan case, where there are practically no studies that address these issues in a systematic manner. There are, nonetheless, a number of works in which these subjects are discussed, however tangentially. On the one hand, there are several scattered approaches to cultural expression, including the work of popular musicians and the development of new musical styles,[56] as well as studies on visual arts.[57] In addition, there are more general reflections on youth culture and identity in analyses of aspects of private life in the second half of the twentieth century.[58] Surprisingly there are no specific explorations of some of the central issues of cultural change in the 1960s, such as the liberation of the body, sexuality, and women's emancipation efforts.[59] It is also surprising that there are very few attempts to understand the more marginal cultural expressions connected with artistic and spiritual experimentation in the same social and political context.[60] Neither are these issues taken up in studies on the 1968 student movement available to date, except through the testimonial inclination of their authors.[61]

On the other hand, as shown above, there is a fairly large, though still exploratory, production regarding the left-wing groups and parties that were active in the years that preceded the 1973 coup d'état. Until very recently, these studies were limited to a strictly political and ideological analysis, with mere glimpses at the relationship to various cultural expressions of the period. This literature was only incidentally interested in the possible connections between the processes of ideological and political renovation embarked on by several left-wing groups and the adoption of new cultural patterns that assigned a leading role to the younger generations, in a way that favored the attitude of permanent quest and experimentation. Its authors referred to such processes of renovation as the trigger for the unification of the Left and its electoral growth and expanding activist base in the early 1970s, especially among youths, while at the same time mentioning the involvement of young people that swelled the ranks of various armed struggle and direct action groups that emerged simultaneously in the country. They did not, however, delve systematically into the forms of socializing that characterized those contingents of leftist youths in connection with the positions of the different groups with respect to the new generational trends and their capacity for integrating them into their agendas of social and political change. The extensive literature on the leading guerrilla movement, the MLN-T, which saw a boom in the new millennium with the presidential election of one of its top leaders, José "Pepe" Mujica, did not in most cases go beyond a stock reference to these aspects.[62] More recent and still few studies on the Communist Party, instead, have begun to show a more evident concern for the spaces of socialization and other cultural aspects, as a result, no doubt, of the very characteristics of a mass party with great penetration in society.[63] Almost none of these studies, however, explore the extent to which these groups considered the potential of young people as agents of revolutionary change in a dependent capitalist society, whether they sought to break with traditional family structures as part of the social transformation they proposed, or if they thought the relaxing of sexual mores could contribute to weakening the structures of domination. In that context, this book starts with the analysis of the 1968 student movement in an effort to begin unraveling these relations between political activism and youth culture, which the leftist groups in other parts of the world were reflecting on during that time.

These preliminary observations, which began with the general historical context and concluded with some considerations of the links between youth, politics, and culture in 1960s Uruguay, seek to specify the scope of the book. Therefore, they are also aimed at clarifying what should not be expected of this book. First, it should be noted that if does not provide an organized history of the different factions of the Uruguayan Left. Fragments of their development will emerge as necessary to present their controversies and debates on the issues that are the focus of this study (an index of names and groups provided in the front matter of the book reconstructs some of their vicissitudes). This structure of the text, which follows individual paths only insofar as they contribute to an understanding of the development of the student movement, also explains why different actors appear late in the account, after the most significant mobilizations of 1968 and their leading features have been presented. Similarly, international events are referred to only when they are relevant to the debates and decisions that affected the spheres of political activism and cultural activity discussed. They are dealt with more systematically in the conclusion so as to examine more generally the categories used to analyze similar phenomena in other geographic contexts. Having offered these explanations and disclaimers, I can only hope they serve as a road map to guide readers through the following pages.

ONE

Mobilizations

STUDENTS TAKE TO THE STREETS

In the Montevideo autumn of 1968, faced with announcements shortly before the beginning of the school year that government-subsidized bus fares would increase, high school students burst onto the public scene as they took to the streets to protest.[1] These protests kicked off the year's great mobilizations, which were some of Latin America's longest and most intense, rivaled only by events in major cities in Mexico and Brazil.[2] In the first days of May, students made headlines as they staged various rallies, occupied school facilities, set up roadblocks with toll collection to raise money, and held spontaneous sit-ins to disrupt traffic around their schools. This activity was, in the words of journalists Roberto Copelmayer and Diego Díaz, "boisterous but peaceful." While demonstrations were led by various actors, activism on a large scale was catalyzed by the Coordinating Unit of High School Students of Uruguay (Coordinadora de Estudiantes de Secundaria del Uruguay, or CESU), which responded to the

Union of Communist Youths (Unión de Juventudes Comunistas, or UJC).[3] Witnesses and commentators alike agree that the levels of violence seen during those days were not very different from what had been experienced in similar situations in previous years. Local newspapers reported sporadic incidents of rocks being thrown at buses and some clashes with police forces that tried to break up the protests, arresting and even slightly injuring some demonstrators. Nobody expected this unrest to maintain its momentum for long. The demonstrators who were arrested were usually set free within hours, and if they were underage they were released to their parents. This was in sharp contrast to reports of a violent police force dispersing demonstrators at the International Workers' Day rally on May 1, where serious incidents had occurred, spurred on by the combative stance of the *cañeros* (sugarcane cutters) of the Union of Sugarcane Cutters of Artigas (Unión de Trabajadores Azucareros de Artigas, or UTAA), who had marched down to Montevideo from the country's northernmost region.[4]

On May 8, just days after President Jorge Pacheco Areco introduced several changes in his cabinet, Interior Minister Augusto Legnani resigned without explanation and was replaced by Eduardo Jiménez de Aréchaga. A week later, Colonel Alberto Aguirre Gestido was appointed chief of police of Montevideo. By then, classes had been suspended in many of the capital's high schools because they were occupied by students, paralyzed by a strike, or temporarily shut down by the authorities. The presence of students in the streets was taking on new dimensions. The number of demonstrations grew, and the various groups of protesters came together in joint marches, often putting up barricades, burning tires, and, according to some observers, hurling makeshift incendiary bombs, or Molotov cocktails, mostly at city buses.[5] At the same time, the number of arrests grew, and the Montevideo police called in the Metropolitan Guard (Guardia Metropolitana) as backup for the regular officers assigned to neighborhood police stations.

Meanwhile, CESU leaders were still hoping to reach a negotiated solution with the mayor of Montevideo to prevent the rise in bus fares. Conflicting rumors surrounding these negotiations escalated the protests, triggering "flash" demonstrations that sought to take repressive forces by surprise. Protesters also organized roadblocks and picket lines intended to inform the public of the situation. This surge of actions also included what were known as "counter-courses," noncurricular classes on various subjects, often held off school premises with the participation of students and teachers who sympathized with their demands. At the end of May, while the municipal authorities announced their commitment to keep student bus fares down, high school students demanded that the benefit be extended to the entire population. The CESU's call to put an end to this stage of the conflict was met with outright rebellion from students, who continued to occupy several high schools.

In early June, the bus fare issue was still unresolved, and student unions found new reasons to protest. Traditionally this time of year brought demands for greater funding for public education as legislators prepared to discuss the budget that was to be adopted by the executive branch. These issues fueled existing conflicts among students and teachers in other public education institutions, such as the polytechnic school, the Universidad del Trabajo del Uruguay (UTU), and the teachers' training college, the Instituto Normal. Student demands were largely connected to an explosive growth in enrollment and the resulting shortage of materials and human resources and the executive branch's attempts to impose solutions. Newspapers across the political spectrum were filled with articles about the crisis in secondary education—the shortage of classrooms, the difficulties of the teaching staff—and the need to take urgent action. This evidenced widespread concern over the deterioration of the country's valued public education system, an indicator that had often been used to support the claim of Uruguay's singularity in the region.

As the country's social and economic crisis reached unprecedented levels, teachers' and students' unions used this public sentiment to their advantage, stepping up their demands and confronting a government set on implementing reforms that were unfavorable to them and limited their participation in governing bodies and decision-making processes. The refusal by governing party legislators to ratify the appointment of Arturo Rodríguez Zorrilla as director of the National Board of Secondary Education further inflamed those who claimed that the government was violating the board's autonomy.[6] Parents also organized to put pressure on both sides, with some supporting the demands of teachers' unions and students and others rejecting this excessive "politicization" of education. The rest of the country was not indifferent to this unrest.[7]

Widespread protests erupted in June when university students joined the demonstrations. On June 6, the Federation of University Students of Uruguay (Federación de Estudiantes Universitarios del Uruguay, or FEUU) called on students to demand that the executive branch release the funds it owed the university and other educational institutions. High school students who were still mobilizing for subsidized bus fares joined FEUU protesters at the steps of the main university building. At the end of the rally, as was often the case in these demonstrations, a group of protesters started marching down the main avenue, 18 de Julio, toward the Old City district. They had advanced only a few steps when they were met with gunfire from a police vehicle. Five students were seriously wounded. Most analysts agree that this incident, which involved shots fired from .38-caliber service revolvers, was the first clear sign that the repressive forces were adopting new methods. There were also mass detentions, with charges filed in court against several of the students arrested.[8]

The way students organized and demonstrated and their aims also changed significantly as of that moment. In the days after the shooting, young people across all levels of education rushed to the streets imbued with "a sort of frenzy," in the words of Gonzalo Varela Petito, who was a direct participant and has a vivid memory of these events.[9] On June 7, students gathered in front of the university to protest the shooting; the rally ended with serious clashes and property damage, as well as the arrest and injury of hundreds of students. Over the next few days, demonstrators adopted tactics that involved gathering in groups, scattering, and regrouping and began to seek out confrontations with the police. The shock effect of these "flash" demonstrations was meant to gain an advantage over the police forces. In addition to actions in Avenida 18 de Julio and other downtown streets, the students staged marches, threw rocks, put up roadblocks, and engaged in violent clashes in the neighborhoods surrounding their schools, many of which were still being occupied.

On June 12, the University of the Republic, the CESU, the FEUU, and the national labor federation (Convención Nacional de Trabajadores, or CNT) called for a demonstration in "defense of freedoms, against repression, and for the release of jailed students." When the rally was over, university authorities asked the demonstrators to disperse, in compliance with the Interior

Ministry's ban on marching to downtown Montevideo. Many participants, the majority of them students, disobeyed the order and confronted the Metropolitan Guard, which was waiting for them armed with tear-gas launchers. Instead of retreating, the young demonstrators put up barricades and began breaking store windows and throwing Molotov cocktails at the police forces, disbanding and regrouping along side streets. The Metropolitan Guard responded violently, leaving dozens injured and almost three hundred students arrested.[10]

The next day, the government issued a decree implementing Prompt Security Measures. These measures—a limited form of state of siege stipulated under the constitution, allowing the government to suspend the rights to strike, freedom of assembly, and freedom of speech, among other repressive actions—had been applied sporadically in previous years (most recently in October 1967) in response to social conflicts and emergency situations such as floods but never for so long or as harshly as they were applied by Pacheco. In justifying the measures, the June 13 decree called attention to the "profound disruption of the social peace and the public order" that could ensue as a result of the several labor conflicts under way, in particular among civil servants and state bank employees, without mentioning the student unrest directly. Only the phrase "unusual climate of street violence," near the end of the decree, alluded to the previous night and similar events.[11]

The ministers of culture, labor, and public health opposed the measures and resigned. These internal differences revealed the initial difficulties encountered by Pacheco as he sought to consolidate the authoritarian shift and to move more decisively toward economic liberalization, the two features that defined his administration from the moment he took office in December

1967 after the unexpected death of President Óscar Gestido. The government sought to contain the wave of mostly labor-related protests, which had swelled over the past decade as real wages dropped and structural inflation set in. The freeze on prices and wages decreed under Prompt Security Measures in June 1968 was another step in that direction as it entailed ignoring collective bargaining mechanisms mediated by the state (which would be formally dismantled by year's end). As of that moment, and except for a brief interruption in March 1969 when the measures were lifted for three months, an unprecedented repressive stance prevailed in the government's approach to the growing social unrest. It was during that period that what Álvaro Rico has termed "conservative liberalism" was consolidated as the ideology that supported the authoritarian restructuring of the Uruguayan state that would culminate with the 1973 coup d'état and that began in 1968 with changes in the political regime.[12]

In the short term, the government's authoritarianism failed in its aim to bring down the level of confrontation, succeeding instead in pushing large sectors of society into joining the protests. Organized labor continued to hold strikes and demonstrations against the government's economic policies (including a general strike on June 18) while resisting harsh repressive actions, such as the militarization and confinement in military facilities of workers who provided services in areas considered "essential." With respect to the student movement, the second fortnight of June was perhaps more turbulent than the first, with a series of demonstrations, roadblocks, rock throwing incidents, and clashes with the police, as well as hundreds of protesters arrested and dozens injured. It would appear that at this stage the younger high school students (those in the first four years of secondary education) took a backseat as their older peers (those in the last two years of high school) began leading the protests along with university students.[13]

On June 27, serious incidents broke out around the School of Medicine. This led the government to accuse university authorities of allowing the institution to be turned into "a rioting center," in the words of the newly appointed culture minister, Federico García Capurro.[14] Two weeks later, on July 11, the police surrounded dozens of students who had taken refuge at the School of Medicine after meeting with workers from nearby factories and demonstrating in the area. This continued until July 14, when, following difficult negotiations between Pacheco and university officials, the police agreed to allow the students to leave the building in the presence of a judge.[15] However, during those four days hundreds of protesters were arrested in the vicinity of the school, and at least one student received a gunshot wound. Reports of injuries suffered by police officers also began to emerge. The skirmishes, street demonstrations, and other forms of protest continued over the following days, with more young people arrested for violating the Prompt Security Measures. Around that time, the FEUU convention met again to decide the steps to be taken after two months of intense street struggle. These discussions, which are considered in greater depth later, were conducted amid growing unrest and escalating confrontations with police forces.

On July 29, architecture students hung a sign in their school building declaring their solidarity with the civil servants who had been militarized. The sign was deemed offensive by the armed forces. After ordering university authorities to take down the sign, the military moved in on the students. They were met with rocks thrown from the roof of the building, to which they responded with volleys of tear gas. The students put up a new sign and took to the streets, where they clashed immediately with the police. The next day a rally was held in front of the main building of the university to protest these incidents, culminating again with a spontaneous march down Avenida 18 de Julio and new clashes with the police, which left three officers injured.[16]

Similar episodes continued until the beginning of August, when the government's repressive actions peaked in response to repeated demonstrations. In the early hours of August 9, the police raided the main building of the university and the buildings of the Schools of Agronomy, Architecture, Fine Arts, Economics, and Medicine, alleging that it was in connection with its investigation into the whereabouts of Ulysses Pereira Reverbel, director of the state power company. Pereira Reverbel had been kidnapped by the MLN-T in one of the first high-profile actions by this group. The raids were conducted with neither a warrant nor any court officers present, and none of the schools' deans were notified. In the morning, when news of the raids spread, a battle involving a large number of students broke out in downtown Montevideo and continued throughout the day, leaving several people seriously injured, including one student with life-threatening wounds from the impact of a tear-gas canister. In other parts of the city there were also demonstrations and serious incidents between protesters and police. That day marked a breaking point in university-government relations, shattering the hopes still harbored by some of finding a negotiated solution to a crisis that had begun as early as March, at the start of the school year. Near the end of the day, the executive branch decided to request authorization from the Senate to remove from office all members of the university's Central Governing Board (Consejo Directivo Central, or CDC). At the same time, the police imposed a prior censorship requirement on all press releases issued by the university. The next day the Tupamaros freed Pereira Reverbel.[17]

These measures prompted immediate reactions from the university community. On August 10, university authorities declared that holding "certain [government] offices" was incompatible with university "teaching positions."[18] Students continued protesting the measures implemented by the government and occupied the Schools of Medicine and Architecture. Run-ins with the authorities became more frequent, and the way these forces dealt with protesters became increasingly violent. On August 12, a dentistry student, Líber Arce, was shot by police; he died two days later. When news of his death broke, the protests that had been erupting spontaneously in different parts of the city stopped and a large number of people began congregating in the main building of the university, where Arce's wake was being held. Nearly two hundred thousand mourners accompanied his remains to the cemetery in what was one of the largest demonstrations anyone could remember. It was the first in a series of funeral processions for activists slain by repressive forces over the coming months and years. After the demonstration, when night fell, a number of violent incidents occurred in downtown Montevideo, including vandalism and looting. The police stayed away, adopting a position that generated much speculation and gave way to conflicting interpretations. The FEUU and other social organizations condemned these incidents and denied any involvement in them, although the participation of leftist activists cannot be completely ruled out.[19]

Over the following weeks, especially after classes resumed in high schools and UTU centers, which had been suspended since Arce's death, students again took to the streets to protest, throwing incendiary bombs, rocks, and other objects, putting up barricades, and setting cars on fire. These new protests left dozens injured and in police custody. In early September, violent skir-

Figure 1. Wake for Líber Arce held outside the main building of the University of the Republic, August 15, 1968. Photographer unknown, *El Popular* private collection, Centro de Fotografía de Montevideo.

mishes occurred after a brief occupation of a night school, Liceo Nocturno No. 1.[20] Students would gather in the vicinity of the main building of the university and the Instituto Alfredo Vázquez Acevedo (IAVA), a large high school located a block away, as well as around other large high schools and the university's Schools of Medicine and Chemistry. From there they would set off on marches and demonstrations that often ended in clashes. The occupations of educational facilities continued, along with class stoppages and teacher strikes, as well as joint actions involving students and workers in some neighborhoods, against a backdrop of ongoing union struggles that were more or less united. On September 19, following an intense day of labor and student protests near the Legislative Palace (the seat of Parliament), the CNT called a general strike that was marked by new violent incidents and clashes with police forces. On September 20, during a demonstration around university headquarters, Hugo de los Santos, an economics student, was gunned down. Under fire from police forces, which made it impossible for medical assistance to reach him, a UTU student, Susana Pintos, tried to carry him to safety and was also shot. Both students died. What distinguished these incidents from those that came before was the use of pellet guns instead of the service weapons employed until then.[21]

To prevent future excesses, the executive branch closed all schools in Montevideo until October 15 and deployed the military to surround school facilities. This was followed by a series of negotiations and tensions between the executive branch and education authorities, especially those of the university (with a request to Parliament to immediately consider a new law regulating the election of its officers by secret and mandatory vote), which ultimately failed to bring the two sides any closer to an agreement, and classes remained suspended. During that time, student actions did in fact appear to dwindle and protests would only start up again with some force at the beginning of the following school year, in a very different context. However, several accounts suggest that during those seemingly calm months the drop in public unrest was inversely proportional to the radicalization of some groups of mobilized youths, many of whom were by then openly embracing confrontational political positions. These developments and a more in-depth examination of the spiral of violence into which the country was plunged between May and October 1968 are the subject of the following sections.

COORDINATES OF A CYCLE OF PROTEST

At first glance, one can identify certain similarities between the 1968 protest cycle and actions taken by student protesters in previous years. According to Gonzalo Varela Petito's description of events at the IAVA high school, union activities usually began "shortly after classes had started for the year, ... reached their peak momentum by May, ... [and] by October they started to die down" as exams drew near. In fact, when high school students began mobilizing in May 1968, their sometimes-violent practices were compared to the combative approach traditionally taken by students in the streets, dating back at least a decade. Earlier protests had been met with police action too.[22] It was not until mid-June, around the time the Prompt Security Measures were implemented, that the nature of the demands changed and the levels of both student belligerence and police responses increased significantly.

Generally speaking, the cycle of action and reaction between mobilized youths and repressive forces truly "escalated," spurred by the government's growing authoritarianism, pushing vast sectors to the streets and making them more predisposed to confrontation. As discussed later in this book, the ideas that encouraged violence in the streets were already present in some minor groups that operated in student (and labor) circles, but their expansion occurred amid widespread outrage at each excessive use of force by the government in its actions to contain social unrest. It seems clear that both the implementation of Prompt Security Measures and the raiding of university facilities as well as the incensed statements hurled by members of the executive branch provoked students and triggered their violent responses. The killing of three young activists in August and September consolidated that context of aggression, conferring legitimacy on their actions and allowing them to attract new recruits. In this way, the demands made by early protesters, which had to do specifically with education, were abandoned in favor of more political issues and demands for radical social change This set the tone for the movement until its relative decline in late October 1968, and established the forms of struggle of the opposition to the Pacheco government in the coming years. Throughout this cycle of protest young people assumed an increasingly confrontational posture. This was striking even when it came to relatively minor problems—such as the differences between IAVA students and their school principal described by Varela Petito— that had formerly been settled peacefully or would have been resolved by applying traditional principles of authority.[23] Similarly, Antonio Romano notes that the "specific educational aspect" of the way in which conflict was approached in educational institutions was diluted "as political confrontation hardened."[24] It is interesting to note here that this challenge to the most basic rules of action in everyday spaces was a process that occurred together with major changes in the material expressions and symbolic significance of the use of political violence in the streets of Montevideo, and it was closely connected to the unprecedented escalation of repression by the government. A detailed examination of such changes in the pages that follow provides insight into the discussions within the movement and the Left over what these practices meant in the short and long term, both in the protests against the policies of the Pacheco government and in the struggle for the revolutionary transformation of society.

Let us begin this analysis by looking at the physical space in which these violent practices unfolded. First, students clearly sought to turn the whole city of Montevideo into the stage for their protests. From May through the first half of June, most demonstrations were held in and around high school buildings where student unions or some left-wing groups were traditionally stronger. The magnitude of these early demonstrations in low-income neighborhoods suggests that the children of the city's working and lower-middle classes felt a high level of discontent. Only on special occasions did they converge toward downtown Montevideo to protest. This happened, for example, on June 6 and 12, two days that marked the beginning of a phase of greater student confrontation and harsher actions by the police.

From that point on, as university students joined in and protests spread, demonstrators moved into downtown Montevideo, where numerous university facilities, high schools, and UTU buildings were located. Demonstrators would typically gather near the IAVA, the largest high school for junior and senior students, and the main building of the university, only a block away, where the largest rallies were held. The students would begin their rock throwing there, with Channel 4 as their target of choice because of the TV station's support of the government. Then they would start down Avenida 18 de Julio, with some students attempting to put up roadblocks or topple a car or two, and march at least a few blocks in the direction of the oldest part of the city. They would resume their rock throwing there, targeting the Pan Am and General Electric offices, which represented U.S. interests in Uruguay. This was usually where the police sprang more decisively into action. Under Prompt Security Measures, the rally itself would usually be expressly authorized, but this second part of the protest would be more or less spontaneous and therefore in violation of the measures. The year's most violent incidents—that is, those that followed the university raids in August and those that resulted in two deaths in September—also occurred in downtown streets, within the twenty blocks from the IAVA and the main building of the university to the centrally located Plaza Libertad.

The area where both the School of Medicine and the School of Chemistry were located, just steps away from the Legislative

Palace and near factories whose workers were involved in labor conflicts, was another district that saw frequent rallies and clashes. The incidents of June 27 and the more serious ones of July 11 through 14, when the police surrounded the School of Medicine, along with the events of late September, were the highest points of mobilization in these areas, which witnessed numerous demonstrations and clashes with repressive forces. Several violent incidents also took place in the working-class neighborhood of El Cerro and in the area around the School of Architecture. There were also many smaller or shorter demonstrations staged around other education centers in various districts of Montevideo, and while it is not possible to review them all here, Varela Petito estimates, based on information from the Interior Ministry, that there were as many as three hundred protests, or an average of two per day, from May to October, the five months with the highest number of actions.[25]

The choice of spaces described very briefly above seems logical, at least at first glance, because they were easily accessible and were natural gathering places for students (and workers in conflict) and because of the increasingly central role the university assumed in the defense of public freedoms, against the government, and in favor of social change. However, when and where to demonstrate was a frequent issue of debate. Analyzing these debates allows us to begin tracing the conflicts that existed within the student movement and its relations with the other groups that opposed Pacheco's authoritarianism. This provides a first understanding of the changes in the forms of protest introduced by the activists who burst onto the public scene in 1968, not only from a political and ideological point of view but also in terms of the impact of the cultural trends embraced by their peers in the rest of the world, which shaped a generational identity.

The characteristics of these student actions were often discussed, for example, by the members of the university's CDC. The exchanges between those who wanted to limit the locations and times of protests, on the one hand, and the young protesters who sought to expand such limits, on the other, challenge the image of intergenerational harmony that is sometimes said to be a defining feature of Uruguay's 1968 student movement. It is often claimed that, in contrast to their peers in France and the United States, activists in this movement did not question either the schools' authorities or their regulations and that the movement was characterized by a strong sense of "university responsibility" based on the students' long-standing participation in the university's joint governing bodies and the cherished autonomy enjoyed by the institution, two typical features of Latin America's university tradition.[26] In general, this is an accurate picture; students, alumni, and faculty often agreed on issues regarding university politics. Because members of all groups participated in joint governing bodies, students did not blame faculty directly for institutional or educational shortcomings. Several sociologists—an emerging field at the time—noted this feature of young Uruguayan university students with surprise. Aldo E. Solari, a pioneer of the discipline in Uruguay, observed this in 1968 with respect to the progressive increase in the number of years required to obtain a degree, which meant students were entering the labor market at a later age, a factor that seemed to go against the repeated calls by students to forge a "popular university."[27] At the same time, with regard specifically to politics, a majority of students, alumni, and faculty (at least those that expressed themselves through the joint government bodies) opposed the national government. This opposition was in line with their traditional defense of the university's autonomy with respect to political power, or drew on more radical ideas regarding the role of intellectuals in what they believed were imminent revolutionary processes.

This, however, should not overshadow the internal differences and the multiple tensions that marked, for example, the relations between organized students and the university rector, Óscar Maggiolo, at the start of his term in 1966. The drafting and discussion of the proposed university reform known as Plan Maggiolo offers a particularly interesting case for understanding the complexity of these relations, as student leaders were actively involved at every stage of the process, continuously questioning both the content of the reform and the motivations of university authorities who supported the proposal.[28] Two other examples of these differences were the adverse reaction of the FEUU to Maggiolo's contacts with president-elect Óscar Gestido in January and February 1967 and the rector's temporary resignation in October over the students' unauthorized placement of a sign on the front of the main building of the university.[29] By the end of the year, after the implementation of the Prompt Security Measures in October and the unexpected death of President Gestido in December, Maggiolo hardened his stance against the Pacheco government, joining the National Movement for the Defense of Public Liberties (Movimiento Nacional de Defensa de las Libertades Públicas, or MNDLP) along with other political, religious, and intellectual figures who sought to form an opposition front. In 1968, relations between the rector and the students improved as the former took a firm stand in defense of university autonomy and allowed the university to participate in demonstrations and assume a key role in furthering progressive social change.[30]

Nevertheless, there were several discussions in the CDC over the use of public spaces, which revealed diverging viewpoints regarding the decision to breach the limits set both by the city's street protest practices and by the unprecedented repression of the government and its new regulations. In early July, for example, student delegates urged the university to hold a public demonstration to show "its militant presence in this struggle that the Uruguayan people as a whole are waging for their freedom." The rector and several members of the CDC approved the spirit of the motion and proposed that, with the aim of joining forces, a call be issued to participate in the rally that was being organized by the MNDLP, "not marching down Avenida 18 de Julio, because we know how [against] it the police were even before the Prompt Security Measures, but from the university to the Legislative Palace, down Sierra Street." A student representative, Luis Carriquiry, agreed on the need to join the rallies but made one important "qualification": "We believe that, despite the difficulties that exist, we should try to first march down 18 de Julio. It has become a tradition for demonstrations as important as this to be staged on 18 de Julio. Not staging it on 18 de Julio would rob the demonstration of some of its strength or shine and it would look like we were doing things a bit on the sly."

Also, when the rector said that demonstrating after 9 p.m. had been "completely ruled out," the students declared that "the demonstration will almost certainly be held at night." As no agreement could be reached, the resolution was postponed. Regardless of what eventually happened (the police denied the authorization to demonstrate in the street and the MNDLP held its rally at the university), what this example highlights is the students' insistence that backing down would, in the words of Pedro Sprechman, a student delegate in the CDC, "seem like a compromise or like we were accepting a status quo and even accepting the violation of a constitutional norm.... What we have here is a matter of principles and that is what we are defending."[31]

These positions were clearly connected to different political stances that are examined in greater detail later. For now, I want to note the generational divide that separated the prudent stance adopted by Maggiolo and other CDC members and the zeal with which students reaffirmed their right to demonstrate when and where they wanted.[32] Some considered it unsafe or unnecessarily confrontational, but it is clear that marching at night down the still elegant Avenida 18 de Julio held strong symbolic value for young people, for whom roaming the city freely, going out at night, and having certain spaces where adults could not control them were synonymous with the passage into adulthood.[33] In denouncing the repression of a Saturday night march, UTU student Raúl Seoane boasted to the *Marcha* reporter interviewing him, "We're the only ones who dare demonstrate on that day and at that hour."[34]

Similarly, the consolidation as of 1968 of street music festivals and other artistic expressions furthered by young left-wing groups, in particular the UJC, can also be interpreted as a generational conquering of public spaces.[35] Another example is the counter-courses that were held, as these were convened by students and were spaces where they interacted with teachers under conditions of greater equality and in what was a clear challenge to the institutional authority expressed in the more formal context of the classroom and the curriculum.[36]

The students' determination to take over certain physical spaces had generational connotations, and this was evident not only in the streets but also within school facilities. Varela Petito observes this with respect to the numerous conflicts sparked between students and IAVA authorities over the use of the school's gym, the placement of signs, and the holding of student assemblies.[37] A high school student interviewed by Copelmayer and Díaz a few months after these events described it eloquently.

> The assemblies were held primarily during school hours. We asked for permission, and if we didn't get it, we tried to hold them anyway. There were classes that went out to a square to hold their assemblies. We even used the auditorium, which until then had been used as a meeting place for the old *pelucones* [conservatives]. We opened the door—when they didn't give us the key—and we had our class assemblies in the room.[38]

Some of the protest strategies can be linked to the age of the participants. Several demonstrations combined the desire to challenge authority with a markedly playful tone that was most likely connected to an old festive tradition of European universities, which was still present in Latin American student life and was frequently associated with political protests.[39] In 1968, this spirit was often expressed through comedy, such as in a humorous sign put up in the School of Architecture in late July that mocked the armed forces and prompted their intervention, or the more absurd one that read, "High school occupied by Nico's gang," mentioned in the weekly *Marcha* in June.[40] The flash demonstrations—one of the preferred actions staged between June and October 1968—were also typically youthful in style, as groups amassed and dispersed quickly to take repressive forces by surprise. The impression that these young activists gave the people of Montevideo was that they were taking over the streets with their disruptive actions. Another common protest practice was the snatching of police caps and holding them up as trophies or as tangible evidence of a victory, however minor. The urge to strip the enemy of such a symbolic element was seen as a form of humiliating the enemy. In at least two accounts from days in which large clashes occurred—including the first shooting on Avenida 18 de Julio on June 6 and the incident that resulted in the death of Líber Arce in August—activists mention cap snatching and a desire to flaunt it as a symbolic victory over the police.[41]

Many photographs from that time show demonstrators, for the most part young men, carrying out these actions with bravado, dressed in clothes that were bolder than those their elders and some of their peers commonly wore. The adults who supported such acts saw them as an exhibition of "virility" that was considered a typical feature of youth activists. Most, however, did not go as far as Hermógenes Álvarez, dean of the School of Medicine, who suggested that the "presence of a young female activist" was the reason a male student was willing to "go unarmed against two policemen who drew their guns at him."[42] With this and other gendered references, such arguments tended to explain leftist activism as a product of the natural outrage that injustice prompted in (male) youths. In this way, they exalted the physical dimension of activism, the image of the body in action, the strength and drive that were commonly associated with an early stage in life, as well as its psychological features of courage, commitment to a cause, and lack of concern for the material consequences of one's actions. This rhetoric usually looked to the past, especially to the Latin American wars for independence, to explain the insurgent roots of 1960s youths. In the words of Carlos Quijano, veteran editor of *Marcha*, these young activists joined the "legion of silent warriors who, in the right or in the wrong, were willing to give their lives for their country."[43] There were points of contact between these interpretations and those of some of the detractors of the student movement, including the interior minister himself, who portrayed young people as idealists or innocents in order to call

Figure 2. Rally at Plaza Libertad, on Avenida 18 de Julio, in downtown Montevideo, 1968. Photographer unknown. *El Popular* private collection, Centro de Fotografía de Montevideo.

attention to the responsibility of the adults who unleashed, encouraged, or took advantage of their rebelliousness (as university authorities were criticized for doing).[44]

The documents of the FEUU categorically rejected these interpretations, with particular force after the death of Líber Arce.

> We are not playing a game when we expose ourselves to tear gas canisters, to jail, and to bullets. Those who have always, out of convenience or hypocrisy, carelessly dismissed our activism, painting it out to be an impulsive reaction, know today that we are willing to risk our own lives to defend the interests of the people.[45]

Some statements by the student movement celebrated the relationship between political commitment and physical action, for example, calling on fellow students to confront the police and advocating a strategy based on "rocks and bodies willing to shout the truth."[46] As I discuss later, this was a controversial view that reflected the political positions at the root of some of the bitterest conflicts within the Left.

ON VIOLENCE

Before analyzing the disagreements prompted by this widespread view of student mobilization, let us look at the evidence available on the actual use of violent methods in 1968 and how it relates to the government's escalating repression. Organized students argued in favor of certain confrontational tactics, such as rock throwing, but they rejected others, especially the use of firearms and anything that could injure others (although a high school activist unabashedly admitted, "It's pretty naive to think that if you throw rocks at a bus you're not going to hurt any passengers").[47] Other tactics, such as the burning of cars, were even more controversial. Although the use of such tactics was generally denied at the time (in the CDC, for example, student delegates tacitly allowed other members to brand those who carried out such actions "outside provocateurs") some later accounts confirm that students did engage in them.[48]

The files of the police agency DNII that are accessible contain numerous references to detentions of young people, many of them underage, who were armed with rocks, flammable chemicals, incendiary bombs, and objects such as sticks, branches, scraps of iron, and pieces of broken sidewalks. Except in those cases in which they had been caught in flagrante, the detainees denied that they meant to use such materials, claiming that they were holding them for someone, that they had forgotten they had them in their pockets, or simply that they did not know why they had them. Students made similar claims when caught with liquids and scarves intended to combat the effects of tear gas, especially after the Metropolitan Guard began to be called in to control demonstrations and protesters perfected their strategies to face these forces. Their obvious aim was to deny any participation in the nonauthorized marches, but the repeated references to certain detainees found in police records and the fact that many of them can be identified as well-known leftist activists suggest that they did in fact participate in such actions and that they frequently resorted to violence.[49] At this stage there were no deaths among the military or police, and none suffered permanent injuries, although in many cases students did target them.[50]

The lack of serious injuries among officers reveals that, despite repeated accusations by police forces and government authorities, the use of firearms was rare among participants in the student movement at this time. In July, when the university rector and the dean of the School of Medicine requested authorization to visit a policeman who had allegedly been shot at one such demonstration, the culture minister and President Pacheco replied that they still had to confirm whether or not he had been wounded by a gun.[51] The interior minister was also unable to give the names of the officers who had allegedly been shot by students in September.[52] Similarly, no handguns or shotguns were included among the weapons seized during the 1968 raids on university buildings. The confiscated items—rocks and other projectiles, chemicals, "explosive cartridges"—were later exhibited to the public in an attempt to show the students' "violent nature."[53] Among the DNII files only one document refers to abundant ammunition supposedly left behind by students after the occupation of Liceo Nocturno No. 1 in September. The investigation led to charges being brought against an individual who had no connection to that school but whom the students had approached for firearms and in whose house the police found a handgun, bullets, gunpowder, and instructions for making Molotov cocktails.[54]

In any case, it is clear that the physical evidence obtained by the police was not enough to justify the use of repressive force on the grounds that the officers were acting in "legitimate self-defense," especially after the three student deaths. As the Blanco Party senator Carlos Furest said in a Senate discussion, "Three to zero is too negative a score to have to keep hearing such nonsense."[55] The governing party thus resorted to portraying the student movement as part of a plan coordinated with trade unions and other political forces to destabilize the country. In the words of Minister Jiménez de Aréchaga, "Agitation spurs repression, which in turn sparks increasing agitation.... I must admit that it is a veritable campaign to bring about the revolution and to do it without much bloodshed."[56] The minister's aim was to evade his responsibility in the incidents that had greatly exceeded the traditional forms of dealing with social conflict, but his statements drew attention to the relationship between student unrest and police repression, an aspect that cannot be avoided when considering the 1968 cycle of protest and violence.

We must consider to what extent each side—demonstrators and repressive forces—modified their attitudes and pushed the limits as the cycle of violence grew, each in response to the actions of the other side. The flash demonstrations, for example, clearly emerged as a form of protest that "because of the ease and discretion with which they were organized" succeeded in "preventing the police from being alerted" and thus from arresting demonstrators.[57] The students were fully aware of the meaning and effect of their actions, and this often sparked internal arguments over the advisability of using this or that method. But let us leave these discussions aside for a moment and highlight instead the level of reflection evidenced by the radicalized young activists interviewed by Copelmayer and Díaz:

F: We wanted a productive violence, one that we could get something out of. If we had a run-in with the police and we damaged a van or one of them was hurt by a rock, it was reported in the newspapers, on the radio.

D: We saw no other method than that to make our opposition more shocking: standing in front of a bus and breaking all its windows ... Our goal was to throw rocks at the bus ... so that the bus driver would go back to the company and say, "Our windows were shattered by students." Management or whoever ran the company was then going to realize that there was a student power, a force that was there, fighting.

J: There is a fundamental difference between the first demonstrations in the month of May and the second demonstrations, which were more violent. I remember that in the first demonstrations students ... were supposed to keep advancing when they tried to stop them, but they weren't supposed to attack those who repressed them.

D: We couldn't go on peacefully demonstrating when we were being repressed with gas and, later, with bullets and shrapnel. That clearly showed that students represented a powerful force, which was playing its triggering role, as we called it, to perfection.[58]

The police, in turn, warned in July that students were looking to confuse repressive forces with their "operative methods" and asked people to "immediately" move away from the hubs of agitation "to avoid being arrested."[59] These examples show that, when faced with unprecedented levels of street violence, both sides sought to gain ground by anticipating the actions of their opponent. The police certainly had a great advantage as intelligence services often enabled them to learn the students' plans in detail and receive military advice to prepare their operations. It should be noted at this time that the military, authorized under Prompt Security Measures to assist in defending the "public order," intervened directly only twice and that its public image was still positive, in contrast to the increasingly discredited police.[60]

In terms of organization, it appears that until mid-September demonstrations were controlled by the local police precincts, which responded when they were alerted that a conflict had broken out in their jurisdiction. One such event ended with the death of Líber Arce as a result of injuries inflicted by a police officer from the Ninth Precinct who was attempting to repress a flash demonstration near the School of Veterinary Medicine.[61] Police officers generally showed up on foot or in police cars or wagons, with their .38-caliber guns and regular nightsticks, and were sometimes backed by firefighters if there were barricades or burning cars; they were careful to document property damage to stores and neighboring houses.[62] At this stage, the Metropolitan Guard, which would later become a symbol of the authoritarianism of the Pacheco government, with their helmets (which earned them the names *casquitos,* or small helmets, and *marcianitos,* or little Martians) and their clubs and vehicles for transporting detainees (known as *roperos,* or wardrobes, and *chanchitas,* or piggies), only stepped in to back the police during large demonstrations or complicated incidents. There were also attempts to use horses and dogs, but these were not as effective as water cannons (known as *guanacos*) and tear gas, although these could backfire depending on the wind. While some student accounts indicate that there were differences in the attitudes of these two forces, it would appear that both the officers from the police precincts and those from "la Metro" (the Metropolitan Guard) were often aggressive and aimed for the body, which would explain the high number of injuries reported once repression was stepped up. It appears also that the weapons used in the first stage were not as lethal as the pellet guns that were used in late September, which, paradoxically, resulted in their use being justified because of their greater accuracy.[63] Two additional deaths that followed would prove just how mistaken, or cynical, that argument was.

The historian Clara Aldrighi argues that the influence of the United States was a key factor in increasing the Uruguayan state's capacity for social control during this period. As of the mid-1960s, the police received training and significant logistical assistance to combat the initial inefficiency diagnosis that had been issued by the U.S. advisers of the Public Security Program (PSP). By mid-1968, according to Aldrighi, the results were palpable, and a growing number of police officers were using the weapons introduced by this program. This included the wooden batons, based on a U.S. design and manufactured domestically, that so many activists were beaten with over subsequent months. Also from the United States came the shotguns used to kill Susana Pintos and Hugo de los Santos in September, which had arrived the previous month in a shipment of fifty riot control weapons ordered by the PSP. Moreover, Alfredo Rivero, the colonel who commanded the Metropolitan Guard and gave the order that day to fire at demonstrators, had been trained in "riot control" under that same program. Although at that time there was no accurate information on the size and forms of PSP operations, much of the opposition to Pacheco linked the presence of U.S. advisers to the rapid increase in the repressive power of the police.[64]

Concerns about escalating violence (and the lack of reliable data) were evident in Senate discussions during this period. After several false starts, legislators finally succeeded in bringing Minister Jiménez de Aréchaga to the Senate to explain the police actions under the Prompt Security Measures. These discussions give us an idea of politicians' positions on these matters. First, the focus on students and the university must be highlighted as it reflects their growing public importance after the issuing of the decree implementing the measures, which made no mention of them. Second, there was a cross-party group of senators (several from the governing Colorado Party, some from the Blanco Party, and the Communist Enrique Rodríguez) who justified or at least explained the students' actions and the positions of the university. From vastly different ideological and philosophical principles, these legislators argued in support of the "idealism" of young people—an idea in vogue at the time—and accused the government of curtailing their ability to fully realize themselves and form part of society. Some drew on their personal experience as parents of students who were participating in the movement; others appealed to their fellow legislators to remember their own rebelliousness in their youth. They all pointed to police brutality and the government's authoritarianism as central to the problem at hand. Accordingly, Zelmar Michelini, the Colorado senator who led the questioning of Minister Jiménez de Aréchaga, asked for his resignation, accusing him of targeting the university and of having turned, together with the chief of police, into a "spur" for students and workers.[65]

On the other side were those who agreed with the minister that the origin of the violence was to be found in certain minority sectors (some three hundred activists backed by university authorities) that were hoping for a conflict in order to destabilize the government. As in the DNII reports, these governing party

Figure 3. Demonstrators resist a tear-gas attack in the area around the School of Medicine and the Legislative Palace, September 5, 1968. Photographer unknown. *El Popular* private collection, Centro de Fotografía de Montevideo.

politicians portrayed the demonstrations of medical and chemistry students and of workers at the Bao soap factory and the Frigorífico Nacional meatpacking plant on September 18 as an attempt to create chaos in parliament, in preparation for the call to "go at it with full force" in downtown Montevideo over the next two days. As proof, they pointed to the items seized by the police and the "first aid room" set up in the main building of the university in anticipation of the September 20 clashes. Although the minister made several attempts to analyze the student movement from a psychological and sociological perspective, his aim was to steer the blame away from the repressive forces and ultimately conclude that the police had acted in "legitimate self-defense" and with the weapons necessary to confront their dangerous attackers. It is worth noting that the origin of the weapons was never clarified. He repeatedly compared the situation in Uruguay to that in France in order to stress the appropriateness of the actions by the police and to highlight the virulence of local youths. Whereas the "universal" issues faced by young people were used to justify the actions of the student movement, the minister drew on foreign examples to claim that the movement was removed from national problems. Thus, one of the movement's leaders was presented as "the Uruguayan Cohn-Bendit," a homegrown "golden youth" with no reason to rebel other than being inspired by Cuba and influenced by Leninism. Adults, and in particular high school teachers and university professors, were similarly presented as instigators of youth violence. It should be noted that the guerrilla group MLN-T was never mentioned as a factor in the protests.[66]

In more general terms, these Senate sessions proved the difficulty of finding common ground and a solution that would halt the cycle of violence. By then—well into October—students had already been back in school for two weeks, following the suspension of classes and the use of military troops to surround school buildings. The government saw the waning of public protests as proof of the immediate effectiveness of the measures. In fact, during the previous months student activists had for that same reason been unwilling to stage strikes or any other form of protest that would have interrupted classes. However, during the weeks when students were forced to stay away from schools and universities, the more militant groups continued to meet and find ways to protest. It was then that many of them realized that they had reached a watershed moment and that they needed to engage in more committed actions and embrace violent methods. Upon returning to class, they began spreading this message among fellow students. This sparked new controversies within the political parties of the Left that had an active presence among students. The ground was laid for a climate of great confrontation that would prevail in the coming years. Chapter 2 assesses the impact of the 1968 student demonstrations within the Left and the resistance movement against Pacheco.

TWO

Discussions

THE UNIONS AND THE MOVEMENT

There is no question that 1968 marked a watershed in Uruguayan politics. Even then, many contemporaries agreed that they were witnessing an unprecedented explosion of participation by students at all levels of education. In Uruguay, as in other countries in Latin America, students had been active in national politics since at least the first decades of the twentieth century, so their political involvement was nothing new in the 1960s. What, then, was so surprising? To begin with, there were the numbers, in terms of both student participation in the demonstrations and the almost uninterrupted presence of these youths on the streets. Another factor was the level of violence deployed. And finally, there was a subjective element added by such fast-paced activity, which operated to create a very short-term "memory effect" that dominated the perception of participants and observers alike, rendering almost unrecognizable the spaces and forms of student activism from just a year before.

Let me try to identify what made the 1968 movement novel vis-à-vis existing unions and previous modes of participation and what elements established continuity with past forms of student activism. Several studies have emphasized that, in contrast to what happened in France and the United States, for example, Uruguay's mobilizations in 1968 did not explicitly challenge old unions, nor did they result in the formation of new ones.[1] On the contrary, the first demonstrations in Montevideo were launched from within the more or less stable organizations of the previous period, such as the CESU and the FEUU. However, the movement soon brought to the forefront a number of explicit criticisms of earlier forms of organizing and fighting, which, in turn, took student activism to new levels within just a few months. As Mercedes Espínola, a member of the CESU governing committee at the time, recalled in 1998, "What characterized '68 was that … it swept all traditional structures away."[2] And this applies both to the CESU, which did not have much influence beyond pro-UJC circles at the high school level, and to the FEUU, which had a long-standing tradition and was well respected within the university and outside it. In the following paragraphs, I provide a brief history of each union and the most significant changes that occurred in 1968.

There are no historical studies of the high school student movement, but scattered references indicate that there was a tradition of organizing by school that can probably be traced to the early twentieth century, when secondary education was still under the purview of the University of the Republic. Until the mid-1950s, the organizations that brought together students from high schools in Montevideo and the rest of the country were still part of the FEUU.[3] Students in the last two years of high school (*preparatorios*, that is, preparation for higher education) were particularly active, but there were several events, such as the demonstrations in support of the Cuban Revolution in the early 1960s, in which students from all grades participated. These years saw growth in high school enrollment, with thousands of students from working-class families gaining access to secondary education for the first time. This, in turn, increased the public visibility of student activism in a wider swath of the city.[4]

There are also no accounts of the history of the CESU. From the documentation that is available, it can be gathered that the CESU was formed in the mid-1960s and held its second national convention in June 1966 amid tensions with some of its member centers.[5] At that time, the CESU focused on coordinating the actions of pro-Communist student groups in several high schools in Montevideo, and in the rest of the country it had regional organizations, at least according to its draft bylaws.[6] A number of small more radical leftist groups were also active in some high schools, while in others groups aligned with the traditional parties predominated as late as 1967. In most cases, there were union organizations—such as the Asociación de Estudiantes de Preparatorios and Agrupación de Estudiantes del Zorrilla (a high school)—that represented the interests and concerns of the student body in areas as diverse as sports, culture, and relations with education authorities. These unions, however, also participated in the wider discussions on national and global affairs that engaged the country's various political parties, which in turn vied for leadership of the student groups in order to extend their influence. To a certain extent, these forms of organization (which for the purposes of this analysis could be called "traditional") were sanctioned or at least tolerated by secondary education authorities, who viewed them as learning grounds for certain citizens' rites and political practices, such as voting, public speaking, debating, and propaganda. In fact, many politicians from parties across the spectrum, including the Blanco and Colorado Parties, had been initiated into politics through participation in the student movement.[7]

It was in those spaces where students began to protest the bus fare increase that led to the 1968 protests. The CESU, as noted earlier, played an important role in this first stage and joined every student action, including some with a clearly violent streak and many that originated in high schools where Communist influence was not strong. It was at this point that the CESU reached its greatest public visibility and activism among secondary school students peaked. Toward mid-May, however, the CESU leadership felt that negotiations with the authorities over subsidized bus fares were going well and called on students to demobilize. Many high schools ignored that call, thus demonstrating that student involvement had exceeded the circles of influence of the CESU and that this organization could no longer make decisions on behalf of the student body. As a student interviewed by Copelmayer and Díaz during those months explained, "The rank and file overran the [CESU]."[8] At the same time, the traditional parties had lost almost all their power of persuasion in the schools that they had previously controlled while the old union associations had taken a backseat.[9] How were high school students' concerns channeled then? Who harnessed their fighting spirit?

Varela Petito's account in the case of the IAVA high school illustrates the dynamics that by mid-1968 would have a major impact on the structures that had existed up to that time both within and outside the CESU. He distinguishes several stages, with a clear turning point occurring as repression was stepped up in June with the Prompt Security Measures: "First, the normal operation of the union's old proceedings and bodies; second, the establishment (as a result of the Prompt Security Measures) of a mobilizations committee that coexisted in conflict with the old structure; third, growing protests that neither respond[ed] to nor care[d] about the statutory regulations of the past."[10]

In contrast to the groups connected with the traditional parties, the CESU and the other unions continued to participate more or less actively in student struggles. But they could no longer claim to be the sole representatives of the movement and had to compete with other, more radical groups, both old and new, whose influence was becoming more widespread. These groups began to act essentially autonomously, furthering various activities, calling for occupying or walking out of school buildings, and coordinating with other student and labor groups with similar ideologies.[11] In contrast to traditional unions and the CESU, whose draft bylaws established that decision making would be in the hands of the governing bodies and that the minority would be subordinate to the majority, these more radical groups did not initially aspire to consolidate a structure or unify all their actions.[12] To a great extent, this resulted in an explicit rejection of the former ways of operation. This is how the students consulted by Copelmayer and Díaz put it:

> The CESU never really existed as such. It was always a stamp, not a structure.... There's no sense in having this new coordinator if it only replaces the CESU with another governing apparatus unconnected with the masses and maintaining an ultra-revolutionary stance. We're not interested in that. The previous system of elections was not working at all, sort of like the national system. Elections have no place here.[13]

These criticisms gradually gave way to alternative forms of organizing. In addition to activists from the vocational schools, who prided themselves on having no permanent authorities of any kind, the most representative example of the new modes of organization adopted by high school students was the Revolutionary Student Front (Frente Estudiantil Revolucionario, or FER). By 1968, the FER had a major presence in the IAVA and was also active in other high schools.[14] According to the very readable and detailed account of Varela Petito, its origins can be traced to 1967, when, spurred by some members of the youth division of the MRO, who were moving away from their alliance with the Communists of the FIDEL, the group participated in the regular IAVA union elections on a separate ticket.[15] These elections divided the FER, and the breakaway sector formed the short-lived Anti-Imperialist Student Group (Grupo Estudiantil Antiimperialista), which openly rejected elections and other "liberal" practices and proclaimed its Latin Americanist inspiration, even in its choice of name. At this point there were other radical leftist groups, including the Proletarian Socialist Unification Movement (Movimiento de Unificación Socialista Proletaria, or MUSP), which had splintered from the Socialist Youth a few years earlier; Christian groups such as Student Union Action (Acción Gremial Estudiantil, or AGE), which took a "third position" (*tercerista*), neither capitalist nor socialist, in international politics; Communist-leaning groups such as Ideas; and groups such as Reaffirmation (Reafirmación) that were linked to the traditional parties. All of these groups had a significant presence in the period immediately preceding the 1968 protests. They were joined at the beginning of that year by the Independent Action Front (Frente de Acción Independiente, or FAI), which was, in Varela Petito's words, "a fresh and open organization with a youthful spirit" that took a centrist position and attracted many Reafirmación followers and students who had no political experience or had just enrolled in the IAVA.[16]

Álvaro Gascue recalls that at an assembly held in May 1968 the remaining FER activists, already dissociated from the MRO, called attention to the struggle of the sugarcane cutters who had marched to Montevideo. They invited them to attend the meeting and convinced fellow students to issue a statement in support of them.[17] In the IAVA elections held that month, the FAI secured a surprising second place, very close behind Reafirmación, which always won in school-wide votes because it attracted the less politicized students. In June, Reafirmación for the first time lost in a general assembly. Shortly after, it was revealed that an important contingent of the FAI had left it to join the FER, which up to that time had been a minority composed of activists of various radical tendencies. From that point forward, and with the Prompt Security Measures in place, the FER consolidated its influence among IAVA students, facing competition only from Communist sectors, amid frequent and heated discussions that bore little resemblance to the "traditional" unionism that had prevailed just a few months before. At the urging of the FER, which had no bylaws or formal leadership, IAVA student activists began operating through a system of class assemblies that sought the direct involvement of the rest of the student body in every discussion and decision. The expansion of this system, which also appears to have operated in other high schools even before it was introduced in the IAVA, was further proof of the weakening of previous union structures during the 1968 mobilizations.[18]

The history of the FER is particularly significant because of the paths taken by its members and its subsequent influence on the more radical Left, which is discussed later. What I would like to highlight here are two factors that made the FER's sudden rise in the IAVA possible and explain to a great extent the explosive public presence of a radicalized student movement as of June 1968.

As Varela Petito aptly shows, there was, on the one hand, a host of new activists with little political experience and, on the other, small ideology-based groups that were critical of the mechanisms of representation of "traditional" unions and whose discourses and forms of organization offered alternatives for these youths. The two elements combined to produce an intricate interweaving of concerns and interests. This can be seen, for example, in an issue of the FER mouthpiece, *Barricada,* where calls to engage in "popular libertarian violence" are featured alongside more mundane demands concerning the use of the school's auditorium and gym, which were framed within the larger issue of student participation in secondary education government.[19]

In this case, the new activists were middle- and upper-middle-class students (the majority of those who reached the final stage of secondary education) who had been attracted to politics through globally circulating ideas that associated youth with protest. The same ideas appear to have influenced young people in lower-class neighborhoods who started to mobilize as they saw their chances of individual and collective fulfillment curtailed in a country that was sinking into a historic social and economic crisis and under a government that responded with unprecedented authoritarianism to the sectors unwilling to pay the costs. This was the gateway to activism for thousands of young people, whose effective radicalization was the result of both government repression and the skill with which some groups were able to channel their discontent.

Something similar occurred in the FEUU, which, in contrast to unions in secondary education, offered a more stable framework for participation and had a legitimate voice because of its involvement in the university's government. The FEUU participated in decision making on matters of direct concern to students and was respected nationally. Along with the increase in the number of university students—22 percent between 1961 and 1965—the 1960s had brought many changes within the FEUU.[20] Near the end of the previous decade, during the struggle for a new university charter, the FEUU had been dominated by anarchist groups and had adopted a *tercerista* position with respect to the two leading world powers of the Cold War. In line with that tradition, several student leaders initially showed little enthusiasm for the path taken by Cuba after the Revolution. Socialist students, however, celebrated the Cuban feat and moved closer to the Communists to consolidate a new Marxist hegemony.[21]

This change in the FEUU's orientation and its many solidarity actions with revolutionary movements across the continent turned it into the target of choice for the diatribes of conservative sectors and right-wing student organizations that employed violent methods.[22] In the late 1960s, its commitment to regional and global issues was strengthened by its involvement in the founding of the Latin American Continental Organization of Students (Organización Continental Latinoamericana de Estudiantes, or OCLAE) in Havana in 1966 and its decision to join the International Union of Students (IUS, headquartered in Prague) in 1967.[23] At the same time, Uruguayan university students protested against the economic policies aligned with IMF guidelines that had been implemented by successive governments since the beginning of the 1960s. They also joined various attempts to expand the social base of support for labor union demands, including most notably the People's Congress in 1965 and the establishment the following year of a unified federation representing all of the country's unions (the CNT).[24] The highest points of student mobilization in 1967 had been the demonstrations against the Organization of American States (OAS) conference held in Punta del Este in April, the demands for a larger education budget in June, and the OCLAE congress held in July in Montevideo.[25] Around that time, a brief period of relatively good relations between university authorities and the national government was followed by raids on university schools and some clashes with the police, which triggered increasingly heated responses from students. The next year, however, the FEUU was slow to join in the actions staged by high school students in the streets. University students held their first demonstration in June, focusing on budgetary demands, often linked to the need to strengthen the university as an institution of social change, a widespread idea in the university community, rooted in a Latin American intellectual tradition that can be traced at least as far back as the 1918 Córdoba university reform.[26] The turning point came when police raided several university buildings in August 1968 under the pretext of looking for a government official who had been kidnapped by the Tupamaros. This episode, which was a gross infringement on the university's traditional independence and self-governance, fueled the spirit of protest and precipitated the announced rupturing of relations between the university and the Pacheco government. In addition to the generational differences seen in joint decision-making bodies, what is interesting to highlight here are the various reactions sparked by these incidents among students and their impact on the way the FEUU operated.

As noted by Jorge Landinelli, who participated in the Communist wing of the federation's leadership, the FEUU was very "loosely" organized and regulated by a "federal agreement" legitimized by almost four decades of uninterrupted operation. The convention, with a representation of eleven delegates per center of study (which at the time included all the colleges and institutes of the university plus the high school teachers' training college, Instituto de Profesores Artigas, or IPA), was the FEUU's highest governing body whose mandate included defining union policies and electing the secretariat, which was tasked with executive duties. The federal council was the decision-making body for day-to-day matters of common interest to all centers, which had two delegates and one vote each. In addition to these, there were central committees that dealt with the different areas of action of the FEUU.[27]

The convention was held twice in 1968: first in June, in response to the Prompt Security Measures, with a call to "take to the streets to agitate in direct and combative confrontation," and then in July, with the aim of assessing the progress of the actions taken.[28] Between these conventions a mobilizations committee was appointed to assist the general secretary in making quick executive decisions in a climate of great conflict. According to journalist Carlos Bañales and Enrique Jara, this committee was composed of seven members representing the different tendencies in the FEUU: "Three positions were filled by Communist activists and the rest by representatives of the radical line, one of them from the MAPU." Based on a list of nine names published in the weekly newspaper *Brecha* in 1998, these seven students can be identified as Rodrigo Arocena, César Baraibar, Barrett Díaz, Marcelino Guerra (who was later arrested and replaced by Jorge Salerno), Raúl Latorre, Roberto Markarian, and Jorge Ramada.[29] For the first time in several years, Communist positions (represented by Díaz, Latorre, and Markarian) began to lose ground to the combined force of the other groups, which, despite their many differences, agreed to support more confrontational methods of struggle.

As of June and July 1968, the differences within the student movement became increasingly evident in the modes of protest themselves. Although formally the direction of the movement continued in the hands of the FEUU, where the Communists retained a relative majority, several observers noted a tendency toward a less centralized mode of decision making with respect to actions. According to Bañales and Jara, many of "the demonstrations that began both at the university's main building and in other areas of the city were decided on impulse by the groups who staged them." This depiction is similar to what Varela Petito says regarding the flash demonstrations of high school students, which he describes as the reflection of a movement that was to a great extent decentralized, lacking a single authority, and riddled with internal differences, so that "minority factions or those unhappy with a majority position" expressed their discontent on their own, without consulting the rest or respecting the limits set in assemblies or decision-making bodies.[30]

As these novel forms of protest spread, the differences among the groups participating in the student movement became more pronounced. As noted above, in the CESU's scope of influence the split became evident toward the end of May. According to Landinelli, by June 1 there were thirteen high schools controlled by groups who accused the CESU of "selling out" and of "trying to stop the struggle by holding back this stage of mobilization."[31] The students interviewed by Copelmayer and Díaz did not hesitate to denounce it for "backing down," "compromising," and "betraying" the cause.[32] Esteban Valenti, CESU general secretary and UJC member, claimed that "these *compañeros* [fellow unionists] who are announcing that they won't clear out of the schools ... all they're doing is fragmenting the CESU and the student movement in general." These controversies began to be aired in street signs.[33] Clearly, high school students no longer operated according to coordinated decisions made from above by any one group. In contrast, at the university level, while some decentralization initiatives were proposed within the FEUU—especially by anarchist groups in the School of Fine Arts—the organization maintained a coherent structure, united behind a common set of demands that touched on both university and national issues.

This can probably be explained by the long tradition of interaction that the various sectors of the Left had in that space, by the university's joint governing system, and by the range of decision-making bodies within the FEUU, which prevented any one group from prevailing for long over the rest.[34] Even the lengthy discussions that culminated in the adoption of a statement condemning the Soviet invasion of Czechoslovakia (to the chagrin of the Communists) did not produce a rift (which did happen in the MNDLP with the withdrawal of the PDC).[35] In September, however, the university rector and several members of the governing councils began to suggest that the FEUU could no longer control the protests.[36] At this point, organizing and decision making at the university student level had become dominated by heated discussions between leftist groups over how the recent student mobilizations could contribute to the shared goal of radical social change.[37]

THE LEFTS AND THE STUDENTS

A series of reports that circulated in late June 1968 among some university students offers a glimpse into a type of document that was not usually read beyond activist circles and of which very few examples have survived for analysis today. Three mimeographed documents recently found in the DNII archive in a file labeled "FEUU Dissidents"—"Draft Manifesto for Federal Activists," "Our Position," and "The Methods of Struggle"—

are the basis for the discussion that follows. They are six pages long in total, and their contents are complementary. They were issued at about the same time and include handwritten annotations that suggest they were drafted or subscribed to by various groups from the architecture, economics, engineering, humanities, notary, and chemistry undergraduate programs.[38]

The first of these texts praises the "street agitation" that had been "spontaneously" deployed by groups of young people inspired by the recent French protests, initially to demand cheap bus fares and later in response to repression. It goes on to denounce the existence of sectors within the FEUU that were trying to stop the "excesses" of that "authentically revolutionary political line" that had been proven "in practice" by the success of the student movement "in the latest stage of its struggle." It accuses those sectors of unnecessarily dragging out assemblies, dispersing in the flash demonstrations, and engaging in other strategies that went against the resolutions of the June 14 convention calling to "defend freedoms by exercising them" and to continue with "street agitation," "direct confrontation," and "combativeness."[39]

The second document moves from tactical differences to address two core and controversial issues: university autonomy and the possibility of a coup. The document's authors claim that the need to preserve the former and avert the latter were used as strong arguments by the more moderate sectors to slow student action. The differences between the various groups were thus becoming more clearly defined, dividing them over matters such as the assessment of the current political situation and the role played by the student struggles in the much-discussed "revolutionary paths." The drafters contend that an "abstract defense" of university autonomy and other "public freedoms does not in itself constitute a revolutionary aim." In practice, they write, "we are already living under a dictatorial regime," and "the aim is not to go back to the old bourgeois democracy" but to "prepare ourselves to forge and live under a new democracy: the democracy of the classes that have until now been exploited."[40]

The "only path of liberation" available to attain this goal, the third document states, is "armed struggle." It was necessary to "prepare in practice, in the day-to-day struggle," through "street agitation" with a "polarizing," "propagandistic," and "didactic" effect.[41] This approach was legitimized by Fidel Castro in the speech delivered at the recent meeting of the OLAS in Havana: "Anyone who stops to wait for ideas to prevail first among the majority of the masses, before initiating revolutionary actions, will never be a revolutionary." More specifically, this quote was used to refute the accusations that activists were "adventurers," "petite bourgeoisie," and "provocateurs" and to combat the "policy of dialogue and peaceful coexistence with the exploiters" that "others" in the FEUU defended.[42]

What did these youthful documents of such markedly dialogical rhetoric say about the divisions and changes within the Left? First, the opponents, who are never explicitly named but are consistently alluded to, were Communist students, with whom the other groups had great ideological and political differences. This opposition to the Communists is also found in the arguments of many contemporaries in other groups within the Left. Given that violence is a focus of this analysis, it is pertinent to note here that the differences were so great that at times they were resolved physically, with political discussions sometimes ending in blows.[43] In general, however, ideological disagreements were settled in drawn-out debates and expressed in convoluted documents such as those quoted above, which strengthened the lasting image of a sharp division between the New Left that burst onto the public scene in 1968 and the old or traditional Left, represented primarily by Communists. These, in turn, also often presented their arguments through the construction of an anonymous adversary, which could be easily identified as the groups that—with increasing force as the decade advanced—were gaining ground within the Left with their strategy and appeal among the younger generations.[44]

These controversies were part of the process of political radicalization that the Uruguayan Left as a whole experienced during this period. I purposely avoid making the distinction between "revolutionaries" and "reformists" that some scholars of this period have made without taking into consideration how language was used at the time.[45] As pointed out by Gerardo Leibner, in the 1960s "the Lefts that hailed themselves as 'revolutionary' ... had diverse political histories and ideological origins." It is, therefore, not a good idea to establish a "direct correlation between the ideological sources of each organization, their political projects, and the revolutionary concepts involved."[46] In fact, many of the internal controversies revolved around what "revolution" or "being a revolutionary" meant for each of the actors involved.

As the documents examined above suggest, part of the new information that those discussions tried to address was the unprecedented scope of 1968 student activism in Uruguay and the world and the original ways in which mobilized students expressed themselves. The Uruguayan Left of that time, which had a long tradition of concern with international affairs, drew on the news and debates on protests in Paris, Rome, Berlin, or Berkeley to argue in favor of the actions that local students were engaging in. The weekly *Marcha*, in particular, as well as its readers, followed these events closely, often referring to them in their analyses of the situation in Uruguay.[47] Coverage began in

April 1968 with a special "Youth Rebellion" issue with informed accounts by local reporters on the student movements in France, Italy, Germany, and the United States.[48] Reports such as these continued to be featured over the coming months, always stressing the element of criticism of the old Left represented by Communist parties and traditional union organizations.[49] The weekly also published texts by and reviews of thinkers who were seen as ideological reference points of the New Left, including Albert Camus, Noam Chomsky, Paul Goodman, Ernesto Guevara, Regis Debray, Frantz Fanon, and Herbert Marcuse, according to a *New York Times Magazine* article translated by the weekly at the end of May.[50] The July issue of its monthly magazine, *Cuadernos de Marcha,* was devoted to students, with articles penned by such intellectuals as Carlos Fuentes, Jean-Paul Sartre, Roger Garaudy, Marcuse, and Raymond Aron, as well as Rudi Dutschke, Daniel Cohn-Bendit, and other student leaders.[51] In line with the Latin Americanist tradition of the weekly, it also included analyses of what was happening at that time among Brazilian and Mexican students.[52]

As reported in *Marcha* articles and disseminated by publishing houses such as Acción Directa, Insurrexit, and Sandino, one of the main ideological innovations of these and other contemporary thinkers was questioning the leading role assigned to the working class by classical Marxism, prioritizing instead the actions of other social sectors.[53] In the United States, for example, the different currents of the so-called New Left debated the issue of "agency" in advancing social change, pointing to the labor movement as having contributed to preserving the status quo in postwar society. This gave rise to responses that assigned a leading role alternatively to African Americans, the poor, the peoples of the Third World, university students, and various alliances formed by these actors. Among the influences that led to viewing young students as potential revolutionary agents were the works of the sociologist C. Wright Mills, who stressed the social mission and political weight of academics, intellectuals, and the university community. The philosopher Herbert Marcuse, a German émigré associated with the Frankfurt school, also highlighted the contribution of minorities and the intelligentsia, along with the need to release individual energies repressed by industrial society and state control. The weakness of Marxist thought and organizations in the United States helped popularize these ideas within the protest movements of the 1960s and prompted a series of internal divisions and subdivisions.[54] Even France, where the Marxist tradition was strong, saw the emergence of theories and explanations for the events of 1968 that questioned the privileged role of the working class. Faced with mass demonstrations of students and their great capacity for protest, the sociologist Alain Touraine and the philosopher Henri Lefebvre, for example, insisted on the importance of students as revolutionary actors in advanced capitalist societies.[55]

The discussions of the Uruguayan Left incorporated these debates on the specific role of students in the development of the revolutionary process. Let us consider first the positions of the Communist Party, the largest sector of the Left, both in terms of its performance in elections and in terms of its political and union participation. Its leaders, much like their comrades around the world, often rejected "bourgeois sociology," generally exemplified by Marcuse, as it provided the "foundations" of the "ultra-leftism that renounces the proletariat" and "blurs the nature of class alliances," in the words of UJC leader José Pedro Massera in August 1968.[56] Two months later, *Estudios*, the PCU magazine that dealt with theoretical matters, published an issue on "youth insurgency." In addition to covering national events, the magazine featured articles by the general secretary of the Spanish Communist Party, Santiago Carrillo, the French Communist philosopher Roger Garaudy, and the Soviet academic Igor Kon, in which they refuted the attempts to play down the classical Marxist view of class struggle as the engine of history. In the introduction, PCU general secretary Rodney Arismendi minimized the uniqueness of "youth insurgency," including it in his assessment of the role of "progressive middle-class intellectuals," especially university intellectuals and students, in the revolutionary process, a long-standing concern of his and a subject on which he had written extensively since the 1950s:

> We do not proclaim—far be it from our theory—the existence of a generational struggle. But we know that a Party that preserves the capital of its old cadres, that is enriched by the new generations, and whose ranks are nourished by the combative torrent of youth, in turn enhancing and shaping much of its stock of cadres, is a Party that thus reflects that it is combating; it is a Party that is not working-class merely in name, rather it can claim that title because it combines the Marxist-Leninist (proletarian) ideological conception with its deep roots in the working class, its proletariat makeup. And it is from there that it builds its influence in the other advanced sectors of society.[57]

In addition to his rejection of the "generational struggle" theories that were in vogue at the time, it is interesting to note how Arismendi, and Communists in general, likened generations to social classes and how he portrayed the Party as a big family where harmony prevailed in the (generational) relations between the "old cadres" (proletariats) and the "combative torrent of youth" (students, the middle classes). I consider later whether such a correlation between social origin and age actually existed and, if so, to what extent. What I want to point out now is Arismedi's implicit refutation of the view of the PCU as an "old" organization, presenting it instead as an intergenerational meeting ground. According to historian Marisa Silva, the rallies held for the Party's anniversary celebrations between 1955 and 1973 presented that same image: the members of the UJC marched in last and saluted their elders (the "old guard," in the vocabulary of the Party), already seated on stage, chanting "Long Live the Party, [the Party] Youth Salutes You."[58] These rites were meant to incorporate young people to activism under the principle that their conflicts were nothing more (and nothing less) than an "objective [reflection] of the conflicts of their society."[59] The Party press often took this idea to extremes, claiming that, in contrast to the capitalist world, socialism (as "territorialized utopia," in Silva's words) had successfully overcome generational conflict.[60] Similarly, relations within the PCU were presented as a preview of what would happen when socialism triumphed, when the elimination of the "essential contradiction" between labor and capital would put an end to all social conflicts.

In an effort to incorporate the idea of generational harmony into the Party's strategy in the 1968 protests, Arismendi argued that it was necessary to "distinguish first of all the revolutionary spirit that stirs young students, to then—shoulder to shoulder and arm in arm with them—elevate protest to theoretical conscience, insurgency to revolutionary praxis, revolt to revolution."[61] The responsibility for this task fell directly on the UJC, the youth wing created in 1955 as part of the party's process of renovation led by Arismendi.[62] As of that moment, which coincided with the expansion of secondary education and university enrollment, the Communists had a strong presence among students and went on to head their union organizations, always in accordance with the Party line. From those positions, in the late 1960s they stressed that the political concerns of students could only acquire meaning if they were framed within organizations that "accumulated forces" to join the revolutionary struggle led by the working class. This was pointed out by a "Communist university student" in a letter to *Marcha:* "A single CESU, guiding high school students; the CEUTU [Coordinator of UTU Students] for vocational students; the AEMM [Montevideo Association of Normal School Students] for teachers in training; the FEUU with university students; all of them united with the CNT!"[63] And this was stated even more clearly by Walter Sanseviero, UJC general secretary from 1965 until his death in 1971: "the necessary action of the masses" cannot be replaced "by the action of any tiny group," and "the efforts to frame [within an organization] the actions of tens of thousands of students against government policies" cannot be substituted by "placing our hopes in the activities of a select group." In other words, the student movement had to be understood as "a social force of the revolution, directly allied with the working class" and not as "an operational group within the popular movement."[64]

By stressing the issue of the "vanguard" of the revolutionary process, the Communists were not just paying tribute to their ideological orthodoxy and combating alternative views. They were also reaffirming their role as leaders of the labor movement, a role that, in contrast to what happened at the student level, was not affected at this stage. Despite the unquestionable growth of more confrontational groups, the PCU retained its power in several important branches of labor activity and in the decision-making bodies of the CNT, the unified workers' federation recently created following a long process of debate and negotiations among the different groups. With a strong presence also in the working-class neighborhoods of Montevideo, the PCU deployed a strategy that, in line with its political postulates, combined work stoppages and strikes with demands and issues raised in official collective bargaining bodies and also at the parliamentary level. In that way, they achieved a presence among various social groups and a territorial scope that exceeded the capacity of all the other leftist groups considered individually, a fact they often called attention to as proof that they were the "vanguard party" of the working class.

The other sectors, also concerned with generating political instruments that would express the popular demands against the Pacheco government and promote radical social change, challenged this claim. Those aligned with the various currents of Marxism—the majority in this period—also assigned a central role to workers and their organizations in their assessment of contemporary history, based on both ideological positions and a certain attraction to the world of labor as a source of "authentic" moral values (it should be noted that more than half of all university students, who were middle and upper middle class, worked "regularly or occasionally").[65] These positions were the groundwork for some direct contacts between groups of students and workers who shared mobilization spaces at the neighborhood level. These included, for example, joint actions furthered by high school and vocational students with workers in the Cerro neighborhood and by students from the Schools of Medicine and Chemistry with workers of the Alpargatas textile factory near the Legislative Palace, in addition to the ongoing coordination with the CNT.[66] These experiences and, more generally, all union activity by anarchist groups, such as the newly formed Worker-Student Resistance (Resistencia Obrero-Estudiantil, or ROE) or those that had more recently embraced the views of the "national Left," such as the old Socialist Party, often clashed with the Communist strategy. As confirmed decades later by Hugo Cores, who was a member of those groups, in response to a "conciliatory" and "reformist" union line that believed in negotiating mechanisms that were "increasingly insensitive to popular demands," these sectors promoted "a methodology of street struggle and agitation" that "encouraged active protest against the abuses," "confronted management and the government and, in furthering their conflicts, did not waver, employing traditional direct action methods."[67]

In 1968, these differences were aggravated by conflicting opinions over the specific importance of the level of activity that students had succeeded in bringing to the streets of Montevideo. The Communists, as seen above, tended to downplay that importance, highlighting instead the "essential contradiction" between the bourgeoisie and the proletariat inherent in capitalist societies and reaffirming the "hegemonic role" of the proletariat in the revolution while rejecting popular theories about other "revolutionary agents" and denying the importance of generational conflict. It is difficult to summarize the positions that existed in the rest of the Left, where groups were influenced by different sources, ranging from Trotsky, Lenin, and Marx to Marcuse. Broadly speaking, the more confrontational groups tended to assign significant weight to student protests and, moreover, were often their leading promoters. This entailed a radical questioning of the dominant forms of organizing and protesting advanced by Communists in labor and student unions. Thus the "street agitation" that the "FEUU dissidents" referred to and the class assemblies that had spread across the high schools of Montevideo—driven by the FER, the ROE, and other groups—were presented as alternatives to a leadership that, according to these sectors, was proving "incapable of taking protests to a truly significant level."[68] In this climate, the Soviet intervention in Czechoslovakia became a trigger for criticizing the "bureaucratic centralism" of the PCU. The declarations repudiating the invasion reveal a taking of sides with respect to conflicts within the Uruguayan Left, including praising "the broad and fruitful discussion on the Czechoslovakian problem in school assemblies, even at the expense of delaying a decision on the matter," which was tantamount to celebrating the defeat of the Communists, who had wanted to avoid the debate.[69]

But while they extolled the novel protest actions of the students, these sectors also failed to refer strictly to the generational issue. Like the PCU, groups such as the MIR, the FAU, the MRO, and the Socialist Party all had relatively autonomous youth wings (the last two operated under their own name, as the MRO Youth and the Socialist Youth).[70] In early 1967, they had formed the Youth Anti-Imperialist University Coordinating Unit (Coordinador Juvenil Universitario Antiimperialista)—which did not gain much visibility—with a manifesto in which they defined themselves as "young members of the people" and explicitly merged their action with "the general struggle for liberation waged by the peoples oppressed by Yankee imperialism."[71]

In 1968, these sectors began referring directly to youth struggles (by which they meant student struggles) as triggers for broader revolutionary action because of their "polarizing," "propagandistic," and "didactic" effect, as described in the documents above. According to several accounts and analyses of the time, this belief in what anarchists would call "pedagogy of action" was shared by relatively broad and scarcely politicized student sectors, which often took to the streets giving little thought to the political consequences in the middle and long term. This was acknowledged by the students interviewed by Copelmayer and Díaz, who praised their first actions for being "spontaneous," "intuitive," and "fresh," guided only by "selflessness" and "abandonment."[72] The Communists pointed to a similar phenomenon when they referred to those "who, attracted by the enormous emotional power of the events that unfolded, were driven to adopt radical positions from which they would soon turn away dejected," in the words of former student leader Jorge Landinelli.[73] In contrast, the "revolutionary potential" of the "vital gesture" was hailed above "doctrinarian attitudes," as a "radical" interviewed by Bañales and Jara in 1968 put it, echoing the Fidel Castro speech quoted by the "FEUU dissidents."[74] As will be seen below, the text by these "dissidents" appears to favor the radicalizing role of small militant groups in the *foquista* line (or *foco* theory of revolutionary war as developed by Debray based on Guevara's experience and writings) that the Tupamaros were starting to defend publicly. But this militant ethos, often found among European and U.S. students, was shared by groups that did not embrace guerrilla warfare, strictly speaking, such as the Association of Students of the School of Fine Arts (Asociación de Estudiantes de Bellas Artes, or AEBA), formed for the most part by anarchists, which defended the "clear actions unconstrained by any form of structure" that characterized the French student protests, against the practices of a "bureaucratic and senile unionism" that they rejected.[75]

In Uruguay this was a controversial issue among the radical groups predominant among students. The vast majority of these groups questioned the PCU's vanguardist conception but believed in union work, felt represented by the CNT labor federation, and adhered to a class-based view of revolutionary struggle. Even some anarchists, such as Rubén G. Prieto (and

AEBA leaders themselves), whose views on the processes of social change can be described as "culturalist," tried to rescue Marcuse from the interpretations of the Communists, who reduced him to an intellectual who championed "student power" as sole agent of the "opposition to advanced industrial society."[76] Looking back on these arguments thirty years later, Hugo Cores, leader of the anarchist sector that founded the ROE in 1968, speaks of an ideological fluidity, which can probably be applied to large sectors of the non-Communist Left of that period: "Without a 'fully formed' doctrine, our theoretical uncertainties determined that discussions in the ROE basically drew on experience.... Marcuse's theses were not of use to us, but that didn't bring us any closer to the positions of the PCU."[77]

A similar "uncertainty" was voiced in a column penned in September 1968 by the veteran Socialist Party leader José Pedro Cardoso in the newspaper *Izquierda,* then published by Vivian Trías, who had been leading the party's renewal efforts since the beginning of the decade. Cardoso began by acknowledging that after reading the *Cuadernos de Marcha* issue on the student movement, it was hard to give an "interpretive opinion" or hazard any "tactical and doctrinarian speculations" with respect to the "French May" events. He expressed, however, his "warm approval" and "enthusiasm" and found common ground between these protests and those of the Latin American student movement of the early twentieth century, which he had taken part in. He also highlighted that students were currently at "the vanguard of the struggle against reactionary and sell-out forces" while at the same time calling on them to "unite with workers," and again proclaimed "the sacred right to insurrection."[78] These statements must be understood in the framework of the Socialist Party's ideological reformulation, which, amid the disillusionment over the outcome of recent elections, had led it to abandon the liberal stamp of its previous leader, Emilio Frugoni, splintering and contributing with its various breakaway factions to the field of the most radical Left. Those internal processes notwithstanding, Cardoso's words (like Cores's three decades later) reveal the extent to which the direction of the revolutionary process was still very much an open discussion among these sectors in the late 1960s.

For the purposes of this analysis, what is noteworthy in these doctrinal quests is the appeal they held for large numbers of new and young activists, who, at least initially, were not too concerned over the consistency of their theoretical references. It is not easy to find firsthand accounts of these early processes of appropriation of texts and ideologies, which were not mediated by party structures or leaders, especially in sectors that, unlike the Communist Party, had yet to adhere to an ideological orthodoxy. The dialogues gathered by Copelmayer and Díaz thus provide a unique window into these issues.

> A: Strategically speaking we can dismiss these guys [the police, the bourgeois press], but not tactically.
>
> J: Like Mao says.
>
> A: No, Mao doesn't say that.
>
> J: Yeah, yeah. He does.
>
> A: Well, it doesn't matter. Confrontations were inevitable. We'd be there on a corner and the *casquitos* [Metropolitan Guard] would turn up and we'd have to confront them, sometimes.[79]

What is interesting in the above dialogue is not the participants' apparent unfamiliarity with Mao's teachings but the "it doesn't matter," which reveals that their direct experience of repression was more important than any attempt to fit into an ideological framework. Similarly, any international influences were filtered through local experiences. As "F" stated:

> I think French students did things right in their struggle, but I don't know much about it because it was at the same time that things were happening here and I didn't have much time to inform myself. They influenced us because they were encouraging, they encouraged the people who were fighting because it showed them that they were not alone, that they weren't just wasting their time.[80]

Copelmayer and Díaz's book also includes discussions by young people on matters such as "continental socialism," the "new man," the role of students in the revolution, and their disagreements with the Soviet Union and Uruguayan Communists, among other common issues debated by factions of the Left at that time. In all these discussions the emphasis is always on the students' experiences in the recent struggles, with doctrine taking a backseat and referred to only as a legitimating framework. In this sense, the explanation offered by "D" was an attempt to define that way of approaching activism:

> The students who came out to fight en masse were mostly around fourteen or fifteen. It was a high school movement and I think those students did not have a clear awareness of what they wanted from society, but they knew very well what they didn't want. And at that age I think that's enough.[81]

PATHS AND PARADOXES OF REVOLUTIONARY ACTION

In the more organic (and adult) spaces, the core issue in all the discussions in the Uruguayan Left in 1968 was that of the "paths to revolution." Several analysts of these issues in Latin America have argued that this was the dividing line between the pro-Soviet

Communists and the New Left, which was inspired in particular by the Cuban example.[82] As historian Gerardo Leibner has rightly noted with respect to Uruguay, while Communists did not remain static in their views over that long decade that began with the Cuban Revolution and ended with the Southern Cone coups of the 1970s, they were always in conflict with the positions of those who advocated the urgency of armed struggle in South America. Generally speaking, the PCU maintained a staunch defense of "the least painful path to socialism," which, in line with the "democratic traditions of the Uruguayan people," would involve forming a political front that would align the proletariat and peasants with the middle classes, a key step toward completing the first, "anti-imperialist and agrarian," stage of the revolution in Uruguay (in line with most of the international Communist movement).[83] In support of this position, many often drew on the well-known advice given by Ernesto "Che" Guevara during his 1961 visit to Uruguay, in which he emphasized the importance of preserving democracy and avoiding any "unnecessary" recourse to armed struggle.[84] It should be noted here that the PCU was the only Communist Party on the continent that had never been banned, and it had enjoyed uninterrupted participation in elections, parliamentary life, and the labor movement since 1921.

But none of that must overshadow the shifts and nuances of its history. In the period considered here, Leibner identifies a major turning point in 1964, when, with the coup in Brazil and rumors of a possible coup in Uruguay, the Party's top leaders began to consider creating an armed apparatus. He notes that around that time there were actual efforts to train activists to engage in certain forms of "revolutionary violence" and that such preparation exceeded the needs of regular "self-defense" or solidarity with the struggles of other peoples as required by "proletarian internationalism." During that time, in a climate already affected by a social and economic crisis, young Uruguayan Communists gained experience in the streets with actions against symbolic targets, such as U.S. companies.[85] It was then that Arismendi suggested that they had to be willing to "shift quickly from one form of struggle to another," according to the demands of each moment.[86]

The general secretary of the PCU returned to these issues in greater depth in *Lenin, la revolución y América Latina*, a book he wrote between January 1968 and January 1970 (and which was published in installments in *Estudios*). In this long book, he chronicled a growing radicalization at the national and regional levels. Arismendi drew on the Russian leader's writings to examine various situations and problems, applying a specific quote from Lenin in the analysis of each. In this way he sought to reappropriate a tradition that was being disputed within the Left and to reaffirm the revolutionary nature of a party line that was often branded as "reformist" for its insistence on legal forms of struggle and the negotiating traditions of Uruguay's political system. Arismendi, who many in the Uruguayan and Latin American Left considered an influential figure in the international Communist movement, tried to strike a delicate balance between ideological arguments and political analysis.[87]

He based his arguments on Soviet definitions from the early 1960s regarding the feasibility of a "peaceful transition to socialism" and suggested some particularities of the "continental revolution," especially taking into account the direct influence of U.S. imperialism, the "distorted" capitalist development, and the expectations opened up by Cuba. He also distanced himself from the positions of many of his comrades in other parts of the world by unreservedly declaring that the "fundamental path to revolution" was armed struggle while at the same time cautioning about the importance of resorting to the methods that were best suited for each place and circumstance (this explains both his active participation in the 1967 OLAS meeting and his opposition to emphatic definitions, such as the one adopted there in favor of taking up arms). This led him to explain in detail the implications of choosing "guerrilla warfare," "revolutionary *foco*" tactics, or "insurrectional armed operations," among other options, setting forth a number of recommendations regarding their pertinence.[88]

These clarifications allowed him to then temper his arguments when it came to Uruguay. He defined the country's current political situation as a stage for "accumulation of forces" and not as a "revolutionary crisis" or a time for "seizing power by force." This conclusion took into account both the "objective conditions" of the revolutionary process, including the "possibilities" that "bourgeois democracy" still offered, and its "subjective conditions," that is, the need to continue the efforts to win over the "support of the people" and then move on to "greater revolutionary battles" led, naturally, by the working class and its "vanguard party," the PCU. The strategy, for the time being, was to continue with "gradual" and "incremental" forms of protest guided by a "propositional program," avoiding the "heroics of a minority that offers up its blood bypassing the great river of popular decisions."[89]

In contrast to other works cited earlier, Arismendi was not looking to determine the exact role of students in these processes but was instead seeking to warn about the consequences of confrontational tactics that could lead the struggle down a path where the repressive forces would have the upper hand, thus shattering any chances of the much-touted "accumulation of forces."[90] On many other occasions the Communists openly criticized the "adventurers" (which they said were a manifestation of the radicalized "petit bourgeois" youth that was a mixture of "impatience, subjectivism, and infantilism")[91] and turned again to Lenin to caution against the thesis that held that a "political sensation" could be a substitute for the "revolutionary political education of the masses."[92] The student unrest in 1968 would appear to have led them to redouble their warnings regarding the real risk that mobilized sectors would "respond to violence with violence," in the words of the Communist leader José Luis Massera, and to adopt a more restrained stance (prudent or cowardly, depending on who was passing judgment) with regard to any form of direct confrontation with repressive forces.[93]

Years later, some former activists from that time have gone as far as to suggest that one of the reasons for forming an armed apparatus that was hidden even from the Party's members (and which was kept in place during that whole period) was to prevent youths who were becoming radicalized in the streets from joining guerrilla groups.[94] This explanation of the incursions of Uruguayan Communists into various forms of political violence as being gestures or tactical moves within the national, Latin American, and even global Left has been applied to other episodes, such as the support for Guevara's Bolivia mission despite the Party's strong misgivings about the project.[95] It seems clear that all of these decisions and opinions were, in fact, framed by the debates of the Left over the role of violence in furthering social change. In 1968, as discussed above, the references to these issues became more specific and familiar, frequently mentioning recent experiences in the streets of Montevideo. In that context, PCU leaders often refuted the accusations of "timidity" or "softness" that were hurled at the Party from other sectors of the Left by pointing out that the three youths killed in that year's student demonstrations, starting with Líber Arce in August, were members of the UJC. How is this apparent paradox to be explained? How are we to interpret the fact that the three fatalities of the 1968 student movement were members of an organization that insisted on the need to avoid confrontation? As noted earlier, most of the answers provided suggest that this was explained merely by the Left's internal dynamics. For example, some have claimed that Communist students participated in demonstrations as a way to maintain their influence and ensure the unity of the student movement, despite having voted against such actions in student union assemblies.[96] The explanations attributed to Arismendi by a U.S. diplomat stationed in Moscow support this position.

> Against strong misgivings, the CP [Communist Party] sent its young cadres to the Montevideo University barricades in 1968 even though the party knew the tactic to be in error. This was necessary, argues Arismendi, to show the students that Communists do not shrink from a fight. The action also served to "neutralize" the "leftists" trying to lead the mass movement, according to Arismendi. But the cost was great—3 Communist students killed and 27 wounded.[97]

Without refuting this explanation, it is interesting to again put the presence of combative young Communists in the 1968 confrontations in the larger context of youth radicalization during this period. As noted above, at both the high school and university levels their positions lost ground in student union organizations toward the middle of the year. This would indicate that they were paying the price for opposing the more confrontational tactics and trying to stop certain forms of student activism. But the UJC continued to grow in those sectors, especially during the most violent incidents of 1968 (according to official figures, membership increased fourfold from 1965 to 1969, with six thousand new members in 1969 alone).[98]

In fact, two of the students killed by the police that year, Hugo de los Santos and Susana Pintos, both in September, had joined the UJC only a month before, in reaction to the slaying of their fellow student Líber Arce in August.[99] This suggests that their attraction to the UJC was a natural development of their recent experience as student activists and that the attitudes of Communist students, including the possibility of dying in the streets, were growing in prestige among some mobilized sectors. The idea that the combative spirit of young Communists stemmed merely from a political decision adopted by PCU and UJC leaders to overcome differences within the Left thus does not hold. It would be more accurate to say that the Party line also absorbed the concerns and expectations of the most recent members, who had been gaining experience in the street struggles under way, the same struggles that led many of their peers to venture into other forms of more openly confrontational political commitment. Perhaps the rest of the explanation for the "paradox" that the three students who had been killed were members of an organization that tried to prevent clashes with the repressive forces can be found in the organization's ability to mobilize so many. It seems evident, however, that most of these young people had taken to the streets before joining the UJC and considered it a suitable space to continue developing their strong militant commitment.

This process was similar to that which allowed very small organizational hubs to pursue more confrontational options, based on a wide range of ideological influences and recent experiences. In addition to the FER, 1968 saw the birth of the ROE, which was strong in some traditionally anarchist unions as well as in UTU centers, the Normal School, and some high schools. The Unifying Action Groups (Grupos de Acción Unificadora, or GAU) also emerged during this year, formed by youths from Catholic left-wing sectors who began organizing in La Teja, a working-class neighborhood of Montevideo. In both cases, their members were activists from organizations such as the FAU and the MAPU that in December 1967 had signed the "*Época* agreement" supporting the OLAS call to take up arms in Latin America and had been banned as a result, in one of Pacheco's first measures as president. Also banned for the same reason were the MIR (a group that had broken away from the UJC in 1963 over the Sino-Soviet conflict), the MRO (with roots in the Blanco Party, strongly influenced by Cuba, and on the verge of abandoning its alliance with the PCU), and the old Socialist Party, which was suffering division and undergoing a doctrinarian shift toward a radical nationalist and Latin Americanist interpretation of its Marxist roots, under the intellectual leadership of Vivian Trías. At a time of heightened fluidity among political organizations and positions, these groups had just jointly reopened the newspaper *Época* as a space for coordinating their actions with the aim of furthering the common goals expressed in the "*Época* agreement". The government shut it down after only five issues (along with the traditional socialist newspaper *El Sol*), and the groups behind the initiative were banned. Thus began another period of reorganization and movement of activists across groups, catalyzed by the events of 1968 and fueled by new contingents from the recently mobilized sectors.[100]

Similarly, many young people who were just starting to participate in student activism went on to join guerrilla organizations, especially the Tupamaros. This group, which had paid little attention to student activism before October, saw a significant growth among students in the last few months of 1968. With few members and still relatively unknown, the Tupamaros were surprised by that year's student mobilizations, which they analyzed from their particular *foquista* perspective, that is, from the belief in the capacity of small committed groups to trigger revolutionary processes, as developed by Guevara and disseminated by Régis Debray but with an emphasis on urban settings.[101] Regarding action in the "field of labor unions," a document issued in May by the MLN-T had highlighted the importance of "stepping up the process of radicalization of the struggles" waged by organized labor. "To do that," it continued, "there is no better way than to apply the tactics of armed struggle," as the sugarcane workers had done in the May 1 rally in Montevideo or as the students were doing in the streets of Paris.[102] In October, they issued the first document that focused on Uruguayan students. In it they held that the contingents of university and high school "independents and anarchists," made up of "some 300 tried-and-true fellows," had succeeded in reviving the fighting spirit in the country and that they were willing to move on to other forms of action: they acted as "spearheads" in response to the "lukewarm actions" proposed by the "Bolshevik bureaucracy and the MAPU" (which was excluded from this new map they traced of the Revolutionary Left).[103]

The number "300" (the same number given by the interior minister in Parliament) and the label "independents and anarchists" probably alluded to the various parties, factions, and groups formed in previous years in the debates over the Cuban experience, the disillusionment with the Uruguayan Left's poor performance in elections (especially the Socialist Party), and, more recently, the problems with the "*Época* agreement." Toward the end of the 1960s, these groups had found substantial common ground in their union and political activities, through their shared questioning of the forms of organization and action of the left-wing parties with a legal and parliamentary tradition. In the first half of the decade, several of these activists had participated in the "Coordinator" experience that gave way to the Tupamaros (most notably the top guerrilla leader, Raúl Sendic, who had been a member of the Socialist Party).[104] In the years that this study focuses on, almost all of them agreed that the Pacheco government was a "legal" or "constitutional" dictatorship and therefore dismissed any approach that believed in the possibilities offered by "bourgeois democracy," as pointed out in the "FEUU dissidents" document.[105] They also agreed on the validity of armed struggle and the need to move forward in the confrontation with management, repressive forces, and all other "enemies of the people." Strong differences persisted, however, with respect to the "paths to revolution," that is, over the best way to achieve a radical transformation at the continental and national levels, which would certainly explain their difficulties in establishing more permanent coordinating mechanisms. While some questioned the *foquista* way and preferred to work on the union front with forms of "direct action," others, whether insurrectional in spirit or not, gradually converged toward armed struggle.[106]

The 1968 protests had a profound impact on this inorganic constellation. At the student level, there were several very small active circles with links to the incipient MLN-T and other groups that had already embraced "direct action" and armed struggle. The most combative educational centers were, in fact, those in which groups of this kind were operating, such as the anarchists in the School of Fine Arts or groups like the Revolutionary Association of Architecture Students 3 (Asociación Revolucionaria Estudiantil de Arquitectura 3, or AREA 3) linked to the Tupamaros in the School of Architecture, which was one of the organizations that signed the series of documents discussed at the beginning of this chapter.[107] The document issued in October by the MLN-T categorized students in each of the university schools as follows: "Agronomy: socialists; Fine Arts: anarchists; Architecture: Tupa-phile; in Medicine there is a strong group but not enough to be a majority."[108] Outside these circles, as the MLN-T became publicly known with the kidnapping of a government official in August, armed struggle began to emerge as a more compelling possibility for many who sympathized with the Cuban experience and its proposal for Latin America. It was to these people that the Tupamaro document was most likely referring when it stated, not without arrogance, "Many, consciously or unconsciously, are waiting for the organization to come out and guide them."[109] With schools closed by the government in late September, a death toll of three students, and the Communists calling for activists to slow down, the "many" already radicalized students that the Tupamaros saw as potential recruits debated how to continue their recent street agitation and whether more structured forms of participation were needed. Around that time, *Barricada,* the newspaper published by the FER, issued a call to fight in "the streets ... with stones today and guns tomorrow," and included a list of "rules of revolutionary conduct" inspired by Mao Zedong.[110] Varela Petito maintains that a certain pessimism that had spread among high school students around that time was "more aimed at taking action than at succumbing to defeatism" and often led to more or less spontaneous acts (e.g., the blocking of traffic by FER members and other IAVA activists in the neighborhood of Pocitos at the end of September) that were meant to trigger "political actions" and go beyond "verbalism," as they called the declarative tendency they criticized in the traditional Left.[111] The Tupamaros took a similar stance ("Words divide us, actions unite us"), and just days after the Pocitos action they hailed it as an example of what needed to be done. In this way, positions increasingly converged and circles grew tighter. Regardless of their actual numbers, which are debatable, the presence of students in the MLN-T would become a determining factor in the coming years.[112]

As for the FER, everything seems to indicate that when classes were resumed in October 1968 several of its activists were already participating in structures that supported MLN-T actions, a process that intensified over the next months. This entailed certain readjustments with respect to the high school students' former relations with the Fine Arts anarchists, who did not share the Tupamaros' conception of guerrilla actions, and would later spark conflicts that led FER activists to disagree with the movement's direction. But that is all part of future developments within the Left that are not relevant to this study.[113]

What is interesting to stress here is that the exponential growth of the MLN-T and other groups that embraced armed struggle and "direct actions" near the end of 1968, as well as the expansion of Communist membership, was a consequence rather than the main cause of the process of youth radicalization in the protests that began in May.[114] In fact, what caught the attention of contemporary observers was the unexpectedness of their unconditional involvement beginning with the very first demonstrations, rather than their commitment to a particular group. It seems clear that there was a direct correlation between the expansion of violent practices and the proliferation of clashes with the police, which in turn brought major changes in the structures, mechanisms of participation, and internal balances of the organizations that furthered the most radical aspects of the student movement and which already had political experience and language they could draw on to coordinate protests. These processes influenced the emergence of a more or less inorganic constellation of confrontational groups that later converged under labels such as "current" and "tendency" at the labor, student, and political levels. Despite the rigidities and tensions of the PCU line, these processes also brought profound changes to what was required of Communists in terms of activism and how it was defined, thus helping explain their enormous growth during this stage, especially among young people, notwithstanding their loss of relative weight in the leadership of students' unions.

This puts into question the usefulness of assuming there was a sharp division between "new" and "old" Lefts (or, even worse, between "revolutionaries" and "reformists"). These labels, which have been used throughout this chapter to explain the leading ideological conflicts of this period, risk obscuring the significant areas of convergence and common ground that characterized the activism of these youths that erupted in 1968 and that led to characterizing them as a unique generation in Uruguay's political history. The next chapter elaborates that idea by drawing on the analysis of militant mystiques and youth cultural expressions that had points of contact with the student movement of 1968.

THREE

Cultural Expressions

MILITANT MYSTIQUES

A brief description of the great epics of the Left, or, as historian Marisa Silva has called them, "místicas de la izquierda" (mystiques of the Left), can give us a better understanding of the points of contact and divergence between the various protest options that emerged for young people.[1] While such options were for the most part associated with the ideological and political discussions under way at the time, it is interesting to note that they were not always fully in line with them. The figure of Ernesto "Che" Guevara, killed in Bolivia in October 1967, serves as a good starting point for this characterization, as all these groups embraced him as a symbol of revolutionary struggle, but each group appropriated him in its own way, underscoring different features to project particular meanings onto him. Examples abound, so let us begin by considering the response prompted by a June 1968 editorial published in *Marcha* under the title "The Image of the Desperate." In it, veteran editor in chief

Carlos Quijano quoted the widely read Marcuse to support the claim that student movements around the world were formed by "desperate" young people reacting to the dearth of economic, social, and cultural opportunities in their respective countries. Quijano also posited that these movements looked not to Moscow but to China and Cuba for inspiration: "Marx, but above all Mao. And also Fidel and Che, whose heroic death has made him shine with unparalleled brilliance." Che, he continued, "is heroism and adventure and glorious life and death, but above all he is the prototype of the 'new man.' The image of the desperate when 'only the desperate can restore hope for us.'"[2]

A few issues later, a "young communist" sent a letter to the weekly in which, in addition to rejecting the influence of the Chinese leader Mao and upholding the Soviet example, he drew on Che Guevara to argue against Quijano (and Marcuse), stating, "We're revolutionaries, not desperate."[3] Although Quijano did not intend to reduce these movements merely to a form of youthful rebellion and instead included that element as an additional analytical dimension, the "young communist" followed the Party line by categorically rejecting the "generational conception" (symptomatically associated with the loss of masculinity):

> Do we as young people have a specific message to convey? My answer, contrary to what *Marcha* says, is that we don't. Does not having a message specific to our generation mean that we don't have any message at all? I also say no to that. We have ... a message that is universal and of the people. We don't have to "set one message against another," "against the message of the generation before us." ... In this era ... , the era of the proletariat, the "generational message" no longer has a place. You may think that's not a very "young" thing to say. Quite the opposite: to generationalize us is to castrate our capacity to use youthful force to get to the root of

the drama.... The problem youth has is not whether it feels represented and with creative capacity in its generation, but ... in the movement. This ..., more than generations, is what defines a youth movement, and one of the factors that defines a revolutionary movement. How right Arismendi is in saying "we're revolutionaries and we don't intend to ... remain a seed"! It transcends the importance of an individual or a group of leaders, it is what defines an entire party. It is not the actions of the desperate, and that is something we also learned from Che! Living or murdered![4]

In his long letter to the editor, the young communist mentioned Guevara two more times, hailing him as an inspiration for revolutionary commitment but not elaborating on his teaching regarding the path to revolution or the ways to achieve victory. As Arismendi explained, "More important than dissecting each of Guevara's statements is understanding the value of his sacrifice ... and the fact that we have thousands and thousands of combatants in our ranks who are as willing to give their lives as this hero of Latin America has."[5] By contrast, the more confrontational youth groups always depicted the Argentine revolutionary as a source of concrete teachings on revolutionary practices. This was true even of those who were critical of his legacy. In 1968, a year after Guevara's death, Carlos María Gutiérrez, another *Marcha* contributor and an exponent of those who disagreed with the Communists over the revolutionary process in Latin America, concluded that what Guevara had proposed was becoming "somewhat anachronistic" in terms of both the "guerrilla warfare" thesis and the efforts to combine Marxism with the Cuban experience. Gutiérrez nonetheless took away a lesson: "What better way to honor Che than by elucidating the meaning of his posthumous tasks and drawing the conclusions that are useful to us?"[6]

Such debates often went beyond Che Guevara to touch on Fidel Castro and Cuba and their impact on the continent at large, but what is important to highlight is that the attraction that Che held for many of the young people who were taking to the streets stemmed, as Quijano noted, from Guevara's call to create a "new man" and from his personal history—from his social background to his heroic death—with which they sought to identify. As scholar Diana Sorensen has observed, Guevara's image contained a "mixture of striking individualism and unconventional personal style, on the one hand, with the will to collective integration," on the other, which was undoubtedly appealing to those who were just emerging into public life.[7] In the words of the Uruguayan writer Jorge Musto, who in 1968 was almost forty years old, "We have to either curse him or thank him, nobody asked him to do what he did and as of October 8, 1967, we have become his casualties. Unless we are able to find similar reasons, a comparable rage, a certain courage to defend them."[8] Other young writers, artists, and intellectuals of the time spoke of feeling challenged or attracted by that same view of Guevara, which recast his defeat and death in Bolivia "from a combative perspective," as shown by historian Aldo Marchesi in his analysis of the importance these political and emotional readings had for armed groups across the region.[9]

The Communists, too, venerated Che's image, but unlike their peers they did not see him as a model of courage and adventurousness, shifting their focus away from these traits as core values of revolutionary activism. As Silva notes, in response to those who extolled "the glory of armed struggle as a path of unconditional commitment" they countered with an epic "of the day-to-day sacrifice and commitment of legal activism."[10] That was no easy task, given the personality and views of Che Guevara himself, and it often meant they had to turn to other figures to prioritize Party-building efforts in their discourses and documents. Discipline and ideological conviction were thus stressed instead of the courage and fearlessness (and also the austerity) that were usually associated with Guevara and highlighted as key attributes of a good militant.[11]

This same distinction between two ways of understanding activism could be posed in terms of "decorum" or "civility," to use less charged expressions. In his analysis of these issues in the United States, Kenneth Cmiel argues that a large part of the political conflicts of the 1960s involved the definition of the limits of "civil behavior." This is evident in the civil rights struggles of African Americans and in the challenging of prevailing social norms by hippies.[12] A similar analysis could be applied to Uruguay. Some conservative sectors, for example, reacted with moral outrage to the 1968 youth protests, branding any behavior that went against what they considered "proper" as "violent."[13] In the Left, many justified the more radical actions of the young protesters as a consequence of the system's "structural violence." They viewed the lack of "civility" as a form of "authenticity" (think, for example, of the radicalizing effect that the marches of the ragged sugarcane cutters from northern Uruguay had on many Montevideo youths). Even those who did not condone confrontational methods, like the Communists and some sectors of the traditional parties, accepted this explanation as a trigger of the "excesses" of mobilized students. "Good manners" were thus considered hypocritical because they tended to cement social limits that were deemed unjust. At the same time, the effectiveness of confronting injustice with a display of "insolence" was questioned, as it risked alienating potential allies in the struggle (the much-touted "accumulation of forces"). The "two epics" could be posed again in these terms, with the Communists defending the "proper ways" to protest and others wanting to push traditional limits and march on Saturday nights down

Montevideo's main avenue, turn over park benches, and throw rocks at repressive forces.

In their speeches and writings, Communist leaders did in fact recommend avoiding excesses and stressed the importance of carrying out the more mundane tasks of organizing, educating, and fund-raising that were vital to the revolutionary future of Uruguay and the world. There was a "productivist conception"— to use Silva's words again—that focused on planning and assessing Party work to later highlight the attainment of aims as a sort of everyday heroism that had little to do with the violent outbursts and the unrestrained actions seen in many street demonstrations in 1968.[14] In line with this conception of activism, political assessments were often accompanied by reports with data on such activities that were presented as evidence of the Party's degree of "penetration in the masses." Weighing up the "great battle" of 1968, for example, Arismendi concluded, "Our Party, which in recent years has expanded its activist base tenfold, saw 11,000 new members joining the Party and the UJC in 1968. Our newspaper increased its print run. Our radio programs have grown in influence, our theoretical journal currently has the largest circulation in the country."[15]

Varela Petito observes that this way of conceiving activism, which was translated into "a highly structured apparatus and ideology," was part of the appeal that the UJC held for many politically aware young people who "did not share the radical ideas" of some of their peers and who were looking for a space to engage in activism.[16] But this contrasting of two forms of activism is not without nuances, especially because, as shown in earlier chapters, young Communists also participated in the unrest in the streets and were even responsible for some of these intemperate actions. For example, an episode that by 1968 had acquired mythical dimensions in the UJC involved one of its members, Rolán Rojas, spitting in U.S. Secretary of State Dean Rusk's face when he visited Montevideo in 1965.[17] In their appeals to Che Guevara, while they avoided mentioning his spirit of adventure, the communists emphasized his willingness to take on the most dangerous tasks and to die for what he believed. His image and his name, as ubiquitous in Communist publications as in those of the more confrontational groups, evoked a shared underlying sentiment that went from invoking the moral component of Guevara's ideal "new man" to highlighting his heroism and capacity for commitment to the cause. The violent days of 1968 strengthened this last aspect of Communist activism, which was heightened over the following years as more and more Communists were jailed and tortured.[18] While UJC members often played a tempering role in protests and clashes with repressive forces, in line with party dictates, they also embraced the now certain possibility of facing extreme consequences, including death.

Alongside the conviction that they were contributing in a decisive way to the birth of a new order and that they were living in "the most transcendent era of humanity," as the general secretary of the UJC Sanseviero put it in 1969, this epic version of the struggle set them apart from the rest of society, which was not willing to make such sacrifices, and drew them closer to the discourse of the more radical groups.[19] The deaths of Líber Arce, Susana Pintos, and Hugo de los Santos were key in this regard. In addition to being held up as proof of the government's repressive intent, they were hailed as examples of the willingness of young people to give themselves entirely to the revolutionary cause, a cause that in promoting radical social change went well beyond typical student demands. This revolutionary exegesis—minus the emphasis on the Party, of course—brought Communist youths closer to the armed and "direct action" groups, which also took up the names of the three "student martyrs" for their brigades and actions.[20] A documentary produced in 1969 by the young filmmakers Mario Handler, Mario Jacob, and Marcos Banchero offered a new reading of the slaying of Líber Arce, turning it into a call to arms in the words of Guevara with which the film closed.[21]

The heroic view of activism that was consolidated in 1968 with the clashes with the police and the deaths of the three students drew on a range of national and foreign sources. It is almost impossible to trace the exact influence of each of these sources. We do not know the extent of the influence of the writings that were actually read and interpreted by activists and their organizations, how much of this view was instigated merely by slogans repeated endlessly as authoritative sources, or the importance of the songs, plays, and movies mentioned frequently in first-person accounts of that time.

With respect to what young people were reading, a brief list of works and authors can be drawn up based on references in opinion pieces and debates on doctrine, as well as in the ads for magazines, books, and publishing houses that were featured in left-wing papers. These references reveal that young Uruguayans in the 1960s fueled their revolutionary heroism—to varying degrees, depending on their cultural background and ideological preferences—with the widely read personal accounts of militants such as the Czech Julius Fucik, the French-Algerian Henri Alleg, and the Vietnamese Nguyen Van Troi (all favored by the Communists); with the more doctrinarian narratives on preparations for revolutionary action by, for example, Lenin (disputed among the various sectors) and Mao Zedong (for almost all sectors, except the Communists); and with manuals or texts calling for action, such as those by the French Régis Debray, the Martinique-born Frenchman Frantz Fanon, and the ever-present Che Guevara (three of the most favored intellectuals among armed struggle advocates).

In addition to these possible readings, the intellectual development of the youths who emerged into public life in the 1960s was marked by a boom of essay writing on the causes of what was diagnosed as a major crisis in the nation's history. The influence was probably greater among those sectors that still lacked a closed ideological framework and were looking for reference points to analyze the situation in Uruguay. As historian José Rilla notes, this trend saw the intersection of "historical revisionism, critical thought, and the emergence of the social sciences."[22] Historical revisionism, in the left-wing version of the Argentine essayist Jorge Abelardo Ramos and the Uruguayan thinker Vivian Trías, was especially persuasive as it proposed a reading of Latin America's wars for independence that lent historical grounds to the call to collective action "from below." These authors went against the grain of most official histories and revisited the nineteenth-century caudillos to find heroes that the Left could identify with based on their resistance to foreign intervention and to pro-European modernization models in the name of a vague "revolutionary nationalism." It was from these new readings that Uruguay's national hero, José Artigas, emerged as a fully consolidated reference for the Left.[23] The dependency theory, in the more radical versions of Paul Baran and André Gunder Frank, also influenced these historical revisions with its contention of the unfeasibility of peripheral capitalism and the need to prompt a break with the metropolis.[24] Several Uruguayan authors thus looked back on the history of the twentieth century to point out the failures of the modernizing project implemented by the governments of José Batlle y Ordóñez. In that project they also identified the consolidation of a number of cultural values and patterns that half a century on were still negatively affecting Uruguayans, primarily because they served as grounds for their refusal to see themselves as Latin Americans.[25]

Despite their many differences, these works "of decline and disbelief," as Rilla has aptly described them, shared a tone of moral criticism of the supposed hedonism, the conciliatory tendency, and the lack of a spirit of sacrifice, which had combined to cement a form of peaceful coexistence and a relatively stable institutional arrangement that were now deemed ineffective for addressing the challenges posed by the crisis or that were exposed as facades concealing an alarming and unjust reality.[26] This criticism was stoked by reports of corruption. Many young people vividly remembered a conference held at the university in which the director of the government-owned national bank, Julio Herrera Vargas, disclosed the circumstances surrounding the April 1968 currency devaluation decree. Vargas accused Jorge Batlle, a leading politician of the Colorado Party, of having used privileged information for his own gain in an episode that came to be known as "la infidencia," or the breach of confidentiality.[27] By this time, authors as varied in their intellectual backgrounds and literary aspirations as Mario Benedetti, whose *El país de la cola de paja* was published in 1960; Carlos Real de Azúa (*El impulso y su freno*, 1964); and Alberto Methol Ferré (*El Uruguay como problema*, 1967) had been mapping out this adverse diagnosis of the prevailing political system and social arrangement for nearly a decade. Many historians and commentators later interpreted these writings as a call to arms.[28]

It would perhaps be more accurate to see these works as part of the same climate of dissatisfaction and criticism that erupted in

1968, without falling into simplified cause-and-effect relationships and reductions of the complex processes of circulation and consumption of cultural products.[29] In any case, in addition to arguments to support their political views and debates on doctrine, they clearly provided many young people with a language of rejection with which to rebel against the perceived complacency and blindness of their social environment, which would soon develop into a militant epic. No accurate figures are available, but contemporaries agree that such texts were among the most widely sold and read during the boom years of publishing. At the same time, *Marcha* and other newspapers distributed in more accessible formats those authors' ideas as well as examples of the "new journalism" practiced by some of their leading contributors.[30] Along with popular music, theater, and films, these publications created a positive image of left-wing activism and revolutionary commitment, with direct appeals to the emotions. Historian Clara Aldrighi argues, based on dozens of interviews and first-person accounts, that these cultural expressions were particularly important for those youths who joined the urban guerrilla ranks in 1968.[31] Peers from other political camps have similar recollections regarding the importance of "protest music," "independent theater," and certain films that portrayed epic episodes from various historical moments or dramatized contemporary experiences.[32]

These cultural products, however, were not necessarily associated with a youth identity tied to global generational trends. As several scholars have posited since the late 1960s, this "militant culture" spread as a result of the sharp turn to the left by intellectuals and artists, which found an echo in the vast sectors mobilizing against the Pacheco government.[33] Much less explored has been the proliferation of cultural and artistic forms that were more characteristic of youth, which also contributed to the militant epic

Figure 4. Sleeve of the album *Canciones para el hombre nuevo* by the singer-songwriter Daniel Viglietti (Orfeo, Montevideo, 1968).

of those who participated in the 1968 protests. Take, for example, the pose, the clothes, and the guitar held almost like a weapon of the singer Daniel Viglietti on the cover of his record *Canciones para el hombre nuevo* (Songs for the New Man). At the height of the student struggles, he invoked Guevara in his lyrics: "His arm, a rifle; / his eyes, the light. / And with the idea / a bullet emerges. / ... / His cry will be / one of war and victory, / like a burst of gunfire / heralding glory."[34]

Viglietti was also paradigmatic in his ability to give voice to the inclination of many mobilized students to embark on guerrilla projects or join direct action groups. This is evident in the song he wrote, also in 1968, for the short documentary film

Me gustan los estudiantes (I Like Students), produced by Mario Handler, on the demonstrations against the OAS Conference held the year before in the Uruguayan resort city of Punta del Este. The film juxtaposes somewhat violent images of street protests (young university students putting up barricades and throwing rocks; policemen waving their batons and brandishing handguns) and scenes of the polite interactions among heads of state inside the meeting venue. The contrast was heightened by the sound track, which used Viglietti's song "Vamos, estudiantes" (Onward, Students) and a song by the Chilean singer-songwriter Violeta Parra (from which the film takes its name) for the outside shots and silence for the indoor footage.[35] This could be interpreted in diverse ways, including a certain exculpatory tone for the police officers who put themselves on the line to protect the politicians. Viglietti's exhortation during the street scenes clearly shows the link between youth violence and revolutionary action that was advocated by many left-wing groups at the time: "Today it's their arms, / what will it be tomorrow? / what will it be? / Today it's rocks, / just imagine, / imagine, imagine!"[36] The film, one of the foundational productions of the country's budding political cinema, premiered at *Marcha*'s eleventh film festival, at the Plaza theater in downtown Montevideo, in a program of documentaries on "the struggles for liberation sparked by peoples of the Third World."[37] According to the account of one of the organizers, "The response we got was exactly what we were aiming for." When the film ended, around midday on Sunday, July 28, "the audience rushed out into the plaza, outraged, and started wrecking park benches. Then they dragged the benches into the middle of the street and staged an improvised demonstration."[38]

In 1968 the connection between student protests and revolutionary struggle that was at the center of this film (and which was probably what spurred such a reaction) was never mentioned in the speeches and official documents of the PCU, which instead called for a less confrontational stance. However, the need to take up arms—or at least an attraction to such a possibility—can be detected in youth culture expressions from the time, especially in spaces associated with Communist activism. These expressions sometimes contradicted the efforts to appropriate the figure of Che Guevara through different interpretations, as described earlier, and painted a picture of armed struggle that was similar to that of those who effectively embraced armed projects.[39]

The references were often subtle. Take, for example, the photographs from the archive of the PCU's official newspaper, *El Popular*, that document the participation of the dance group directed by the young choreographer Mary Minetti in a performance titled "La noche de Vietnam" (Night Falls on Vietnam) organized in 1968 by the Movement of Culture Workers of FIDEL, the coalition formed by Communists and their allies.[40] The stills show several young dancers starkly dressed in canvas shirts and jeans with leather belts. The clothes were unisex (a term that began to be used then), blurring distinctions between men and women, but the hairstyles and makeup mark gender differences, in line with the fashions of the time: sculpted eyebrows for the women and long sideburns for the men. The outfits and personal grooming choices clearly revealed the adoption of features of a generational identity that was spreading globally while at the same time alluding to the clothing adopted by certain Third World guerrilla movements. The stills suggest choreography defined by severe and emphatic movements, with the dancers ending in a fighting pose, knees bent and fists raised, evoking the propaganda posters of socialist countries. The title of the dance itself, "Ballet guerrillero," leaves no doubt as to its

Figure 5. Photograph of the "Ballet guerrillero" choreographed by Mary Minetti, at "La noche de Vietnam" organized by the Movimiento de Trabajadores de la Cultura del Frente Izquierda de Liberación (FIDEL), staged in front of the Municipal Government building in downtown Montevideo, March 26, 1968. Photographer unknown. *El Popular* private collection, Centro de Fotografía de Montevideo.

intention to artistically depict revolutionary violence, ostensibly as a way of expressing solidarity with the struggle of the Vietnamese people but also obviously echoing local undercurrents. What is interesting in this example is not the depiction of violence, which is common to other artistic expressions of the time, but its circulation among Communists. It was in 1968 that these more or less veiled calls to arms, almost always featured in youth cultural expressions, began to coexist with other references that were more in line with the official militant mystique of the PCU, such as the singer-songwriter Alfredo Zitarrosa's insistent praise of "the compañero who fights without carrying a gun."[41] This political and generational tension was most likely the result of the exponential increase in the youngest activists in the ranks of the UJC. These new members were not as politicized as the older ones but rapidly became radicalized during the course of that year, similar in many aspects to those who joined other sectors of the Left. This shared backdrop of political experiences and epic references may perhaps explain a certain fluidity among the various groups, that is, the relative mobility of sympathies and the shifting of activists from one group to another, with some activists starting out in the UJC and moving on to the FER and others taking the opposite path, among the many moves that were common then.[42] A brief examination of the new forms of expression in youth culture during those years provides greater insight on this.

YOUTH CULTURES

In 1966, Alfredo Zitarrosa, who was nearing his thirties, declared that he did not feel part of "this turbulent generation" and its cultural expressions. He saw the Beatles as merely "a sociological phenomenon" and mocked the band's local fans.[43] Viglietti, who was only slightly younger, stated a few months later in *Época* (the short-lived paper of the more radical groups) that "the Fab Four" were "a constant joy, who inject a dose of life, of confidence in things," and the fact that they were "capitalist" and "rich" was irrelevant as they were part of "a struggle that I hope grows stronger every day, a struggle against prejudices and stereotypes, against the establishment. In that sense, they have been revolutionary."[44] The opposing views of these singer-songwriters would appear to suggest a political rift, a confrontation along doctrinarian lines that has been repeatedly pointed out by contemporaries and scholars.[45] However, as I show below, the receptivity to the new youth culture revealed by Viglietti did not stem from any defined political affiliation. Such openness was typical in the early 1960s in certain circles with strong artistic and intellectual interests developed outside political parties or groups. Many in these circles ended up joining the protest movement that erupted in 1968 via a range of channels, changing in the process the political identities of the various sectors of the Left.

At least as of the early 1960s, many Uruguayan intellectuals began adopting increasingly critical positions that can be situated within the Left, in a process of incorporation into activism that the so-called 1945 Generation (including the boom essayists) patently embodied.[46] In the field of youth culture, however, the more systematic contacts between the spheres of cultural consumption and production, on the one hand, and formal political activism, on the other, appear to have been a by-product of the mass radicalization of 1968 that has been overlooked in the narratives of that time. Even for the Communists, who had been taking a deliberate political approach to such spaces since the 1950s, the second half of the 1960s saw a boost in their ability to attract large contingents of young people and bring into their ranks some of the most daring experimental artists.[47] Other sectors of the Left also experienced a growth in creative spheres marked by global youth culture. A look at some individual and collective exponents supports these observations.

The first case is that of Ibero Gutiérrez, a student who was killed by a paramilitary group in 1972 when he was only twenty-two. Until very recently, his memory was circumscribed by his death, presented as an example of the period's young martyrs, almost completely obliterating his artistic oeuvre and his interest in the cultural expressions of his peers (or subordinating them to the narrative of his revolutionary commitment).[48] In recent years, however, a number of publications and exhibitions have underscored his artistic production in close connection with the political choices that, to some extent, determined his tragic end.[49] The abundant material on his short artistic life that is now available (hundreds of pages of journal entries, poems, photographs, drawings, and paintings) opens a window onto the diversity of paths that led young people to activism in the 1960s, not in contradiction to other life choices and concerns but in combination with them.

First, the cultural imprint of the middle class of 1960s Montevideo, which was Gutiérrez's social background, is visible in his work. His father was a bank clerk and a high school literature teacher; his mother was a homemaker with musical inclinations. Growing up in a two-child family—common in a country with near-zero population growth—meant that as teenagers the Gutiérrezes could spend all their time studying and pursuing their interests, activities that were stimulated by their access to newspapers and magazines, literature, art books, concerts, movies, and television, as is reflected in Ibero's journals. An early interest in the fine arts was cultivated thanks to an allowance he used to buy art supplies and to the encouragement of memorable high school teachers who, like the painter Germán Cabrera in this case, motivated their students to pursue their talents and creative interests. A major influence in his immediate circle of friends and family was his maternal uncle Alberto Methol Ferré, who was by then a leading representative of the country's "historical revisionism" and one of the most important lay intellectuals of Uruguay's Catholic Church.[50]

This brings us to Gutiérrez's religious education, first with his family as a practicing Catholic, later as a believer in Christian morality, which provided ethical grounds for his intellectual quests, and finally as a critic of the church in response to contemporary events. In 1968, the year Ibero turned nineteen, the second plenary meeting of the Latin American Episcopal Council (Consejo Episcopal Latinoamericano, or CELAM) was held in Medellín, Colombia, with the primary aim of bringing to the region the changes proposed by the Second Vatican Council. The discussions and documents produced at that meeting, with the support of the 120 participating bishops, marked a shift to the left for the church in Latin America, which can be traced back to a number of progressive priests in different countries in the region, many of whom would later embrace liberation theology and openly support socialism.[51] Pope Paul VI attended the opening ceremony and repeatedly expressed the church's commitment to combating "the unjust economic inequalities between the rich and the poor." At the same time, he called on Colombian peasants to "refrain from placing their trust in violence or revolution," thus revealing the pragmatism of the church hierarchy with respect to the process of radicalization that Latin America was experiencing.[52] These last words by the pope convinced young Ibero Gutiérrez to move away from Catholicism, as he saw in them a "message of resignation." This disillusionment had probably been building up as a result of other experiences and contacts with the world of Uruguayan Catholics frequented by his father.[53]

By then, Gutiérrez was studying law at the university and had joined the student union, participating ("reluctantly," according to his cousin Fernando González Guyer) in the demonstrations, and he had been briefly jailed for violating the Prompt Security Measures imposed in June 1968.[54] Many other young people with a Catholic upbringing also began participating in student unions and political activities at this time but without abandoning their faith. On the contrary, they were able to harmonize the two commitments by joining the growing number of "reflection groups" and "grassroots communities" where the Medellín documents and other religious issues were discussed. This, in many cases, swelled the ranks of Christian-based leftist organizations, such as the MAPU and the GAU, in addition to the Christian Democrat Youth (Juventud Demócrata Cristiana, or JDC), the youth division of the PDC, which pushed for the party's turn to the Left. There were also priests and nuns who began expressing their explicit support for the MLN-T and other armed organizations, while the University Parish attracted many Catholic students who would later gravitate to various radical political options.[55]

In the case of Ibero Gutiérrez, who does not appear to have been part of any of those circles in 1968, religiosity persisted in the iconography that populated his works: Christ was portrayed as a fighter, a guerrilla almost, and in any case a symbol of the sacrifice necessary to change people's lives.[56] In these images we can see the same shifts in meaning from revolutionary struggle to religious devotion that were expressed in the song Viglietti

Figure 6. *Cristo: Si es posible, aparta de mi este Cáliz* (oil on canvas, 50 × 60 cm), by Íbero Gutiérrez, undated. Museo de la Memoria, Intendencia de Montevideo.

wrote in honor of the Colombian "guerrilla priest," Camilo Torres, slain in 1966:

> They say that after the bullet a voice
> was heard.
> It was God's voice shouting:
> Revolution!
> …
> They nailed him with bullets to the
> cross, called him a bandit like Jesus.
> And as they went for his rifle,
> they found the people had one hundred
> thousand.
> One hundred thousand Camilos ready to
> combat.[57]

Besides marking a turning point in his religious life and the beginning of his student activism, 1968 was a key year in Gutiérrez's growth as a writer, after honing his literary skills in journals and early poems. It was then that he was awarded first prize in an international essay contest organized by Radio La Habana on the subject of the first ten years of the Cuban Revolution, and he traveled first to Madrid and Paris (where he met students who had participated in the May mobilizations) and then to Cuba to receive the award. According to Luis Bravo, as of that moment his poetry reflected "the contrast . . . between the 'old world' that was in turmoil and the revolution of the 'new man' in Cuba, and his return to a Uruguay in the midst of a political crisis." While he was traveling and shortly after returning home he wrote several texts countering "aspects of affluent society with aspects of the underdeveloped world." In later works he conveyed an "apocalyptic view of technocratic society" and ventured into erotic themes, experimenting with the avant-garde artistic languages already present in his adolescent writings.[58] Over the following years, in the brief time he had left, he was prolific, creating in a range of artistic forms and languages. Death robbed him of the possibility of reaching his full potential, at least as a painter and photographer, according to the more recent critics of his work. Only in literature—what he shared less during his lifetime—does he appear to have found his own voice.

Beyond these considerations, those who have begun studying his works highlight Ibero Gutiérrez's ability to incorporate, from his place in Uruguay, the various trends of the youth protest movement that was spreading across the world: quotes from the Beatles and Bob Dylan; references to Flower Power, Marcuse's writings, and the surrealists; views on sex, consumerism, and technocracy; opinions on the "French May," the Soviet invasion of Czechoslovakia, and the anti-imperialist struggles in Vietnam and Cuba, among other issues and subjects. For these reasons, and most of all because of his searching spirit and the belief that the revolution involved a profound transformation of every aspect of life, always from the perspective of culture, Bravo has called him "one of the most compelling voices of the 'counterculture' trend" of the 1960s.[59]

Gutiérrez cultivated his talents and avidly consumed the new cultural developments of the times as he moved closer to the Left and suffered the consequences of his activism. After he returned from his trip and until his death, that is to say, during his most artistically fruitful years, he participated in radical student groups and was in contact with those who supported the urban guerrilla movement. While he never actually joined that movement, his association nonetheless earned him harassment by the police and led to repeated arrests.[60] In the early 1970s, several young people who had a similar "peripheral" relationship with armed groups were killed by death squads, perhaps as a brutal warning to the politically engaged young people of that era. For the purposes of this analysis it is interesting to highlight Ibero Gutiérrez's story as an example of the intersections of political inclinations and cultural renewal efforts that first occurred in the climate of radicalization of the 1960s outside the Left and later shaped new ways of understanding activism, by then more formal and systematic, within the frameworks and structures of left-wing groups and parties.

Another paradigmatic example of this attitude, which combined an interest in politics with aesthetic quests and which ultimately fueled the protest movement, was *Los Huevos del Plata* (*HDP*), a magazine published by young writers and poets who were joining in the rebellious mood of the 1960s without having first made a commitment to a particular party or organization. The "hachepientos," as they liked to be called, playing on the magazine's abbreviation, adopted an aggressive tone from its beginning in 1965. The name of the magazine itself (*Eggs of the Plata* and its abbreviation, *HDP,* which can be confused with the abbreviation for *hijo de puta,* or son of a bitch) lampooned the pretentious titles of earlier cultural publications (*Escritura, Asir, Número, Nexo,* and *Marcha*) and posed a challenge in terms of masculinity, a sort of virile confrontation over the control of spaces of power (in addition to the primitive vulgarity of *HDP*).

The magazine's first target was the 1945 Generation, which had set itself up as the country's "critical conscience," to use critic Ángel Rama's well-known phrase, but whose institutions and spaces of expression were by then widely accepted. Such spaces included the prestigious weekly *Marcha,* which the younger generation had begun reading as teenagers, and the high school and university courses that the members of this generation taught and that many 1960s youths had attended. The literary taste and the Latin Americanism of some members of the older generation were rejected by *HDP,* which identified itself instead with what young people were doing around the world and with literary trends considered marginal, "damned," or "strange" (to use Rama's words again). Moreover, the translation of rock lyrics, penned by musicians such as Bob Dylan, and the repeated references to rock and to a host of other cultural expressions and consumption trends were meant to desacralize the poetic and literary experience and place it at the same level as pop culture originating in developed capitalist countries. These operations within the intellectual field were clear manifestations of a generational commitment aimed at opening up spaces for innovative artists.[61]

With the same inquisitiveness that attracted them to the new cultural developments that characterized their peers in other parts of the world, the *hachepientos* participated in the concerns and debates of the Left. Thus, for example, the magazine celebrated the Cuban Revolution, publishing works by its youngest and less orthodox poets, and it referenced the French student movement of 1968 in numerous reproductions of graffiti, a still novel form of expression.[62] Similarly, the political rifts expressed in the pages of the magazine echoed youth protest movements in other countries, as is evidenced by the following exchange between Horacio Buscaglia and Juan José Iturriberry. It began with Buscaglia in late 1967, when he had already become an habitué of the spaces that spawned what would later be known as "national rock."[63] In his first contribution to *HDP* he defined the guitar as an "instrument used by a bunch of socially embittered, filthy, lazy, homosexual, communist or reactionary youths to try to convince idiots that peace is the world's only salvation" and "protest song" as "antirevolutionary propaganda produced by capitalist pigs; communist propaganda produced by filthy Marxists." In the next issue, published in March 1968, Iturriberry, at the time a music and musicology student at the University of the Republic, responded with two definitions of his own: "Machine gun: An instrument that plays the only music imperialism understands. It can fit comfortably in a guitar case"; and "Protest Song: Rifles, machine guns, bazookas, traps, and Molotov cocktails form the basic instrument quintet necessary to play these songs. A very fine tune was played in Cuba and today more like it are sprouting up everywhere, in embryonic or fully formed versions: Vietnam, Laos, Guatemala, Colombia, Venezuela, Yemen, etc."[64]

The ironic tone and the familiarity with basic themes of youth culture (particularly music) were almost unprecedented in the ideological and political discussions of the Uruguayan Left. At the same time, the arguments wielded by the two polemicists blurred the line between those who opposed armed struggle and those who supported it, which could usually be equated with communists versus radicals. Buscaglia adopted the pacifist tradition of some youth groups in the United States who rejected war in the abstract (although in the immediate context they opposed the war in Vietnam) and proposed a path of understanding based on a personal search for harmony. He also denounced the two-pronged attack faced by these groups: from conservative sectors, for serving leftist discourses; and from the Left, for turning it into a fashion and a consumer good. This view shaped Buscaglia's intense relations with the cultural spaces of the PCU over the following years and forced him to take an anti-imperialistic stance to deal with the tensions underlying the dissemination of the cultural influences of the English-speaking world.[65] Iturriberry's contribution also revealed his close attention to the youth movement in the United States, although at first glance it would appear to be a classic defense of armed struggle. This was evident especially in his reference to Stokely Carmichael, the student leader who became the most radical advocate of Pan-Africanism and Black nationalism, whom Iturriberry called "the sanest of black men," continuing: "He holds that U.S. troops in Vietnam should not withdraw from the war, because he believes in the need to see them defeated there and everywhere else, to then wage the final battle within the United States."[66]

Besides allowing us to identify typically young ways of being leftist in 1960s Uruguay, Buscaglia's and Iturriberry's pieces, along with other texts featured in *HDP*, reveal the importance that the subject of revolutionary violence was gaining for many writers and poets of their generation. This was connected with a key discussion among Latin American left-wing intellectuals regarding their specific role in the processes of social change. Claudia Gilman has pointed out that "by stressing the 'revolutionary' requirements (as opposed to simply critical, aesthetic, or scientific requirements) of intellectual practice," they "compromised their legitimacy and validity criteria." Thus the "transition myth" that had served to explain the "precarious nature ... of both aesthetic formulas and intellectual behaviors" was debunked and rigid criteria began to be applied to determine who "could be or was worthy of being considered a revolutionary."[67] This increasing politicization of intellectuals led paradoxically to an anti-intellectual discourse that opposed words to actions or, more precisely, distrusted the former in favor of the latter. This brought back the old artistic vanguard/political vanguard dichotomy around which turn-of-the-century discussions had revolved and which once again created divisions in the 1960s.

HDP editors and writers addressed this dilemma from a clearly generational perspective, participating in a unique way in the debates of the Uruguayan and Latin American Left. Another example that supports this idea involves the cover of the October 1968 issue of *HDP*. This issue was devoted entirely to commemorating the hundredth anniversary of the publication of the first canto of Comte de Lautréamont's *Les Chants de Maldoror*, a nineteenth-century poem in six cantos written by the Montevideo-born French writer Isidore-Lucien Ducasse, which was a major inspiration for surrealism, dadaism, and symbolism. The front cover, however, featured the caption, "Heroic Guerrilla Week," and Guevara's famous statement praising Uruguay's democratic conditions was printed on the back cover with no mention of the first anniversary of his death in Bolivia. The only context for the quote was a series of communiqués on press

Figure 7. Cover of the magazine *Los Huevos del Plata,* no. 12 (October 1968).

censorship issued by the Montevideo police. Inside the magazine there was a box with a black band across the left-hand cor-
ner and the words, "Glory to the combatants Líber Arce, Susana
Pintos, Hugo de los Santos," the three young Communists
recently killed by the police. This was immediately followed by
a long editorial and other critical essays on *Les Chants de Maldoror,* with no further comments.[68]

All of these references can be read as part of the discussions
that the Uruguayan Left was engaging in at that time.[69] On
the one hand, the "heroic guerrilla" and the "combatants" had a

DE LA PRENSA

Montevideo, 9 de agosto de 1968.

Señor Redactor Responsable:

Se pone en conocimiento de esa Redacción, que cualquier comunicado o remitido, que la Universidad de la República u organismo integrantes, como ser Facultades, Institutos, Escuelas, etc., envíe a ese órgano de publicidad, debe ser sometido previamente a su publicación, a contralor por parte de esta Jefaturá de Policía, no incluyéndolo en la edición respectiva sin obtener la correspondiente aprobación.

Saluda a usted atentamente, el Jefe de Policía de Montevideo.

Montevideo, 22 de setiembre de 1968.

Señor Dedactor Responsable:

Comunico a Ud. que por resolución del Poder Ejecutivo y a fin de asegurar el cumplimiento del Decreto N? 383/968 del 13 de junio último, el contralor de este periódico se ejercerá en lo posible y hasta nueva orden, con anterioridad a la salida de la edición a la calle.

A los fines indicados se aplicará el régimen establecido en la comunicación enviada a ese periódico en el día de ayer.

Saluda a usted atentamente,

El Sub Jefe de Policía de Montevideo.

Montevideo, 27 de setiembre de 1968.

Señor Redactor Responsable:

Comunico a Ud. que a partir del día de mañana, se restablece el régimen para las publicaciones periodísticas, de lectura posterior a la aparicion, quedando, en un todo vigentes las limitaciones impuestas por el Decreto 383/968, del 13 de junio de 1968, y las interdicciones que fúeron comunicadas por nota de 17 de julio del corriente año, según instrucciones aprobadas oportunamente por el Poder Ejecutivo.

Saluda a usted atentamente.

El Sub Jefe de Policía de Móntevideo.

"Ustedes tienen algo que hay que cuidar que es, precisamente, la posibilidad de expresar sus ideas; la posibilidad de avanzar por cauces democráticos hasta donde se pueda ir; la posibilidad, en fin, de ir creando esas condiciones que todos esperamos algun dia se logren en América, para que podamos ser todos hermanos, para que no haya la explotación del hombre por el hombre ni siga la explotación del hombre por el hombre..."

FRAGMENTO DEL DISCURSO PRONUNCIADO POR EL COMANDANTE ERNESTO "CHE" GUEVARA EL 17 DE AGOSTO DE 1961, EN EL PARANINFO DE LA UNIVERSIDAD DE LA REPUBLICA ORIENTAL DEL URUGUAY.

LOS HUEVOS DEL PLATA

Deseamos Canje
Exchange Desired

aparece cada tres meses, impresa en la Imprenta GADI, Florida-Uruguay; editada y dirigida por Clemente Padín y redactada por Carlos Buratosi, Horacio Buscaglia, Néstor Curbelo, Edgardo S. Juan José Iturriberry y Mario Levrero. El dibujo de la tapa pertenece a Enrique Patiño. Pór razones de espacio se publicarán las colaboraciones solicitadas. Este número corresponde al último de la suscripción 1968. A partir del próximo éstas deberán ser renovadas.

Nueva Dirección: Casilla 2454 La Cruz de Carrasco - Montevideo, Uruguay

Acusen Recibo

Figure 8. Back cover of *Los Huevos del Plata*, no. 12 (October 1968).

radical tone reinforced by the ironic context lent by the inclusion of Guevara's statement, which was typically used by the Communists to legitimize their opposition to armed struggle. On the other hand, it recognized the sacrifice of the young, unarmed Communists who had been slain in the streets. The *hachepientos* not only moved deftly in the debates within Uruguay's Left, but their revolutionary commitment seeped into their literary obsessions, without necessarily having to clarify exactly which side they were on. They thus moved away from

Gloria a los Combatientes

LIBER ARCE

SUSANA PINTOS

HUGO DE LOS SANTOS

I CENTENARIO   CANTO I MALDOROR del CONDE de LAUTREAMONT

LOS HUEVOS DEL PLATA cumplen, al festejar en este número el Primer Centenario de la publicación del Canto I de "Los Cantos de Maldoror" de Isidore Ducasse, con uno de sus propósitos esenciales: divulgar a autores y obras que, de una u otra manera, han significado un nuevo eslabón en la lucha del hombre contra el orden y lo establecido.

En Agosto de 1868, aparecía, en un pequeño fascículo signado por tres asteriscos, el Canto I de la obra más inquietante y efervescente de la literatura francesa. Al año siguiente se edita la versión definitiva, esta vez firmada con el seudónimo "El Conde de Lautréamont" que no ve prácticamente la luz hasta una nueva edición en 1890 y, sólo 30 años después, se comienza a descubrir a este autor, merced al esfuerzo anterior de los iluminados León Bloy, Remy de Gourmont, Rubén Darío y otros, y, más recientemente, al entusiasmo que su obra despertó entre los surrealistas quienes iniciaron una exhaustiva investigación en torno a su vida.

LOS HUEVOS DEL PLATA han querido contribuir en la dilucidación de su obra, tan poco conocida, publicando desde el viejo artículo de nuestro Darío (1896) hasta otros más cercanos de André Bretón, Anna Balaklan y Gastón Bachelard; el testimonio personal de un condiscípulo de Ducasse: Paul Lespés, recogido por F Alicot e incluido en la obra de M. Pleynet "Lautréamont par lui meme"; trabajos inéditos de nuestros colaboradores Carlos Cullére y Ruben Kanalenstein; y el homenaje poético de André Bretón y Jules Supervielle.

Figure 9. First page of *Los Huevos del Plata*, no. 12 (October 1968).

the theorizations that occupied most left-wing intellectuals, whom they accused of having "turned the revolution into a bunch of papers."[70] On occasion they seriously and explicitly challenged the public statements of this "izquierdina esnóbica" (a sardonic distortion of the expression "snobbish Left"), as they sometimes referred to these left-wing intellectuals.[71] At other times they resorted to more creative satirical devices, as with the fake communiqué against a "coup in anyplace" signed by a group of "Uruguayan intellectuals convinced of the devastating effect that words or shouting have from a distance," instructing the editors to substitute dates and places every time there was a military coup somewhere on the planet.[72]

These and other similar spoofs proclaimed *HDP*'s contempt for those who expressed their social and political views from positions of privilege. Cristina Peri Rossi, a young writer whose work was occasionally featured in the magazine, put it clearly: "The 'present' generation ... does not limit itself to signing manifestos, almost always eloquent and respectable, or writing their little poems to Che, working from the comfort of their desks."[73] The idea was to call attention to the split between sporadic expressions of commitment and the apathy they saw in the everyday actions of most "committed intellectuals." Slowly but surely this criticism spread to cover all that "pestilent and inferior product that is culture," or "La Gran Puta" (literally, "The Great Whore," but also an expletive similar to "Motherfucker!"), as they dubbed it in their last issue, published in 1969.[74] Peri Rossi again revealed something similar when she dedicated her short story collection *Los museos abandonados* "to guerrillas, to their unsung heroes, to their martyrs, to their dead, to the New Man who is being spawned by them," noting at the same time that literature was "the crudest tribute" that could be paid to them.[75] In the case of the collective project *HDP*, the prevalence of this ambivalent sentiment expressed a greater shift in its cultural critique: the magazine was born as a satire of the 1945 Generation, it later turned into a virulent (and often vulgar) attack on the "izquierdina esnóbica," and it finally resulted in a call, inspired by Guevara, to abandon "the freedom to romp around like a monkey in the more or less narrow cage of cultural activity."[76]

HDP ended its run with an exhortation to engage more fully in the struggles of the time. It sounded like a call to arms, especially considering that it occurred at the same time that the ranks of the

Tupamaros and similar groups were growing. The final issue's editorial and several pieces by contributors contained direct references to revolutionary violence.[77] Although the fact that this was the magazine's last issue lent more seriousness to these combative references, similar calls had been featured before in the magazine without leading those who made them to actually take up arms. In many cases, they were more a reflection of an aesthetic attraction to violence than of a real will to embark on guerrilla projects, similar to what was seen in some youth expressions connected with the PCU. Initially, the *hachepientos* had conceived their contribution to the renewal of cultural and artistic activities as a socially and politically committed task, in a way reconciling the avant-garde aspirations of both fields. They gradually began to realize that they were trapped by their own approach: they had started out as a virulent critique to dominant cultural circles and had ended up reproducing some of those very same logics, with a stable magazine (even if it had an iconoclastic name and changed its format with every issue), and a relatively broad readership (at its height the magazine had a print run of five hundred and as many as eighty-nine subscribers).[78] The publication of a special issue titled *La vaca sagrada* (The Sacred Cow) in late 1967 was an attempt to break that stability with an even more caustic and direct intervention. But it was not enough, and they finally discontinued the magazine in 1969 with a call to action that suggested the decision to take up arms, this time effectively. The year 1968 had left its mark.

A month later, however, it was clear that the new project embraced by several former hachepientos, including Clemente Padín, the main force behind the magazine, was of a very different sort, involving visual poetry, an art form that very few had seriously attempted before in the country. The war cry of the last issue of *HDP*, then, had been a call to inaugurate a space for experimenting in poetry. Just that. It was thus that *OVUM 10* was born, a publication that sought to combine formal innovation, aesthetic provocation, and political protest. Its editors and contributors were somewhere between poetry and fine arts, with avant-garde experiments in hybrid forms such as mail art and performance art. What is interesting for the purposes of this study is that the decision to close the *HDP* stage, with the exhortation to move on to higher levels of struggle, was actually a shift in artistic language, in the belief that the written word had lost its convening power.

As with the founding of *HDP* five years earlier (and many aspects of Ibero Gutiérrez's work), this initiative revealed that certain ideas and practices that were circulating globally regarding what it meant to be young were having a decisive influence on the shaping of local political identities. This was initially translated into the articulation of a discourse for working out political positions that was more "performative" than "ideological," a rejection of certain aesthetic traditions and national pantheons, a shedding of the Latin Americanist creed in favor of a generational identification, and a general conception of culture and art more open to mass and commercial products, especially those originating in the English-speaking world. Last, this approach was accompanied by a unique way of resolving the words/action dilemma, which baffled many at the time, by opting to abandon writing in favor of other forms of expression characterized by a spirit of continuous experimentation (and, in this sense, they were surprised to discover, far too late, that there were similar experiences in the region, such as the Tucumán Arde exhibit in Argentina).[79]

In the next few years, the *hachepientos* embraced different political projects, with varying degrees of zeal. Describing the particular paths chosen by each of them would exceed the purposes of this book, but it is interesting to note here that several played a minor role supporting armed struggle and at least two of the more prominent contributors of *HDP,* Padín and Buscaglia, went on to participate regularly in Communist-supported cultural spaces, where there was considerable receptivity to eccentric interests, styles, and behaviors.[80] Both men contributed to the PCU mouthpiece, *El Popular.* Padín wrote a regular column on visual poetry and other avant-garde art. Buscaglia edited "La Morsa," the newspaper's music page aimed at a young readership, which in its very name, "The Walrus," paid tribute to the Beatles, and he was actively involved in *Magazine,* the Sunday supplement.[81] These were all young people who, like Ibero Gutiérrez, expressed political views and artistic tastes long before they decided to commit themselves to any one left-wing group and who in the heat of the 1968 protests engaged in more formal activism without abandoning other activities.

It may be argued that because of their talents and artistic skills they are not representative of most young people who became activists in the late 1960s in Uruguay. However, the great demonstrations of 1968 had a similar effect on hundreds or even thousands of other young men and women who had been absorbing a political, cultural, and ideological atmosphere conducive to protest, and who then found concrete languages and spaces to express that commitment.[82]

It could also be argued that some young people became politically involved without any such mediation and that they considered activism an all-consuming affair, leaving no room to pursue other interests considered "trivial." This is reflected, for example, in the words of Carlos Liscano, who joined the MLN-T at a very young age and only began his writing career after he was released from political imprisonment in the 1980s.

I had vague illusions about my intellectual and artistic prospects, but I put them all off for some day in the future. The present, music, the movies, the theater, fashion, these were not excluded for reasons of discipline, but because they were seen as trivial aspects, circumstantial, and they all receded in the face of the enormity of the task before us, which was changing the world.[83]

I would venture that this sense of incompatibility, this demand for more complete devotion, became more widespread toward the early 1970s, as repression escalated and discipline within these groups was stepped up.

The experiences described in the previous pages suggest that, at least in and around 1968, there were more points of coincidence between the militant Left and young people more attuned to the cultural developments typical of their peers in other parts of the world than is generally acknowledged. A way of "being young" was thus gradually forged, combining a readiness to experiment in life, a rebellious attitude toward the knowledge and traditions of older generations, and a critical view of contemporary social and political conditions. This identification of youth with a desire for change in all aspects of life could be considered part of the "structure of feelings" of that time, to use a concept coined by Raymond Williams, that is, the set of shared perceptions and values "which gives the sense of a generation or of a period" and is most clearly expressed in art and literature.[84] By 1968 young people had consolidated their role as political actors, and the impact of their views and ideas spread beyond the field of culture and was clearly seen in the political actions of most left-wing groups. These differences in the way of defining what it meant to be young in 1960s Uruguay were determined not only by ideological concerns but also by class and gender divisions to which we now turn.

MORE NUANCES

I have argued that Uruguayan Communists in the late 1960s were especially open to new expressions of youth culture originating in Europe and the United States. The other sectors of the Left also attracted young people who participated in such cultural trends, as evidenced by Ibero Gutiérrez's experience, but for the most part they did not explicitly include them in their publications or spaces of socialization. In these contexts, anything directed specifically at young people took the form of rebel icons (Che Guevara), implicit references to hairstyles and clothing popular among young people, repeated praise for generational protest movements (particularly in France), and the constant urging to transgress street protest rules. In the texts of these groups, young people as political actors were generally subsumed within popular struggles and assigned the role of renewing them, spurring them on, and radicalizing their revolutionary content. The Communists, in contrast, did not attribute this or any other specific role to youths—whom they saw as representatives of the "progressive" middle class—and they recognized the revolutionary potential of young people only insofar as they "accumulated forces" in a movement that was necessarily led by the working class. However, the broad cultural influence of the PCU, forged as early as the 1950s, opened a privileged space for the expression of youth practices and ideas that were circulating globally. Here I want to explain these differences within the Left by looking at the ways in which such groups represented their social makeup.

A common spoof of the slogan "Join and Fight" that the UJC began to use around that time can serve to illustrate such differences. The slogan had been recast sarcastically as "Join and Dance" by some of the other groups to mock the Communist strategy for securing new recruits. Since the early 1960s, the UJC had, in fact, been organizing dances and *peñas* (musical gatherings) for young people, where they mixed beat tunes and other popular rhythms with folk music.[85] Evidence suggests that these music festivals were effective in attracting sectors that were not very politicized. For example, in their statements to the police, several young people arrested in 1967 for painting graffiti with UJC messages protesting the OAS Conference in Punta del Este pointed to these cultural events as the origin of their political involvement. They claimed that their contacts with the organization had begun at dances and other parties where they had been invited to participate in more specifically political tasks.[86] While these explanations may have been intended to conceal more formal Party commitments, the fact that they came up in several statements indicates a recruitment pattern, the same strategy that prompted members of other leftist groups to poke fun at the UJC slogan, whose authors, convinced of its effectiveness, continued to use it.[87]

In mocking the slogan, however, these groups were not just being humorous. Behind their spoof there was a serious critique of the UJC for its willingness to accept into its ranks anyone wishing to join, without requiring any prior preparation or a proven commitment, in the belief that new recruits would be trained and educated once inside the organization.[88] In many cases, these other groups either had a restricted admittance policy for security reasons or they operated much like sects, so that to them indiscriminate recruitment was proof of the ideological weakness of the Communists. The growth of the Tupamaros in the student movement occurred, as noted earlier, among radicalized youths who had been gravitating toward the views and forms of action of the more confrontational groups. Through shared experiences and ideas these young people established personal contacts that enabled their incorporation into the organization. Many of them first collaborated in support structures and only then went on to join the MLN-T itself with the aim of participating in armed actions. According to several commentators, this process was more widespread and began earlier among high school students, where "traditional" organizations were weaker, than in the university, where these organizations were able to continue channeling student concerns.[89] The greatest difference with the Communists did not, in any case, lie in their ideological education of new recruits, which often consisted of little more than a veneer of slogans and general concepts. Rather, it was the difficulty of reaching people who had not previously shown an interest in certain forms of struggle, a problem symptomatic of their clandestine organization. Varela Petito, however, describes similar instances around the radical groups that helped swell the ranks of the MLN-T as of 1968: "People who without being involved in strictly militant activities … hung around these circles because of their social appeal. They exchanged ideas, had friends there (with whom they did not necessarily agree in terms of ideology), frequented cafés with them, etc."[90]

It is possible, then, to identify more reasons for these groups' sarcastic take on Communist recruitment practices. Varela suggests that the "outrage" that the "Saturday dances" held at UJC facilities sparked among the "radicals" had to do with a "puritanism" that prevailed in those circles.[91] A brief review of the available sources reveals that at this stage such "puritanism" did not stem from a greater conservativeness in their behavior as compared to that of other youth groups such as the UJC. On the contrary, it would appear that all these sectors challenged and defied, albeit within certain limits, the socially repressive context of the time. Some experts in psychology and sexuality—professions that were experiencing a boom during those years—were openly leftist and often wrote opinion pieces for these groups' publications (with abundant references to European and U.S. scholarship).[92] But there is no indication that these organizations analyzed how the relaxation of social norms could affect the structures of domination, nor did they discuss texts on that subject that were popular at the time. Neither was there any interest in feminist positions, at least not formally.[93] Such issues took a backseat to the groups' political priorities, in line with the prevailing conception that the transformation of the public sphere would bring about a transformation in private life. Two statements by women—a former Communist and a former member of the Tupamaros, respectively—encapsulate this conviction among activists: "Revolution was a magic act that would solve every problem"; "We had to first seize power to only then worry about such matters."[94]

Broadly speaking, politicized youth sectors rejected the idea that experimenting in one's private life would lead to collective liberation, a key issue of the "cultural revolution" of the 1960s in Europe and the United States, and one that had a great impact on the practices of some small leftist armed groups such as the Weather Underground that aimed to break with "bourgeois morality."[95] In Uruguay, politicized youths do not appear to have been interested in drugs, not even as a topic of conversation, except for very small circles that were only marginally connected with activism.[96] With respect to sex, the situation was more nuanced. Some writers of this militant generation addressed the relationships between sexual exploration and political commitment. For example, Cristina Peri Rossi wrote about such issues with poetic skill in her 1968 and 1969 texts.[97] But on the whole, and while these concerns may have spread into other spheres, the views and behaviors of leftist youths do not appear to have led them to explicitly and systematically reflect on sexual or social liberation; rather, they promoted an atmosphere of greater plasticity and capacity for challenging traditional morality.[98]

When asked about these issues three or four decades later, the young activists of the 1960s recall very different experiences, ranging from frank acceptance of tradition (courting, marriage, procreative sex, strict gender roles in a couple) to explicit rebellion against its rules (frequent change of partners, casual sex, attempts at gender equality in couples). Aldrighi's interviews with individuals who were members of the MLN-T at that time allow us to begin drawing an outline of these memories. The men remember diverse relationships in terms of length, stability, and conditions. Among the oldest, some mention a first formal girlfriend or marriage outside their circle of activism followed by one or more "relationships" with "compañeras" (partners who were also fellow activists). Several of the younger men describe a transition from teenage "girlfriends" to mature "partners" who were also members of the organization. Almost all recall that private life was subordinated to the demands of their political activities. This included child rearing, which was generally left to the mothers, who engaged in what is referred to as "peripheral activism." These matters usually take up only a few lines or paragraphs of the interviews; mostly, the interviews contain political reflections and discussions on doctrine.[99]

In the memories of the women, in contrast, these issues acquire greater significance, revealing ambivalence to the new roles they were assigned or the choices they made during those years: renouncing motherhood, having children in precarious conditions (because, as Viglietti sang, "we need children for the new dawn"), being separated from them, accepting abortion, the double load of taking on political and household tasks, the growing control of the organization over their bodies and behaviors.[100] There are also narratives, from those and later years, that construct the mythical figure of the sensual guerrilla woman who enjoyed sexual freedom—almost the exact opposite of the traditional sexist ideal.[101]

These are extreme accounts, in which the memories of a period of experimentation, when everything seemed possible, are mixed with the harsh experiences of clandestine life, prison, torture, and exile that came later. Based on the evidence available, in 1968 endogamy requirements and penalties for individual behaviors imposed for security reasons on militants, especially women, were still lax. Also, the practices aimed at regulating militant morality through "proletarianization" (with its local variant coined by the MLN-T, the "peludización," in reference to the sugarcane cutters from northern Uruguay who were known as "peludos," or hairy ones) were not yet widespread.[102] This is probably because the tight cluster of militants that existed then adopted these patterns willingly and because the persecution from repressive forces had not yet reached the acute levels of intensity that would later both force individuals to make "short-term personal life" choices—in the words of leader Yessie Macchi—and prompt the group to attempt to discipline such attitudes.[103] Sources on this first stage describe an organization with conflicting ideas regarding the roles of the young women who were joining the struggle and in some cases occupying political and military leadership positions: from the supposedly equalizing function of taking up arms to the usefulness of exploiting feminine "charms" or "abilities" in certain actions (following advice given by Guevara in his manual *Guerrilla Warfare*), and also the "compañera" and "guerrillera" that Viglietti saw as a "whole woman," complementing the "new man" (austere, honest, and brave but "without ever losing the capacity for tenderness") that Che proposed as the masculine ideal.[104]

Only in the case of the small Proletariat-Socialist Unification Movement (Movimiento de Unificación Socialista Proletaria, or MUSP), splintered from the Socialist Youth in 1965 and dismantled by repressive forces in late 1968, did practices aimed at controlling the private lives of militants appear to have been a major problem during this period.[105] The accounts and documents regarding the other sectors of the Left speak of diversity and frequent ambiguity in the behaviors that were assigned to or allowed in men and women, both by the organizations and the activists' social background. It was common for these groups to proclaim equal rights for men and women in the understanding that they were partners (*compañeros*) in their public and private lives. It was also common to criticize virginity, courtship, and marriage because they were hypocritical and went against the necessary "authenticity" that had to prevail in matters of the heart.[106] This insistence on "authenticity" entailed a prescriptive image of "healthy" sexuality, which was heterosexual, based on mutual love, and responsible for the consequences (i.e., concerned with both contraception and child rearing). It was also common to bemoan the lack of "sexual education" and speak negatively of the commercialization of sex and the female body through pornography, prostitution, and advertising.[107] That is not to say that, as evidenced in accounts by Tupamaros, the experiences of actual militants lived up to the models derived from documents, as there is proof of tensions between what was prescribed and what was experienced.[108]

Milton Romani, who at the time had been gravitating toward anarchist-inspired radical groups, relates an anecdote that reveals both the desire for relaxed social norms and the limits that still prevented it, especially for the youngest activists, who still had to answer to their parents. His recollection is also eloquent because it equates sex and political actions with signs of adulthood in a context where the lines between political involvement and private life were blurred. In retrospect, then, activism emerges as an opportunity for transgression in all areas:

> We threw ourselves into activism and we had problems at home because of our relationship. But it was mostly because ... we were fucking, and neither Mónica's family nor mine—both so progressive—could tolerate that.... We got married to liberate ourselves without causing a rift, we didn't know how else to do it. In 1968, over the New Year's ... I was supposed to be participating in an action that my group was preparing; that is, an adult thing, you know? In the end, the action was canceled, so I was free to do whatever I wanted and Mónica and I decided to spend the night together. I went to pick her up at her house and we told her folks we were going to welcome the new year with my parents. So we went to an apartment a friend loaned us. We had a fantastic night.... In the morning, I hear: toc toc toc. And when I open the door, it was my father!! "C'mon, get dressed and let's go," he said.... I was fuming, but I didn't have the guts to say, "Don't be such a ball-buster!" Of course, what had happened is that our parents had called each other to exchange good wishes for the new year and that's how they found out we weren't in either house. All hell broke loose. And meanwhile we were already doing our thing.[109]

Similar descriptions of moments in which rebellion was expressed in all spheres of life crop up repeatedly in the memories of those who were young activists during that period. Rebelliousness was a way to distance themselves from the older generations who were not undergoing a cultural change. Again, this must be understood in the framework of a social environment that was still conservative and in spaces—the spaces specific to activism—

where the relaxing of social norms resulted more from new forms of socializing, which were unfolding away from the watchful eyes of the adults, than from an intellectual interest in individual liberation or sexual experimentation. The references to homosexuality are particularly useful in demonstrating the limits of the 1960s "sexual revolution" in Uruguay. In interviews conducted decades later in a climate of greater acceptance, there are frequent spontaneous references to the "prejudices" of the "cultural environment we were in" and also a guilty acknowledgment that, when repression began, homosexuals were labeled as "fragile" and "insecure" and often forced out of the organizations because they were seen as "a weak spot that could be exploited by the enemy."[110]

One conclusion that can be drawn preliminarily from this overview of perspectives on sexuality and gender is that these political sectors became stricter in such matters after 1968. As state repression intensified, many groups began to define appropriate behaviors for their members as a way of confronting it. It was then that endogamy, control over the female body, and the dangers that both women and homosexuals supposedly represented for the safety of the group became issues more rigorously dictated by the organizations. This was compounded, in the newer groups that were consolidated during that time, by intense efforts to implement more stable and structured forms of organization, which in turn led to the imposition of stricter rules to govern their members' private lives.[111] But during the period of interest here, ideological factors do not appear to have determined marked differences in the attitudes of the various groups toward sexuality and sexual behavior, other than certain norms imposed by the nature of activism within each sector.

What exactly did Varela Petito mean, then, by the "puritanism" he attributes to the "radicals"? According to him, the "activist morality" of these sectors was "austere," "opposed to sentimental concessions and liberal and legal values," including "formal academic training" and "professional and conventional family life," as well as "distrustful of amusements typical of young people."[112]

As seen earlier, socializing was part of the UJC's growth strategy, implemented since its beginnings in 1955, as part of the PCU's efforts to actively combat the anti-Communist sentiment of the Cold War. At the same time, the UJC's receptiveness to different forms of popular culture, including its more "conventional" and "sentimental" aspects, reflected a willingness to expand in socially and culturally diverse spheres.[113] The UJC presented itself as space for "regular youths" who combined activism with their other interests, excluding only those who—again according to Leibner's analysis—were considered "pitucos" (a pejorative term for high-class people) or "lúmpenes" (lumpen), that is, the "two extremes of the social imaginary" presented as adversaries of the organization. An "integrating social narrative" was thus built that "camouflaged or softened any social contradictions" that could exist within the Party.[114]

The ideological implications of such transformations were not analyzed in Party documents, except in general considerations regarding the need to attract "the great masses" to further the aim of social change, always in the interest of the working class. Becoming a member of the PCU or the UJC meant joining organizations that were continuously reaffirming their working-class identity and that had a long tradition in the labor movement. However, a quick look at issues of *El Popular* from the late 1960s and early 1970s reveals the diversification of what Leibner calls "social ideology": "the ideas about society shared by a group or sector regardless of the ideology it expressly professes."[115] This is evident in the new sections of the paper whose form and content appealed to various social sectors, which were not necessarily politicized, with a prevailing sensibility that could be characterized as "middle-class." Thus, the Sunday supplement featured recipes, child-rearing advice, and movie and theater reviews, as well as pages devoted to global youth culture.

With respect to youth culture from Europe and the United States, the supplement *UJOTACE* struck a defensive tone, describing global pop culture as "authentic" in its context of production and representative of the concerns of large sectors of young people in the societies in which they originated. At the same time, it recognized how the circulation of such products in the market and their uncritical adoption in social contexts that were not their own weakened their subversive potential. In any case, the approach to such new cultural expressions in Communist youth spaces was casual, with their importance as symbols of consumerist society being downplayed, provided that those who followed such cultural trends were willing to combine them with activism. This is eloquently illustrated by Alicia, an eighteen-year-old university student, in her defense of miniskirts: "Can you imagine having to run in a maxi[skirt] in a flash demonstration?"[116]

Numbers available on the growth of the UJC during those years provide clues for understanding such attitudes. According to official data, 78 percent of the six thousand new members recruited in 1969 defined themselves as manual or white-collar workers, 22 percent as students, and 18 percent as unemployed. Among the more committed activists, who participated as delegates in the 1971 National Convention, 47 percent described themselves as students (27 percent of these also worked), 41 percent as workers, and 12 percent as unemployed. Sixty-one percent had joined the UJC less than three years earlier.[117] Even allowing for possible inaccuracies in these figures, it was clearly a diverse organization that enabled the interaction of people from very different social backgrounds. Most members worked, but the prevalence of students among the more active militants suggests that the sectors that set the tone of the organization were not strictly working-class but rather wage-earning middle-class youths.[118] This was evident, as noted earlier, both in their publications and in the numerous recreational activities common to this period, which prompted a sarcastic response from other activist groups.

Data available on the class makeup of radical sectors is very scattered. It comes from a range sources and does not allow for a systematic comparison with the records available for the UJC. In the Tupamaros' case, however, it is clear that the organization allowed for contacts among militants from diverse social backgrounds, with a significant proportion of its membership, or a majority according to several sources, composed of students and university professionals. Other crucial members came from specific clusters of workers, such as the northern sugarcane cutters.[119] As with the Communists, such numbers point to the "shift to the left" of the urban middle classes in the 1960s, which was a major topic of discussion at the time.[120]

In the 1960s it was common to use the social origins of radical militants to make a case in political arguments. For conservatives, including the interior minister himself, it was a way of discrediting militants by highlighting their disconnection from the majority of Uruguayan society. Thus a 1968 student leader was portrayed as a "golden youth" living in the affluent neighborhood of Pocitos and vacationing in the even more exclusive resort of Punta del Este.[121] The Communists, for their part, often used labels such as "adventurers," "provocateurs," and "infantile" to describe militants from radicalized middle sectors, without denying their revolutionary potential. In fact, several PCU leaders underscored the importance of the university community as allies of the working class. This was not only in line with their ideology, but it was also meant to explain the "originality" of Latin American experiences, such as Cuba's, where those sectors had played a key role.[122] The social background of some of these leaders was also a factor. Arismendi, for example, came from a middle-class family from outside the capital, and José Luis Massera had been raised in Montevideo in a bourgeois home. This information was used by some radical sectors to criticize Communist leaders.[123]

All of this suggests that what led young radicals to mock the recruitment efforts of the Communists was not so much the actual social makeup of each group as the way each group linked social identity to political commitment. Leibner argues that for "the radicalized revolutionary organizations" politicization emerged from their members' will to "place themselves outside established society, be it through armed struggle, or by seeking out violent clashes with the police." Activism was presented as "the intersection of class and culture, the discovery of the social other, and a personal transformation." This provides insight into both the weight of the sugarcane cutter mobilizations in the founding of the MLN-T and the significance of the solidarity tasks and social work carried out in poor neighborhoods by activists with a Catholic background. For many young students, coming into contact with urban labor struggles was critical to their political awakening.[124] In short, the "radicalized activists were politicized and became revolutionaries by breaking away from their original social setting, defying cultural norms, and exhibiting their transgression." Leibner contrasts this movement with the Communists' tendency to "reimmerse themselves in the social world they came from ... , often accepting its conventions, many of its prejudices, participating in their customs, practices, and other ingredients of social psychology ... with the aim of politicizing them and pushing them toward revolution."[125] This contrast helps us understand the various conceptions of militant commitment that existed in the Uruguayan Left in the late 1960s.

Conclusion

1968 and the Emergence of a "New Left"

When thinking about 1968 in Uruguay, we must consider a longer time line and the year's broader connection to the rise of authoritarian regimes throughout the Southern Cone of Latin America. There is a vast literature, dating as far back as the 1960s, devoted to the study of the "new authoritarianism" that emerged in Brazil, Argentina, Chile, and Uruguay during those years. All of these countries were relatively developed, and large percentages of their populations were urban, educated, and politically engaged. These characteristics set them apart from other Latin American cases. Early explanations of the rise of this new authoritarianism stressed structural and socioeconomic conditions. Such explanations were abandoned as the study of politics began to dominate an academic field greatly concerned with the role of political systems and the alliances between the actors who brokered the democratic transitions of the 1980s. In the 1990s there was a broadening of the interpretive framework and other issues and approaches came into play, especially amid a growing interest in human rights and truth and reconciliation processes. Scholarship from this period emphasized memory studies in order to deal with the most traumatic aspects of these regimes and their systematic patterns of abuse that affected everyday life. More recently, historians have claimed for themselves the study of an era that, despite its importance in the present, is beginning to look more suited to the distance in which our discipline thrives.[1] The scholarly traditions that have dominated the study of Southern Cone dictatorships, and the fact that many aspects remained unexplored, motivated me to research and write this book.

One of my concerns with existing scholarship is the exaggerated tendency to think of the 1960s as a mere preamble to these authoritarian experiences and to find in that decade all the features that would later be consolidated under dictatorships and societal control systems that entailed the loss of social and political rights for most citizens in these countries. This has resulted in the privileging of the study of violent forms of protest as necessary (and even sufficient) preconditions for such repressive practices. By analyzing this process from the perspective of the 1968 events in Uruguay my aim was, instead, to reaffirm the idea that the violence deployed in these protests is an effect to be explained and not merely a causal factor of the deterioration of the country's democratic institutions leading to their final collapse with the 1973 coup d'état.[2] Similarly, I sought to emphasize that confrontation and street unrest were forms of struggle employed by the opposition, which gained greater significance as they met with escalating repression from the Pacheco government. The violent protests of 1968 were innovative, but the novelty arose largely from the relatively widespread use of strategies, slogans, and even forms of organization that were already present in various sectors of the Uruguayan Left (mostly in minor groups) and from the call to take up modes of protest that were spreading across the world on the shoulders of a new youth cultural movement.

In line with this last assertion, I set out to show the diversity of paths to political activism and radicalization undertaken by this generation. As noted in the introduction, this has not been considered for the Uruguayan case specifically. My approach acknowledges the tensions involved in adopting new cultural trends from youth movements in Europe and the United States as part of the forging of a strong local protest movement. My research findings shed light on the paradoxical role played by some traditionally anti-imperialist groups and parties in the shaping of a youth audience and a market for certain products we might collectively describe as mass culture. This approach involves, in turn, significant changes in the way the links between social movements and political parties in this period have been analyzed. Through a detailed account of the timing of the protests of 1968 and the diverse ways of engaging in politics in the late 1960s, this book establishes that the student movement was the milieu where young people became radicalized, encountered leftist groups, and decided to become political activists—and not the other way around. These findings support what historical sociologists have concluded about other national cases, but it goes against the grain of widespread assumptions by many scholars and witnesses of the 1960s in Latin America, particularly in Uruguay, who regard student movements and the radicalization of youth as the result of a persistent call for action by leftist groups and parties.

The study by Donatella della Porta on groups that embraced political violence in Italy and Germany, which emerged from social movements developed in the 1970s, offers a useful framework to set forth these conclusions.[3] In line with that framework, my analysis of the relationship of the 1968 student movement to political violence takes into account macrolevel politics, where the determining factor was the political system's inability to respond in a nonrepressive way to the protests of the sectors that were being most affected by the social and economic crisis. What came after can be explained using a middle (or meso, as della Porta calls it) level analysis that takes into consideration the movement's internal processes, from the disruption of "traditional" forms of participation to the expansion of innovative modalities of political action that in many cases ultimately veered toward armed struggle. I have already suggested two factors as triggers for that passage: on the one hand, the influence of a number of radical left-wing groups that already existed and supplied alternative organizational traditions and languages; and on the other, the general impact of a youth culture that was spreading across the world and spurred young generations to demand their place in national decision-making processes. The micro level—that is, the scale of individuals and their networks of relations—only appears tangentially through some first-person accounts and case studies, providing a glimpse into paradigmatic, although not widespread, experiences, such as that of the *hachepientos* and of young Ibero Gutiérrez.

In my study, in contrast to della Porta, I argue that going beyond what were strictly armed options provides greater insight into the impact and subsequent development of political violence. The 1968 student movement, with its major radicalizing effect, was the realm where the country's various left-wing options grew, including those that challenged the urgency of taking up arms but that nonetheless engaged in some forms of street violence. This points to large areas of coincidence within the Left broadly understood, and it explains a certain ideological fluidity experienced by those who were just starting to participate in political life. While this needs to be corroborated with further evidence, I would venture that it was not by chance that the most serious attempts made until that time to unite left-wing forces in a common front were underpinned by the joint participation of thousands of young (and not so young) people in the intense protests of 1968. The trigger was the Pacheco government, with its harsh stabilization programs and brutal authoritarianism. While often disagreeing on the strategies and ultimate aims of popular mobilization, the various groups cooperated in organizing an opposition that would finally overcome the traditional limits that confined the Left to workers and intellectual circles. Just two years later, with the founding of the left-wing coalition Frente Amplio, these forces were able to offer a realistic alternative of legal struggle and electoral participation, although that did not entail categorically ruling out the possibility of resorting to revolutionary violence. The MLN-T, in fact, halted actions in the lead-up to the 1971 national elections, in which the Frente Amplio ran for the first time. The defeat in the elections and the exacerbation of repression opened up a new period of political radicalization, with greater confrontation within the Left as well, which culminated in the 1973 coup amid the authoritarian wave that swept across the Southern Cone of Latin America.

As for 1968, I am particularly interested in emphasizing that its contribution to those subsequent developments had to do with a process that occurred in parallel and was not without similarities to what in much of the literature on these issues is termed the "New Left" or "Revolutionary Left" and which was at that time being forged in opposition to the "Traditional Left," made up primarily of the old Socialist and Communist Parties. In Uruguay, however, it is more difficult to detect the sharp division between the different traditions that marked the development of a New Left in Europe and, even more clearly, in the United States in the

1960s, following the hiatus created by the fierce anti-Communism of the early post–World War II years. This was especially evident in the Socialist Party, which has not been mentioned much in these pages precisely because it fragmented and splintered into subgroups. The Socialist Party's long-standing faith in electoral politics existed in conflict with emerging internal discussions over the option of taking up arms and pursuing other forms of organization and mobilization. Even the Communists, who became almost paradigmatic opponents of violent alternatives, maintained wide areas of contact with the rest of the protest movement and participated actively in its most violent actions, bringing thousands of slightly politicized youths into the struggle and thus marking a different route from that taken by their comrades in the region. Last, the anarchist groups were decisive in the new configuration of the Left in the country, with their two-pronged approach that supported both union work and "direct action." At the same time, it would appear that at least some aspects of the "cultural revolution" permeated the full scope of political options in the Left, primarily by urging political leaders to take the generational issue into account and to include young people as political actors. This was true even if student activists were assimilated under the "people" or as "allies" of the working class. This ultimately led to the exaltation of certain forms of activism that required the skills and energy associated with being young.

For all these reasons, reinterpreting the meaning of the New Left and the Revolutionary Left in the case of Uruguay involves several threads of analysis. First, it entails stressing the multiplicity of ideological and political relations that existed among all the sectors converging in the opposition to Pacheco, without which the founding of the Frente Amplio in 1971 could not be explained, but neither could the persistence of the FEUU and the many instances of coordination among students and the labor movement united in the CNT. Second, it requires maintaining a certain awareness of the varied and intertwined meanings ascribed to the notion of "revolutionary" in their disputes, such as in their appropriations of the figure of Che Guevara (the two "mystiques"), so as to include among their ranks those who did not opt for armed struggle. Third, it calls for focusing on the different ways of incorporating globally circulating ideas about what it meant to "be young," from the cult of the body in motion to "beat" music and a certain relaxation of social norms.

My interest in these last two aspects has much to do with the extensive literature on the U.S. case, which skillfully analyzes the links between political dissidence and cultural rebellion in the emergence of the New Left. In doing so, this scholarship emphasizes the political meaning of a decade that had been reduced to mere fashion and a market phenomenon. In Latin America, instead, the expression has almost always been used to refer to groups that advocated or engaged in armed struggle and "direct action," those who demonstrated, in Greg Grandin's words, "a will to act."[4] As noted in the introduction, until very recently that tendency had reduced the impact of cultural influences—in the broad sense of the term—involved in protest movements. In a recent article, Eric Zolov proposes a more inclusive use of the term that comprises both "the pursuit of a strict self-discipline evident in the myriad, factionalist-ridden revolutionary movements that erupted across the hemisphere" and "the equally myriad cultural practices that eschewed a narrow self-discipline, though no less so the pursuit of a revolutionary aesthetic."[5] This book examines the Uruguayan case from this inclusive perspective—for the first time in local historiography—proposing an approach to 1968 that can be put in dialogue with the more recent literature on these subjects in other parts of the world.

With respect to the assimilation of the New Left to the Revolutionary Left in exclusion of classic Marxist traditions, primarily the Communist Parties, the literature on the United States offers instead few elements to reflect on the Uruguayan and Latin American cases. The protest groups that emerged on U.S. university campuses first employed a liberal language that enabled their growth in a political climate wary of Marxism or any appeal to Soviet-style socialism. They were gradually joined by various religious traditions engaged in solidarity actions focused on social justice. This movement also contained a significant element of cultural resistance, in the broad sense of the term, which could be traced back, for example, to the beatniks of the 1950s. Only at a second stage, well into the decade, did these mostly student groups filter into other left-wing traditions—which in many cases had originated in the Third World—spreading a more diverse attitude, radically open to the rest of the world and greatly concerned with explaining multiple social contradictions regarding race, gender, age, and class.

The combination of distinct ideologies, cultural traditions, and direct influences from prominent intellectuals like C. Wright Mills and Herbert Marcuse gradually influenced diverse political groups, coalitions, and movements. Many of these groups focused on a set of interconnected issues, such as the Vietnam War, racism, and consumer society, which brought sectors with more clearly political concerns closer to different countercultural protest expressions. In the rich literature available on these issues there are few attempts to explain how revolutionary violence emerged in this context. Jeremy Varon has made the most thorough and interesting attempt to place the violent group known as the Weather Underground within the protest family that can be traced back at least to the most important group of the 1960s student revolt, Students for a Democratic Society.[6]

The social, political, economic, and cultural differences between both cases are many and perhaps too evident to list here. However, it is also clear that during this period a "language of dissent," to borrow a term coined by Jeremi Suri,[7] and a spirit of revolt spread across various regions, channeling the frustrations felt by the new generations who reacted to restrictions imposed on them by their specific social environments. Suri has made the most systematic effort to show the global rise in political expectations among young people in the 1960s and their frustration with the authoritarian turn at the end of the decade. His explanation focuses on foreign policy and how world leaders of dominant nations developed a "containment" policy during the Cold War as a way of preventing domestic disruptions. Such an approach, which explains the events in China, the United States, France, Germany, Czechoslovakia, and the Soviet Union as being part of the same movement, has the enormous advantage of showing great similarities among different student activist movements around the globe. While such political conflicts were sparked by relatively comparable local problems, this perspective suggests that historical actors soon saw these events as part of a transnational movement based on globally disseminated languages that articulated dissent and lent arguments for the often-violent rebellion in the streets of Wuhan, Berkeley, Paris, Berlin, Prague, and Moscow. Part of the shared perceptions had to do with the exhaustion of previous discourses and forms of protest, primarily those of pro-Soviet Communist Parties.[8]

Something similar occurred in the streets of Mexico City, Rio de Janeiro, and Montevideo. Among the common features of these experiences was—in Latin America as well—the expansion of public university systems that fostered a crucial environment for youth dissent. There was, for the first time ever, a large contingent of young people who were not fully incorporated into the job market and whose prospects for the future were uncertain. These students were coming of age at a moment when their respective societies were showing the first signs of breakdown of a development model that had until then proven relatively successful. It is thus no surprise that educational reform was a key issue in the public debates of both rich and poor countries.[9] In Uruguay, these discussions and protests, which touched its uniqueness as a relatively educated and cultured country in the context of Latin America—one of the great myths of the national identity—intersected with a large resistance movement against the measures of the Pacheco government, which were aimed at transferring the burden of the crisis to wage-earning sectors and dismantling the conflict resolution mechanisms implemented in previous years. Upon those bases, the much-touted student-worker unity was manifested in repeated instances during 1968, bringing together different positions and modes of protest. In the case of students, the demands combined a radical language advocating for revolutionary change, which was heavily influenced by Marxism and had an anti-imperialist and pro-Cuban inspiration, with calls to dissent originating in Europe and the United States that were able to articulate their discontent with forms of activism that had prevailed until then. In Uruguay, this combination, characteristic of 1968, cut across the dividing lines between the PCU and the groups that, with their power of persuasion among young people, competed within the Left.

On the one hand, the discussions on the vanguard of the revolution, the lack of internal democracy, the shortcomings of countries where "real socialism" prevailed, and the specific role of the proletariat in the processes of social change caused rifts in the Left and prompted bitter discussions. On the other hand, however, the most important protests that took place in 1968 in Latin America, including in Uruguay, cannot be understood without taking into account the active role of Communists. This allows us to test the general thesis put forward by Suri regarding the local implications of the policy of containment of the great powers. Seen from the perspective of the protest movement, Uruguay presented more complex cleavages and systems of alliances since the PCU remained pro-Soviet throughout the period and continued to uphold the "peaceful coexistence" thesis while participating in all the protests of 1968 and converging with the broad constellation of groups inspired by the Cuban or Chinese examples.

In this sense, recent reflections by Jeffrey Gould on the 1968 protest movements in Brazil, Mexico, and Uruguay are worth noting here. Gould concludes his analysis by arguing that "to suggest that they [the Communists] blocked or opposed the movements is palpably wrong." Neither would it be correct to suppose that "the core values of the 'traditional left' were also tossed out with the bathwater of vanguardism and authoritarianism." On the contrary, according to Gould, the commitment to mass organizations, primarily of workers, that struggled for structural transformations in society was not really challenged by the New Left that was consolidated during those violent days. Rather it was systematically repressed by the sectors on the Right that ultimately took power.[10] To put it in Suri's terms, the challenge posed by these movements spurred a search for sources of authority outside the domestic sphere.[11] In Uruguay, as in many other Latin American countries, this meant an exacerbation of the friend-enemy logic of the Cold War, a polarization of sides, and the tightening of ties with all those who could boost the repressive capacity of the state. This included building regional alliances and accepting increasing U.S. support. In sum, the fertile events of 1968 gain renewed meaning when examined from the perspective of a longer time line that explains the strengthening of right-wing authoritarianism across the region in the years immediately after.

Notes

INTRODUCTION

1. For a more extensive overview of the historical context, see the first chapter of Vania Markarian, *Left in Transformation: Uruguayan Exiles and the Latin American Human Rights Networks, 1967–1984* (New York: Routledge, 2005).

2. This is true even taking into account the brief disruptions of the 1930s and 1940s by Presidents Gabriel Terra and Alfredo Baldomir. See Juan Oddone, *Uruguay en los años 30* (Montevideo: CID/FCU, 1989) and *Uruguay entre la depresión y la guerra, 1929–1945* (Montevideo: FCU, 1990); Gerardo Caetano and Raúl Jacob, *El nacimiento del terrismo, 1930–1933,* 3 vols. (Montevideo: EBO, 1989–91); and Ana Frega, Mónica Maronna, and Ivette Trochón, *Baldomir y la restauración democrática* (Montevideo: EBO, 1987).

3. "Batllista" and "Batllismo" are derived from the name of the most important leader of the Colorado Party in the early twentieth century, José Batlle y Ordóñez, who served as president from 1903 to 1907 and from 1911 to 1915. The use of these terms is not intended to downplay the role of other social and political actors, in particular, the National (Blanco) Party, in the consolidation of many distinctive features of that era.

4. The "foundational myths" of this "happy country" are described in Juan Rial, "El 'imaginario social' uruguayo y la dictadura: Los mitos políticos de [re]construcción," in Carina Perelli and Juan Rial, eds., *De mitos y memorias políticas: La represión, el miedo y después* … (Montevideo: EBO, 1986), 22–25. The victory of the national soccer team in the 1950 World Cup fueled that illusion. See Gerardo Caetano and José Rilla, *Historia contemporánea del Uruguay: De la colonia al MERCOSUR* (Montevideo: CLAEH/Fin de Siglo, 1994), 180–81. Regarding the idea of a "happy Uruguay" as a "Batllista creation," see Francisco Panizza, *Uruguay, Batllismo y después: Pacheco, militares y Tupamaros en la crisis del Uruguay batllista* (Montevideo: EBO, 1990), 79–82.

5. The end of the 1950s marked the beginning of "structural inflation" in Uruguay. See, e.g., Samuel Lichtensztejn, *Comercio internacional y problemas monetarios* (Montevideo: Nuestra Tierra, 1969).

6. See Benjamín Nahum, *Manual de historia del Uruguay*, 2 vols. (Montevideo: EBO, 1995), 2:202–4; and Caetano and Rilla, *Historia contemporánea del Uruguay*, 205.

7. See Nahum, *Manual de historia del Uruguay*, 2:250–55; and Caetano and Rilla, *Historia contemporánea del Uruguay*, 211. On the Reform, see Benjamín Nahum, Ana Frega, Mónica Maronna, and Ivonne Trochón, *Historia uruguaya*, vol. 8, *El fin del Uruguay liberal, 1959–1973* (Montevideo: EBO, 1990), 106–11. On the economic situation, see Walter Cancela and Alicia Melgar, *El desarrollo frustrado: 30 años de economía uruguaya, 1955–1985* (Montevideo: CLAEH/EBO, 1985).

8. See Thomas O'Brien, *The Century of U.S. Capitalism in Latin America* (Albuquerque: University of New Mexico Press, 1999), 137–58; and Peter H. Smith, *Talons of the Eagle: Dynamics of U.S.–Latin American Relations* (New York: Oxford University Press, 2000), 148–55.

9. See Nahum et al., *Historia uruguaya*, 18–24.

10. See Adolfo Garcé, *Ideas y competencia política en Uruguay, 1960–1973: Revisando el "fracaso" de la CIDE* (Montevideo: Trilce, 2002). See also Nahum et al., *Historia uruguaya*, 124–28; and Henry Finch, *A Political Economy of Uruguay since 1870* (New York: St. Martin's Press, 1981), 241.

11. On the second government of the Blanco Party, see Nahum et al., *Historia uruguaya*, 25–35; on the stagnation of the rural sector and the end of the import-substitution model, see 99–104, 129–37.

12. See Cancela and Melgar, *El desarrollo frustrado;* Alicia Melgar, *Distribución del ingreso en el Uruguay* (Montevideo: CLAEH, 1981); Alfredo Errandonea, *Las clases sociales en el Uruguay* (Montevideo: CLAEH/EBO, 1989); and Israel Wonsewer and Ana Maria Teja, *La emigración uruguaya, 1963–1975: Sus condicionantes económicas* (Montevideo: CINVE/EBO, 1985).

13. For secondary schools, see Antonio Romano, *De la reforma al proceso: Una historia de la Enseñanza Secundaria, 1955–1977* (Montevideo: Trilce/CSIC/Udelar, 2010); for the university, see M. Blanca París de Oddone, *La Universidad de la República de la crisis a la intervención, 1958–1973* (Montevideo: Universidad de la República, 2011), 71.

14. On the new constitution and that year's elections, see Nahum et al., *Historia uruguaya,* 44–54.

15. On the Gestido administration, see Nahum et al., *Historia uruguaya,* 55–56.

16. In 1966 it presented a moderate left-wing agenda and obtained 3 percent of the total votes (three seats in Congress). On the evolution of the PDC, see Carlos Zubillaga, "Los partidos políticos ante la crisis (1958–1983)," in Gerardo Caetano, José Rilla, Pablo Mieres, and Carlos Zubillaga, *De la tradición a la crisis: Pasado y presente de nuestro sistema de partidos* (Montevideo: CLAEH/EBO, 1991), 73–74. See also José M. Quijano, "Entre Kiesinger y Camilo Torres," *Marcha,* May 16, 1969, 13; and "Crisis en la democracia cristiana," *Marcha,* May 23, 1969, 13.

17. After wrangling over parliamentary representation, the coalition formed by Erro and the Socialists split up in 1963. In 1966, the Socialists obtained 0.9 percent of the vote and Erro only 0.2 percent. Figures drawn from Gerardo Caetano, Javier Gallardo, and José Rilla, *La izquierda uruguaya: Tradición, innovación y política* (Montevideo: Trilce, 1995), 149.

18. See Jorge Castañeda, *La vida en rojo: Una biografía del Che Guevara* (Madrid: Alfaguara, 1997), 445–61.

19. The OLAS was founded in Havana in 1966, after the failure of a more ambitious attempt to bring together all of the revolutionary forces of the "third world." The goal was to coordinate armed revolutionary actions in the continent. See Marta Harnecker, *Haciendo posible lo imposible: La izquierda en el umbral del siglo XXI* (Mexico: Siglo XXI,

1999), 24–25. At the 1966 meeting, Fidel Castro criticized most Latin American Communist Parties (and in particular Venezuela's) for opposing guerrilla movements. See reports of the OLAS meeting in *Marcha,* August 8, 1967, 20–21.

20. For more information on this subject, including the bitter arguments over the appointment of the Uruguayan delegation, see Eduardo Rey Tristán, "La Organización Latinoamericana de Solidaridad (OLAS) y la polémica sobre las formas de la revolución latinoamericana: El caso uruguayo," in Antonio Gutiérrez Escudero and María Luisa Laviana Cuetos, eds., *Estudios sobre América siglo XVI– XX* (Seville: Asociación Española de Americanistas, 2005).

21. The activists and groups that founded the MLN-T in 1965 had begun coordinating their activities in 1962. Many activists were socialists and anarchists who had worked with rural workers in northern Uruguay, helping them unionize. In 1967 they were operating as an urban guerrilla group. For more information, see Clara Aldrighi, *La izquierda armada: Ideología, ética e identidad en el MLN-Tupamaros* (Montevideo: Trilce, 2001).

22. On these groups in relation to the OLAS meeting, see Eduardo Rey Tristán, *A la vuelta de la esquina: La izquierda revolucionaria uruguaya, 1955–1973* (Montevideo: Fin de Siglo, 2006), 108–22.

23. Until the 1950s, Frugoni headed the PS and remained close to sectors of the traditional parties. As of that decade, a younger generation challenged this reformist stance of the party. While this faction came to agreements with other radical, Christian, and nationalist groups—which eventually proved unsuccessful—Frugoni and his followers left the PS. See Zubillaga, "Los partidos políticos ante la crisis," 72–75. On Frugoni's role, see Eduardo Jaurena, "Violencia y legalidad," *Cuadernos de Marcha* 39 (July 1970): 39–40. For more information on the process of radicalization in the PS, see Rey Tristán, *A la vuelta de la esquina,* 114–15.

24. On the background of this process, see Nicolás Duffau, "El Coordinador, 1963–1965: La participación de los militantes del Partido Socialista en los inicios de la violencia revolucionaria en Uruguay," in *Colección Estudiantes* 30 (Montevideo: FHCE, 2008).

25. See Yamandú González, *Continuidad y cambio en el movimiento sindical uruguayo: Una perspectiva histórica de su problemática actual* (Montevideo: CIEDUR/DATES, 1993), 36–39.

26. The "tendency" was a name used primarily among unions. It more or less included activists from the groups that had been banned in December 1967 and their offshoots formed in the period immediately after. For an analysis of these groups in the student movement, see Gonzalo Varela Petito, *De la república liberal al Estado militar: Uruguay 1968–1973* (Montevideo: Ediciones del Nuevo Mundo, 1988), 56–70. See also Hugo Cores, *El 68 uruguayo: Los antecedentes, los hechos, los debates* (Montevideo: Ediciones de la Banda Oriental, 1997), 57–65.

27. For a similar approach for the French case, see Kristin Ross, *May 68 and Its Afterlives* (Chicago: University of Chicago Press, 2002), 26.

28. On the student movement of that period, see Mark Van Aken, *Los militantes: Una historia del movimiento estudiantil universitario uruguayo desde sus orígenes hasta 1966* (Montevideo: Fundación de Cultura Universitaria, 1990); and Vania Markarian, María Eugenia Jung, and Isabel Wschebor, *1958: El cogobierno autonómico* and *1968: La insurgencia estudiantil* (Montevideo: Archivo General de la Universidad de la República, 2008).

29. For a review of the history of the student movement until that time, see Van Aken, *Los militantes*. For the playful component of some protests, see, e.g., the description of the 1963 mobilizations demanding a larger budget, in París de Oddone, *La Universidad de la República de la crisis a la intervención,* 71.

30. See, e.g., "Jóvenes: Entre la violencia y la sociedad ideal," *Marcha,* June 13, 1969, 12.

31. For Argentina, see, e.g., Sergio A. Pujol, "Rebeldes y modernos: Una cultura de los jóvenes," in Daniel James, ed., *Nueva historia argentina,* vol. 9, *Violencia, proscripción y autoritarismo, 1955–1976* (Buenos Aires: Sudamericana, 2003); for Chile, see, e.g., Patrick Barr-Melej, "Siloísmo and the Self in Allende's Chile: Youth, 'Total Revolution,' and the Roots of the Humanist Movement," *Hispanic American Historical Review* 86, no. 4 (November 2006).

32. For an overview of this new literature on the "global sixties" in Latin America, see the January 2014 special issue of *The Americas* 70, no. 3, especially the introduction by Eric Zolov, 349–62.

33. Pierre Nora, "La génération," in Pierre Nora, ed., *Les lieux de mémoire* (Sèvres: Gallimard, 1992), 3:956.

34. See Norbert Elias, "El terrorismo en la República Federal Alemana: Expresión de un conflicto social intergeneracional," in Norbert Elias, *Los alemanes* (Mexico City: Instituto Mora, 1999).

35. See Philippe Ariès, "Las edades de la vida," in Philippe Ariès, *Ensayos de la memoria* (Bogotá: Norma, 1996).

36. For a preliminary review of the studies on youth rebellion and generational conflict produced globally while the events of the 1960s were still recent, see, for example, Konrad H. Jarausch, "Essay Review: Restoring Youth to Its Own History," *History of Education Quarterly* 15, no. 4 (Winter 1975); and John R. Gillis, "Youth and History: Progress and Prospects," *Journal of Social History* 7, no. 2 (1974).

37. See Raymond Williams, *Keywords: A Vocabulary of Culture and Society*, rev. ed. (New York: Oxford University Press, 1985), 90–91.

38. Pierre Bourdieu, "Algunas propiedades de los campos," in Pierre Bourdieu, *Campo de poder, campo intelectual: Itinerario de un concepto* (Buenos Aires: Quadrata, 2003), 120.

39. Claudia Gilman, *Entre la pluma y el fusil: Debates y dilemas del escritor revolucionario en América Latina* (Buenos Aires: Siglo XXI, 2003), 33, 35–56.

40. See Theodore Roszak, *The Making of a Counterculture: Reflections on the Technocratic Society and Its Youthful Opposition* (Garden City, NY: Doubleday, 1969). For more recent debates and definitions, see Milton Younger, *Counterculture* (New York: Free Press, 1982); and Peter Braunsten and Michael William Doyle, eds., *The American Counterculture of the 1960s and 1970s* (New York: Routledge, 2001).

41. See, e.g., Thomas Frank, *The Conquest of Cool: Business Culture, Counterculture, and the Rise of Hip Consumerism* (Chicago: University of Chicago Press, 1997).

42. For more on this subject, see Vania Markarian, "To the Beat of 'The Walrus': Uruguayan Communists and Youth Culture in the Global Sixties," *The Americas* 70, no. 3 (2014).

43. On student mobilizations, see, e.g., Todd Gitlin, *The Sixties: Years of Hope, Days of Rage* (New York: Bantam Books, 1993); and Douglas C. Rossinow, *The Politics of Authenticity: Liberalism, Christianity, and the New Left in America* (New York: Columbia University Press, 1998). On the civil rights movement, see, e.g., Sara Evans, *Personal Politics: The Roots of Women's Liberation in the Civil Rights Movement and the New Left* (New York: Vintage Books, 1980). On various aspects of the 1960s and 1970s "counterculture," see, e.g., Braunsten and Doyle, *The American Counterculture of the 1960s and 1970s.*

44. Eric Hobsbawm, *The Age of Extremes: The Short Twentieth Century, 1914–1991* (London: Michael Joseph, 1994). See also "May 68," in Eric Hobsbawm, *Uncommon People: Resistance, Rebellion, and Jazz* (New York: New Press, 1998).

45. Eric Zolov, *Refried Elvis: The Rise of the Mexican Counterculture* (Berkeley: University of California Press, 1999).

46. For an introduction to the debates on "cultural imperialism," see John Tomlinson, *Cultural Imperialism: A Critical Introduction* (Baltimore, MD: Johns Hopkins University Press, 1993).

47. See Zolov, *Refried Elvis,* chap. 4.

48. See Vania Markarian, "Treinta años de debates públicos sobre el movimiento estudiantil de 1968," in *Anuario de Espacios Urbanos 2001* (Mexico City: Universidad Autónoma Metropolitana/Azcapotzalco, 2001).

49. See Jaime M. Pensado, *Rebel Mexico: Student Unrest and Authoritarian Political Culture during the Long Sixties* (Stanford, CA: Stanford University Press, 2013).

50. See Marcelo Ridenti, *Em busca do povo brasileiro: Artistas da revoluçao do CPC a era da tv* (Rio de Janeiro: Editora Record, 2000); Christopher Dunn, *Brutality Garden: Tropicalia and the Emergence of a Brazilian Counterculture* (Chapel Hill: University of North Carolina Press, 2001); and Victoria Langland, *Speaking of Flowers: Student Movements and the Making and Remembering of 1968 in Military Brazil* (Durham, NC: Duke University Press, 2013).

51. On this issue, see also Denise Milstein, "The Interactions of Musicians, Mass Media and the State in the Context of Brazilian and

Uruguayan Authoritarianism," *Estudios Interdisciplinarios de América Latina y el Caribe* 17, no. 1 (2006).

52. The two classic studies on culture, intellectuals, and politics in 1960s Argentina are Óscar Terán, *Nuestros años sesentas* (Buenos Aires: Puntosur, 1991); and Silvia Sigal, *Intelectuales y política en Argentina: La década del sesenta* (Buenos Aires: Siglo XXI, 2002). The book that most aptly addresses the diversity of issues that characterized the intersections between culture and politics in that decade is Enrique Oteiza, ed., *Cultura y política en los años 60* (Buenos Aires: Facultad de Ciencias Sociales, 1997). This book includes several essays that pose key issues that were later elaborated in Andrea Giunta, *Vanguardia, internacionalismo y política: Arte argentino en los años sesenta* (Buenos Aires: Paidós, 2001); and Ana Longoni and Mariano Mestman, *Del Di Tella a Tucumán Arde: Vanguardia artística y política en el 68 argentino* (Buenos Aires: El Cielo por Asalto, 2000). For discussions on youth culture in the 1960s, see Sergio A. Pujol, *La década rebelde: Los años 60 en la Argentina* (Buenos Aires: Emecé, 2002); and Pujol, "Rebeldes y modernos." For approaches that incorporate the gender dimension, see Isabella Cosse, Karina Felitti, and Valeria Manzano, eds., *Los 60 de otra manera: Vida cotidiana, género y sexualidades en la Argentina* (Buenos Aires: Prometeo, 2010).

53. See, e.g., Eduardo Anguita and Martín Caparrós, *La voluntad: Una historia de la militancia revolucionaria en la Argentina, 1966–1973* (Buenos Aires: Grupo Editor Norma, 1997).

54. See Valeria Manzano, *The Age of Youth in Argentina: Culture, Politics, and Sexuality from Perón to Videla* (Chapel Hill: University of North Carolina Press, 2014); and Isabella Cosse, *Pareja, sexualidad y familia en los sesenta* (Buenos Aires: Siglo XXI, 2010).

55. See, e.g, Ezequiel Adamovsky, *Historia de la clase media argentina: Apogeo y decadencia de una ilusión, 1919–2003* (Buenos Aires: Planeta, 2009); Sebastián Carassai, *The Argentine Silent Majority: Middle Classes, Politics, Violence, and Memory in the Seventies* (Durham, NC: Duke University Press, 2014); and the dossier coordinated by Isabella Cosse in *Contemporánea* 5 (2014).

56. See Guilherme de Alencar Pinto, *Razones locas: El paso de Eduardo Mateo por la música uruguaya* (Montevideo: Ediciones del TUMP,

1995); and Fernando Peláez, *De las cuevas al Solís: Cronología del rock en el Uruguay, 1960–1975*, 2 vols. (Montevideo: Perro Andaluz Ediciones, 2002–4).

57. See, e.g., Gabriel Peluffo, "Instituto General Electric de Montevideo: Medios masivos, poder transnacional y arte contemporáneo," in Oteiza, *Cultura y política en los años 60*.

58. See the articles by Alicia Haber, Hugo Achugar, Vania Markarian, Esther Ruiz, and Juana Paris in José Pedro Barrán, Gerardo Caetano, and Teresa Porzecanski, eds., *Historias de la vida privada en el Uruguay III: Individuo y soledades, 1920–1990* (Montevideo: Taurus, 1998).

59. See, e.g., Graciela Sapriza, "Feminismo y revolución: Sobre el 'infeliz matrimonio,' indagatoria sobre feminismos e izquierdas" (paper presented at the Red Temática de Género conference, Universidad de la República, Montevideo, September 2006).

60. An exception (partial because of its brevity and monographic approach) is Alfredo Alpini, "Juventud divino tesoro: El 68, los hachepientos y después" (unpublished manuscript, Facultad de Humanidades y Ciencias de la Educación, Universidad de la República, 1996). More recently, and more in tune with this book, see Luis Bravo, "La vida es una caída en el presente," prologue to *Obra junta, 1966–1972: Ibero Gutiérrez* (Montevideo: Estuario, 2009); and "La contracultura sicodélica en los cuadernos carcelarios de Ibero Gutiérrez," prologue to Ibero Gutiérrez, *La pipa de tinta china: Cuadernos carcelarios 1970* (Montevideo: Estuario-Biblioteca Nacional, 2014).

61. See, e.g., Gonzalo Varela Petito, *El movimiento estudiantil de 1968: El IAVA, una recapitulación personal* (Montevideo: Trilce, 2002); and Cores, *El 68 uruguayo*.

62. Aldrighi's *La izquierda armada* is the study that delves most deeply into these aspects.

63. See, e.g., Marisa Silva, *Aquellos comunistas, 1955–1973* (Montevideo: Taurus, 2009); and Gerardo Leibner, *Camaradas y compañeros: Una historia política y social de los comunistas del Uruguay* (Montevideo: Trilce, 2011). See also Sara López, "La cultura toma partido," *Revista Encuentros* 7 (July 2001). Other texts include Communists and Tupamaros in analyses of the young activists of the 1960s with a more impressionistic tone.

See Ana Laura de Giorgi, *Las tribus de la izquierda en los sesenta: Tupas, latas y bolches* (Montevideo: Fin de Siglo, 2011); and Esther Ruiz and Juana Paris, "Ser militante en los sesenta," in Barrán, Caetano, and Porzecanski, *Historias de la vida privada en el Uruguay.*

CHAPTER ONE: MOBILIZATIONS

1. This section draws on basic literature that is in agreement regarding the general development of the 1968 student movement. Specific texts are cited when reference is made to an author's views or opinions or when the facts discussed are either not widely accepted or clearly controversial. As the literature available is relatively scarce, news reports and accounts by the actors themselves were also used, in addition to studies based on primary sources. The works used most extensively were Carlos Bañales and Enrique Jara, *La rebelión estudiantil* (Montevideo: Arca, 1968); Roberto Copelmayer and Diego Díaz, *Montevideo 68: La lucha estudiantil* (Montevideo: Diaco, 1969); Carlos Demasi, ed., *La caída de la democracia: Cronología comparada de la historia del Uruguay, 1967–1973* (Montevideo: Fondo de Cultura Universitaria/CEIU/FHUCE, 2001); Jorge Landinelli, *1968: La revuelta estudiantil* (Montevideo: Facultad de Humanidades y Ciencias–Ediciones de la Banda Oriental, 1989); Vania Markarian, María Eugenia Jung, and Isabel Wschebor, *1958: El cogobierno autonómico* and *1968: La insurgencia estudiantil* (Montevideo: Archivo General de la Universidad de la República, 2008); Eduardo Rey Tristán, *A la vuelta de la esquina: La izquierda revolucionaria uruguaya, 1955–1973* (Montevideo: Fin de Siglo, 2006); and Gonzalo Varela Petito, *El movimiento estudiantil de 1968: El IAVA, una recapitulación personal* (Montevideo: Trilce, 2002).

2. See Jeffrey L. Gould, "Solidarity under Siege: The Latin American Left, 1968," *American Historical Review* 114, no. 2 (April 2009): 348–75.

3. See Copelmayer and Díaz, *Montevideo 68: La lucha estudiantil,* 81; Landinelli, *1968: La revuelta estudiantil,* 31–32.

4. See, e.g., Varela Petito, *El movimiento estudiantil de 1968,* 66–67; "Ya son tres los muertos," *Marcha,* September 27, 1968, 13.

5. On the use of Molotov cocktails at this stage, see Bañales and Jara, *La rebelión estudiantil*, III.

6. For an analysis of this episode framed in the longer-term process of the "dismantling of [Uruguay's] pedagogical tradition," see Antonio Romano, *De la reforma al proceso: Una historia de la Enseñanza Secundaria (1955–1977)* (Montevideo: Trilce/CSIC/UDELAR, 2010), esp. 68–73.

7. Protests outside the capital were most likely different from those in Montevideo. Some clues to what they were like can be found in the repeated demands from parents and students against the "politicization" of teachers, which were not as frequently seen in the capital. While there is no systematic research on this subject, it should be noted that the climate of protest was also felt outside Montevideo. See, e.g., "Estudiantes de Vichadero desocupan liceo," *Acción*, April 3, 1968, 4; and "Medidas en secundaria por hechos ocurridos en liceos del interior," *El País*, September 11, 1968, 4.

8. See, e.g., Landinelli, *1968: La revuelta estudiantil*, 34; Rey Tristán, *A la vuelta de la esquina*, 384; and Varela Petito, *El movimiento estudiantil de 1968*, 70.

9. Varela Petito, *El movimiento estudiantil de 1968*, 60.

10. See, e.g., Landinelli, *1968: la revuelta estudiantil*, 35–37; and Bañales and Jara, *La rebelión estudiantil*, 117.

11. See Decreto 383/968, June 13, 1968, in Uruguay, Poder Ejecutivo, Registro Nacional de Leyes y Decretos.

12. See Álvaro Rico, *1968: El liberalismo conservador* (Montevideo: FHC/UDELAR and Ediciones de la Banda Oriental, 1989).

13. See, e.g., Landinelli, *1968: La revuelta estudiantil*, 39; and Bañales and Jara, *La rebelión estudiantil*, 74–75.

14. Quoted in Landinelli, *1968: La revuelta estudiantil*, 45.

15. For a detailed account of these days from the perspective of university authorities, see María Blanca París de Oddone, *La Universidad de la República de la crisis a la intervención 1958–1973* (Montevideo: Universidad de la República, 2011), 115–17.

16. See, e.g., París de Oddone, *La Universidad de la República*, 42–43; and Bañales and Jara, *La rebelión estudiantil*, 121. See also "Bombas de gas contra la Facultad de Arquitectura," *Jornada*, July 30, 1968; and "Los

incidentes frente a arquitectura," *Gaceta de la Universidad,* July–August 1968. General Líber Seregni, who would later become the top leader of the leftist coalition Broad Front (Frente Amplio, or FA), lived at the time in an apartment across the street from the School of Architecture and promptly alerted university authorities of the students' actions. See Consejo Directivo Central (CDC), *Actas de Sesiones,* July 29, 1968, Archivo General de la Universidad de la República (AGU), Montevideo.

17. See, e.g., Landinelli, *1968: La revuelta estudiantil,* 48–50; Bañales and Jara, *La rebelión estudiantil,* 123; and Markarian, Jung, and Wschebor, *1968: La insurgencia estudiantil,* 102–3.

18. Asamblea General del Claustro Universitario, *Actas,* August 10, 1968, AGU. For a detailed account of these events, see París de Oddone, *La Universidad de la República,* 116–17.

19. See, e.g., Landinelli, *1968: La revuelta estudiantil,* 54–60; Bañales and Jara, *La rebelión estudiantil,* 123–24; and *Chasque,* August 28, 1968 (a weekly publication issued briefly as a substitute for *Marcha* when it was closed for three issues on August 21). For an interesting interpretation of that night's incidents in Avenida 18 de Julio, see Samuel Blixen, *Seregni: La mañana siguiente* (Montevideo: Ediciones de Brecha, 1997), 55–56.

20. See "Ya son tres los muertos," *Marcha,* September 27, 1968, 13; and the police file labeled "Incidentes y desalojo del liceo Zorrilla de San Martín, Set. 68" (Folder 3314), in Uruguay, Ministerio del Interior, Archivo de la Dirección Nacional de Información e Inteligencia (ADNII), Montevideo (hereafter cited as ADNII).

21. See, e.g., Varela Petito, *El movimiento estudiantil de 1968,* 113–15. See also "A la opinión pública," Statement by the Uruguayan Association of Medical Doctors (Sindicato Médico del Uruguay), September 21, 1968, in Archivo Maggiolo (Box 10, Folder 212), AGU; CDC, *Actas de Sesiones,* September 21, 1968, AGU; file labeled "Sucesos 18 y 20 Set. 1968, Universidad, Medicina y Cerro" (Folders 5093 A and B), ADNII.

22. See, e.g., "Educación: el boleto estudiantil," *Vanguardia,* May 21, 1968, 14. See also the descriptions of university mobilizations and police responses between 1958 and the first half of the 1960s in París de Oddone, *La Universidad de la República,* 62–81, 107–19.

23. See Varela Petito, *El movimiento estudiantil de 1968*, 96, 125.

24. Romano, *De la reforma al proceso*, 53.

25. See Varela Petito, *El movimiento estudiantil de 1968*, 113.

26. See, e.g., Landinelli, *1968: La revuelta estudiantil*, 10–18; and the more nuanced views in Varela Petito, *El movimiento estudiantil de 1968*, 135. This is also what Romano meant with the "dissolution of the specific educational aspect of the confrontation" in the case of secondary education, in Romano, *De la reforma al proceso*, 48.

27. See Aldo E. Solari, "La universidad en transición en una sociedad estancada: El caso de Uruguay," in Aldo E. Solari, ed., *Estudiantes y política en América Latina* (Caracas: Monte Ávila Editores, 1968), 201–4. A few years earlier, another sociologist, Isaac Ganón, had been similarly surprised at the intergenerational harmony reflected in students' opinions on family life. See his conclusions from a survey conducted in 1964 by the Institute of Social Sciences of the Law School of the University of the Republic published as "Nuestro estudiante contemporáneo," in Isaac Ganón, *Estructura social del Uruguay* (Montevideo: Editorial As, 1966), 183–86.

28. For an approach to these issues, see Vania Markarian, "Apogeo y crisis del reformismo universitario: Algunos debates en torno al plan Maggiolo en la UDELAR," *Pensamiento Universitario* 14 (2011).

29. See Markarian, Jung, and Wschebor, *1968: la insurgencia estudiantil*, pp. 17–25. Regarding the sign, see CDC, *Actas de Sesiones*, October 20, 1967, AGU.

30. See Markarian, Jung, and Wschebor, *1968: la insurgencia estudiantil*, 27–28.

31. See CDC, *Actas de Sesiones*, July 5 and 12, 1968, AGU.

32. As was the case with the July 1968 incident at the School of Architecture mentioned above and another that led the rector to resign for a few days in October 1967 (see notes 16, 30). There was a marked increase in this type of conflict as of 1967. In her detailed study of this period in the history of the university, París de Oddone gives an account of only two similarly serious instances prior to that year: one in 1961 and another in 1965. See París de Oddone, *La Universidad de la República*, 69, 78–81.

33. For the lack of safety in large central marches, see Bañales and Jara, *La rebelión estudiantil*, 100; Varela Petito, *El movimiento estudiantil de 1968*, 73.

34. Quoted in Carlos Bañales, "Qué pasa cuando los veinteañeros alzan la voz," *Marcha,* June 7, 1968, 8–9.

35. On the importance of urban public spaces for youth-generated protest music in the United States, see George Lipsitz, "Who'll Stop the Rain? Youth Culture, Rock 'n' Roll, and Social Crisis," in David Farber, ed., *The Sixties: From Memory to History* (Chapel Hill: University of North Carolina Press, 1994), 213–14.

36. The counter-course experience has not been studied in depth. See some references in Cores, *El 68 uruguayo,* pt. 3, chap. 3;; Romano, *De la reforma al proceso,* 88–89; Bañales and Jara, *La rebelión estudiantil,* 112–13; Copelmayer and Díaz, *Montevideo 68,* 28–29.

37. See Varela Petito, *El movimiento estudiantil de 1968,* 98–101.

38. Quoted in Copelmayer and Díaz, *Montevideo 68,* 34.

39. See, e.g., the description of the budget-related protests of 1963 in París de Oddone, *La Universidad de la República,* 71. This same aspect appears in the demonstrations filmed by Mario Handler for the university's film institute, Instituto de Cinematografía de la Universidad de la República (ICUR), in 1965. See *El "entierro" de la Universidad,* 2 mins., directed by Mario Handler (Montevideo: ICUR, 1967), in Fondo ICUR/DMCT, AGU.

40. There is no account of the content of the School of Architecture sign in any of the sources, but there is a reference to its "great sense of humor" in CDC, *Actas de Sesiones,* July 29 and August 5, 1968, AGU; and to its "dramatic irony" in the July 30, 1968, issue of the FEUU newspaper, *Jornada.* The high school sign is referred to in Carlos Bañales, "Qué pasa cuando los veinteañeros alzan la voz," *Marcha,* June 7, 1968, 8–9.

41. See, e.g., Varela Petito, *El movimiento estudiantil de 1968,* 70, 88.

42. Quoted in Bañales and Jara, *La rebelión estudiantil,* 32–33. On the importance of political participation and virility in the U.S. "New Left" (and the criticism by feminists), see Doug Rossinow, *The Politics of Authenticity: Liberalism, Christianity, and the New Left in America* (New York: Columbia University Press), 16–18, 297–333.

43. Carlos Quijano, "La tierra purpúrea," *Marcha,* October 17, 1969.

44. Something similar can also be seen in later analyses of these processes of radicalization, such as Herbert Gatto, *El cielo por asalto:*

El Movimiento de Liberación Nacional (Tupamaros) y la izquierda uruguaya (Montevideo: Taurus, 2004).

45. Quoted in *Jornada*, August 22, 1968, 1, taken from Landinelli, *1968: La revuelta estudiantil*, 60.

46. Quoted in *Jornada*, June 20, 1968, 1, taken from Landinelli, *1968: La revuelta estudiantil*, 40.

47. Quoted in Copelmayer and Díaz, *Montevideo 68*, 18.

48. See, e.g., CDC, *Actas de Sesiones*, September 21, 1968, AGU. The student movement was apparently divided on this matter over the "concept of private property," according to statements quoted in Bañales and Jara, *La rebelión estudiantil*, 99.

49. See the records of arrests in the file labeled "Acto público y manifestación de FEUU. Daños en 18 de Julio y detenciones 7/6/68" (Folder 2495), ADNII. For the strategies deployed by students to confront police actions, in particular tear gas, see Bañales and Jara, *La rebelión estudiantil*, 97–98.

50. In this regard, the information contained in the DNII files is taken as truthful given that there was no reason to minimize the injuries suffered by the police in clashes with students. As in other records of the time, there is information on injured police officers, but no deaths or permanent damage are reported. See, e.g., the unlabeled file on the incidents of September 18 and 20 at the School of Medicine, the Cerro neighborhood, and the main building of the university (Folders 5093 A and B, Fourteenth Police Division), ADNII. For a student account on "serious" injuries inflicted on a police officer, see Copelmayer and Díaz, *Montevideo 68*, 41.

51. See CDC, *Actas de Sesiones*, July 12, 1968, AGU. See also Varela Petito, *El movimiento estudiantil de 1968*, 75.

52. See "Ya son tres los muertos," *Marcha*, September 27, 1968, 13–15. See also Varela Petito, *El movimiento estudiantil de 1968*, 75.

53. See, e.g., "Falta de autoridad Universitaria," *Acción*, August 9, 1968, 1.

54. See the file labeled "Incidentes y desalojo del Liceo Zorrilla de San Martín, Set. 68" (Folder 3314), ADNII; and "Remitido por dar armas a estudiantes," *Acción*, September 14, 1968, 1. See also Bañales and Jara, *La rebelión estudiantil*, 127.

55. In the Senate session held October 8 and 9, 1968, quoted in Información Documental de América Latina (INDAL), ed., *Las Medidas Prontas de Seguridad: Actas de la Cámara de Senadores del Uruguay* (Caracas: INDAL, 1973), III.

56. Ibid., 96.

57. Varela Petito, G., *El movimiento estudiantil de 1968*, 73.

58. Quoted in Copelmayer and Díaz, *Montevideo 68*, 7–19, 37–38, 40, 43–44.

59. Quote from *El País,* July 14, 1968, 1, taken from Landinelli, *1968: La revuelta estudiantil*, 42.

60. The two instances in which they participated directly and that are most remembered with respect to the student movement were the removal on July 29 of the sign put up in the School of Architecture and the surrounding of education facilities starting on September 22. Many students still had a favorable opinion of the military. See, e.g., Copelmayer and Díaz, *Montevideo 68*, 39. These attitudes toward the military, shared by many sectors of the Left, had major political consequences in the following years, when the armed forces increased their political participation. See, e.g., Vania Markarian, *Idos y recién llegados: La izquierda uruguaya en el exilio y las redes transnacionales de derechos humanos, 1967–1984* (Mexico City: Ediciones La Vasija/Correo del Maestro–CEIU, 2006), 30–40.

61. There are different versions of what happened in the lead-up to Líber Arce's death, but there is no doubt at all as to the identity of the shooter, a police officer from the Ninth Precinct who, moreover, was charged and sentenced to a short term in prison. See, e.g., the reference to the officer having used a .22-caliber gun, which was not his service gun, in "Los presos del penal golpearon al oficial que mató a Líber Arce," *Extra,* November 8, 1968, 9. For an eyewitness account, see Héctor Lezcano, quoted in César Di Candia, *El camino de la violencia uruguaya, 1940–1973* (Montevideo: Ediciones El País, 2006), 25–26.

62. See, e.g., the operation documented in the file labeled "Incidentes y desalojo del Liceo Zorrilla de San Martín, Set. 68" (Folder 3314), ADNII.

63. For a description of repressive strategies, see Varela Petito, *El movimiento estudiantil de 1968*, 74–75, 92, 108, 113–14; Bañales and Jara,

La rebelión estudiantil, 103–4; and Copelmayer and Díaz, *Montevideo 68,* 38–44.

64. See Clara Aldrighi, *El caso Mitrione: La intervención de los Estados Unidos en Uruguay, 1965–1973* (Montevideo: Trilce, 2007), 387, 390–93.

65. In the Senate session of October 8 and 9, 1968, cited in INDAL, *Las Medidas Prontas de Seguridad,* 77; and for the speeches by the other senators in that session and in the October 29 session, also with Minister Jiménez de Aréchaga present, 70–158.

66. Ibid., 70–153; and for the reference to the "Uruguayan Cohn-Bendit," 89. With respect to the Tupamaros, it is interesting to note that until that moment the press did not systematically link them to the general social and political protest movement. See, e.g., "Tupamaros: Conmoción," *Extra,* October 9, 1968, 1.

CHAPTER TWO: DISCUSSIONS

1. See, e.g., Jorge Landinelli, *1968: la revuelta estudiantil* (Montevideo: Facultad de Humanidades y Ciencias–Ediciones de la Banda Oriental, 1989), 8–10.

2. Interview with Mercedes Espínola, in *Brecha,* "1968: La pasión por el poder (4)," August 8, 1998, 8.

3. See, e.g., Landinelli, *1968: la revuelta estudiantil,* 9.

4. The number of high school students doubled from 1950 to 1960, following similar growth in the previous decade. See Germán Rama, *Grupos sociales y enseñanza secundaria* (Montevideo: Arca, 1963), 15–17.

5. See the documents included in the file labeled "Coordinadora de Estudiantes de Secundaria del Uruguay—CESU" (Folder 1928), in Uruguay, Ministerio del Interior, Archivo de la Dirección Nacional de Información e Inteligencia (ADNII), Montevideo.

6. See "Proyecto de Estatutos de la Coordinadora de Estudiantes de Secundaria del Uruguay (que será discutido en la 2ª Convención Nacional)" in the file labeled "Coordinadora de Estudiantes de Secundaria del Uruguay—CESU" (Folder 1928), and other documents in the file labeled "Agrupaciones de estudiantes—FEUU y otras organizaciones" (Folder 1318), ADNII. See also Gonzalo Varela Petito, *El movimiento estudiantil de 1968: El IAVA, una recapitulación personal*

(Montevideo: Trilce, 2002), 47; and Eduardo Rey Tristán, *A la vuelta de la esquina: La izquierda revolucionaria uruguaya, 1955–1973* (Montevideo: Fin de Siglo, 2006), 388.

7. See, e.g., Varela Petito, *El movimiento estudiantil de 1968*, 50–52. For a similar process at the university level and its significant changes during that time, see Aldo E. Solari, "La Universidad en transición en una sociedad estancada: el caso de Uruguay," in Aldo E. Solari, ed., *Estudiantes y política en América Latina* (Caracas: Monte Ávila Editores, 1968), 180–205.

8. Quoted in Roberto Copelmayer and Diego Díaz, *Montevideo 68: La lucha estudiantil* (Montevideo: Diaco, 1969), 16.

9. Varela Petito, *El movimiento estudiantil de 1968*, 102.

10. Ibid., 145.

11. See, e.g., Carlos Bañales and Enrique Jara, *La rebelión estudiantil* (Montevideo: Arca, 1968), 73–75.

12. For the CESU, see "Proyecto de Estatutos de la Coordinadora de Estudiantes de Secundaria del Uruguay (que será discutido en la 2a Convención Nacional)," in the file labeled "Coordinadora de Estudiantes de Secundaria del Uruguay—CESU" (Folder 1928), ADNII.

13. Quoted in Copelmayer and Díaz, *Montevideo 68*, 25, 27.

14. For UTU students, see Bañales and Jara, *La rebelión estudiantil*, 71–72. See also the flyer with the message "Ante la represión del gobierno, UTU responde con la violencia revolucionaria en la calle" (The UTU responds to government repression with revolutionary violence in the streets), in the file labeled "Incidentes y desalojo del Liceo Zorrilla de San Martín, Set. 68" (Folder 3314), ADNII. Álvaro Gascue recalls that there were FER groups "in the IAVA, in the last two years ... of the Miranda [high school], in the Cerro high school, and in the Zorrilla night school." See Álvaro Gascue, "Apuntes para una historia del Frente Estudiantil Revolucionario (FER)," *Cuadernos de la Historia Reciente 6* (2010): 26.

15. See Varela Petito, *El movimiento estudiantil de 1968*, 60–65. A report found in the DNII files also traces the origins of the FER to the IAVA elections of May 1967 and indicates the influence of the Uruguayan Anarchist Federation (Federación Anarquista Uruguaya, or FAU) and of the "Chinese communist tendency." The latter may refer to the

effect that the Sino-Soviet conflict (and the Cuban experience) had on some members of the UJC who broke away and joined the MRO in 1966. See the file labeled "FER: Informe 1508 del D-2 del 28/10/70 sobre nómina de fundadores del FER, participantes en las elecciones del 24/5/67" (Folder 3404 A), ADNII. For the history of the MRO, including its shaky alliance with the Communists, see Rey Tristán, *A la vuelta de la esquina,* 262–83. A similar version of the FER's origins in the MRO and its alliance with the FAU and some "independent" activists (although with small differences regarding groups and dates) can be found in Gascue, "Apuntes para una historia del FER," 26–27.

16. See Varela Petito, *El movimiento estudiantil de 1968,* 60, 65. For more on the MRO and the MUSP, see Rey Tristán, *A la vuelta de la esquina,* 262–83, 293–301.

17. See Gascue, "Apuntes para una historia del FER," 29. This episode, like the May 1 demonstration mentioned earlier, is part of the multiple (political, cultural, and symbolic) repercussions that the five "sugarcane marches" staged between 1962 and 1971 had in Montevideo, especially in the Left. For an in-depth analysis of these issues, see Silvina Merenson, "'A mí me llaman peludo': Cultura, política y nación en los márgenes del Uruguay" (PhD diss., IDES/Universidad Nacional de General Sarmiento, 2010), 108–40.

18. See Varela Petito, *El movimiento estudiantil de 1968,* 60–65, 127–35. On the assemblies, see also "Implementar asambleas de clases," in an undated issue of *Barricada* found in the file labeled *"Barricada,* órgano del FER" (Folder 3), ADNII; Rey Tristán, *A la vuelta de la esquina,* 390–91; Hugo Cores, *El 68 uruguayo: Los antecedentes, los hechos, los debates* (Montevideo: Ediciones de la Banda Oriental, 1997), 60; Gascue, "Apuntes para una historia del FER," 30; and Copelmayer and Díaz, *Montevideo 68,* 33–36. On the FER's operating mode, see esp. Eduardo Rey Tristán, "Movilización estudiantil e izquierda revolucionaria en el Uruguay (1968–1973)," *Revista Complutense de Historia de América* 28 (2002).

19. See, e.g., *Barricada,* "Un proceso, una vanguardia" and "Por qué planteamos el cogobierno," undated, found in the file labeled "Barricada, órgano del FER" (Folder 3), ADNII.

20. Enrollment in the university increased by 54 percent between 1955 and 1966. These percentages are calculated based on tables 2 and 3

of a document in which the rector proposed a university restructure plan, titled Distribuido 396/67 ("Plan de Reestructuración de la Universidad presentado por el Rector de la Universidad Óscar J. Maggiolo"), issued in July 1967, AGU.

21. See Mark Van Aken, *Los militantes: Una historia del movimiento estudiantil universitario uruguayo desde sus orígenes hasta 1966* (Montevideo: Fundación de Cultura Universitaria, 1990), 174. For internal differences at this stage, see also documents in the file labeled "Agrupaciones de estudiantes—FEUU y otras organizaciones" (Folder 1318), ADNII.

22. A CIA agent stationed in Montevideo during those years describes the efforts to encourage right-wing student groups and influence unions, in particular, the FEUU. See Philip Agee, *Inside the Company: CIA Diary* (New York: Bantam Books, 1976), 405. On the continued interest of various U.S. government officials in Uruguayan youth organizations see, e.g., "Amembassy Montevideo to State Department: Embassy Youth Program," April 21, 1970, National Archives and Records Administration (NARA), College Park, MD.

23. See, e.g., Landinelli, *1968: La revuelta estudiantil,* 22–23.

24. See, e.g., Héctor Rodríguez, "El arraigo de los sindicatos," *Enciclopedia Uruguaya* 51 (1969).

25. See the files labeled "Detenidos en actos no autorizados y por fijación de murales con motivo de la conferencia de Punta del Este" (Folder 2218) and "Encuentro Latinoamericano de Estudiantes" (Folder 2257), ADNII.

26. A contemporary and widely read example of this way of thinking can be found in Darcy Ribeiro, *La universidad latinoamericana* (Montevideo: Departamento de Publicaciones de la Universidad de la República, 1968).

27. See, e.g., Landinelli, *1968: La revuelta estudiantil,* 101; and Bañales and Jara, *La rebelión estudiantil,* 75–76.

28. See Landinelli, *1968: La revuelta estudiantil,* 39–44.

29. List based on personal communications with Roberto Markarian and Rodrigo Arocena. See also Vania Markarian, María Eugenia Jung, and Isabel Wschebor, *1968: La insurgencia estudiantil* (Montevideo: Archivo General de la Universidad de la República, 2008), 102; Bañales

and Jara, *La rebelión estudiantil,* 75–76; and "La FEUU en 1968: Nosotros los de entonces . . . ," *Brecha,* August 21, 1998.

30. Varela Petito, *El movimiento estudiantil de 1968,* 73.

31. Quoted in Landinelli, *1968: La revuelta estudiantil,* 32.

32. Quoted in Copelmayer and Díaz, *Montevideo 68,* 15, 16, 23.

33. Quoted in Bañales and Jara, *La rebelión estudiantil,* 74–75.

34. See, e.g., Landinelli, *1968: La revuelta estudiantil,* 96; and Varela Petito, *El movimiento estudiantil de 1968,* 135.

35. See "La FEUU condena la intervención," *Marcha,* September 13, 1968; and "Del Centro de Estudiantes de Arquitectura," *Izquierda,* September 13, 1968. See also Landinelli, *1968: la revuelta estudiantil,* p. 92.

36. See Consejo Directivo Central (CDC), *Actas de Sesiones,* September 21, 1968, AGU.

37. See, e.g., Landinelli, *1968: La revuelta estudiantil,* 44, 89–99; and Varela Petito, *El movimiento estudiantil de 1968,* 124–25.

38. See the file labeled "Disidentes de FEUU" (Folder 3224), ADNII. One of these documents is mentioned in passing in Cores, *El 68 uruguayo,* pt. 3, chap. 6. He also includes a group from the School of Medicine among the students who signed the document.

39. See "Proyecto de manifiesto a la militancia federal," in the file labeled "Disidentes de FEUU" (Folder 3224), ADNII. For similar criticism of the FEUU leadership, see statements by medical students quoted in Bañales and Jara, *La rebelión estudiantil,* 84–86.

40. See "Nuestra posición" in the file labeled "Disidentes de FEUU" (Folder 3224), ADNII.

41. See "Los métodos de lucha" in the file labeled "Disidentes de FEUU" (Folder 3224), ADNII. For similar positions of "radical" students, see the statements quoted in Bañales and Jara, *La rebelión estudiantil,* 82–83.

42. See "Los métodos de lucha" in the file labeled "Disidentes de FEUU" (Folder 3224), ADNII.

43. See Varela Petito, *El movimiento estudiantil de 1968,* 51, 138–39, 141; and Cores, *El 68 uruguayo,* pt. 3, chap. 3.

44. See Gerardo Leibner, *Camaradas y compañeros: Una historia política y social de los comunistas del Uruguay* (Montevideo: Trilce, 2011), 461–514.

45. See, e.g., Rey Tristán, *A la vuelta de la esquina*, 15, 382.

46. Gerardo Leibner, "Las ideologías sociales de los revoluciona-rios uruguayos de los 60," *Nuevo Mundo Mundos Nuevos* (2007), http://nuevomundo.revues.org//index11682.html.

47. See, e.g., "La protesta estudiantil," *Marcha,* June 7, 1968; and the following in *Marcha*'s "Cartas de los lectores": "Los estudiantes galle-gos también se rebelan" and "Los estudiantes franceses y las estructu-ras decrépitas," May 31, 1968; "La imagen de los revolucionarios," June 7, 1968; "La protesta estudiantil," July 5, 1968; and "Marcuse y los estu-diantes," December 20, 1968.

48. See, e.g., Jean-Francois Kahn, "Europa: la juventud se rebela," and Meri Franco-Lao, "Sobre el movimiento estudiantil en Italia," *Marcha,* April 26, 1968.

49. See, e.g., Christian Hebert, "Aux armes, étudiants," *Marcha,* May 11, 1968; Alberto Ciria, "El poder estudiantil en EEUU," and Luis Cam-podónico, "Sangre y fuego en el barrio latino," *Marcha,* May 17, 1968; "La encrucijada de Francia," *Marcha,* May 24, 1968; Lucien Mercier, "¿Revolu-ción cultural en París?," *Marcha,* May 31, 1968; and Carlos Fuentes, "La Francia revolucionaria: imágenes e ideas," *Marcha,* July 25, 1968.

50. See "Los siete héroes de la nueva izquierda," *Marcha,* May 31, 1968; and "Herbert Marcuse, el ídolo de los estudiantes rebeldes," *Marcha,* May 17, 1968.

51. See "Los Estudiantes," *Cuadernos de Marcha,* July 15, 1968. Other authors popular at the time, such as C. Wright Mills and Louis Althus-ser, were also featured in *Cuadernos de Marcha* in 1968, along with clas-sic Marxist texts and writings by Uruguayan and Latin American left-wing intellectuals, protest movement leaders from around the world, and representatives of European political liberalism, among other tendencies and schools of thought.

52. See, e.g., Carlos Núñez, "Brasil: Por qué luchan los estudiantes," *Marcha,* July 25, 1968; and Hiner Conteris, "México, nuevo brote de la rebelión estudiantil," *Marcha,* September 27, 1968.

53. See, e.g., the announcements for books such as *Insurgencia estu-diantil* published by Editorial Acción Directa of Montevideo with texts by Daniel Cohn-Bendit and Rudi Dutschke and documents of the U.S., Dutch, and Italian student movements (*Chasque,* August 28, 1968);

La imaginación al poder: La revolución estudiantil, published by Insurrexit of Buenos Aires, with writings by Cohn-Bendit, Marcuse, and Sartre (*Marcha,* November 1, 1968). These selections were published in advance of book distribution in the Uruguayan market and were most likely more widely read. Varela Petito notes, for example, that the "two most important (and difficult to digest) books" by Marcuse were not found in Montevideo bookstores until 1969 (Varela Petito, *El movimiento estudiantil de 1968,* 111).

54. See Jeremy Varon, *Bringing the War Home: The Weather Underground, the Red Army Faction, and Revolutionary Violence in the Sixties and Seventies* (Berkeley: University of California Press, 2004), 166–68, 188–89; Jeremi Suri, *Power and Protest: Global Revolution and the Rise of Détente* (Cambridge, MA: Harvard University Press, 2003), 121–30; and Douglas C. Rossinow, "'The Revolution Is about Our Lives': The New Left's Counterculture," in Peter Braunstein and M. W. Doyle, eds., *Imagine Nation: The American Counterculture of the 1960s and 1970s* (New York: Routledge, 2001), 99–124.

55. See, e.g., Michael Seidman, *The Imaginary Revolution: Parisian Students and Workers in 1968* (New York: Berghahn Books, 2004), 2–3.

56. José Pedro Massera, "Al señor A.O.," Cartas de los Lectores, *Marcha,* August 2, 1968, 2–3.

57. Rodney Arismendi, "Sobre la insurgencia juvenil," *Estudios* 47 (October 1968).

58. Marisa Silva, *Aquellos comunistas, 1955–1973* (Montevideo: Taurus, 2009), 37–48.

59. Juan Flo, "La universidad agredida responde junto con todo el pueblo," *Estudios* 48 (December 1968). This philosopher offered a sophisticated version of the argument by pointing out as a particularity of young people "a more lax commitment with the dominant ideology as ... they begin their intellectual life when the power of attraction of that ideology is starting to wane" and the fact that "they experience the social crisis more directly as a personal crisis." Flo formed part of ideological and philosophical aggiornamento efforts that emerged in 1967 and 1968 within the intellectual circles of the PCU and were expressed in the magazine *Praxis,* whose editing staff also included Julio Rodríguez and Alberto Oreggioni. See Magadalena Broquetas,

"La revista *Praxis* (Uruguay, 1967–1968): Marxismo como ciencia y compromiso, 'dos caras inseparables de la misma actitud'" (unpublished MS, courtesy of the author in 2009).

60. Silva, *Aquellos comunistas,* 159–76.

61. Arismendi, "Sobre la insurgencia juvenil." On the role of the middle sectors, and in particular students, and criticism of other positions, including Garaudy's and Marcuse's, see José Luis Massera, "A manera de presentación," in Rodney Arismendi, ed., *Insurgencia juvenil: ¿Revuelta o revolución?* (Montevideo: EPU, 1972).

62. The first youth groups connected with the Communist Party were founded in the 1920s, following the student mobilizations spurred by the university reform movement in Córdoba, Argentina. They were members of the Moscow-based Young Communist International and participated in the activities of the Red Sports Federation (Federación Roja del Deporte). According to some activists of those early years, young Communists were particularly concerned with international issues, mobilizing in defense of the Soviet Union and the Spanish Republic. Domestically, they were especially active in protesting against mandatory conscription in the 1940s. Around that time, with Eugenio Gómez at the helm of the Party, many young people were expelled or withdrew from activism in rejection to his sectarianism and rigidity, and the Communist Youth Federation (Federación Juvenil Comunista) was dissolved in 1946. The refounding of the federation as the UJC in 1955 was done by members of a PCU student division and "a few labor activists." At the end of 1967, with fourteen divisions in the capital and at least one division in each of the eighteen departments outside Montevideo, it prided itself on being "the country's largest political youth organization." See "Los jóvenes y la conferencia de la OLAS," *Marcha,* September 8, 1967; "Era imperioso formar la fuerza de avanzada de la juventud uruguaya," *UJOTACE,* August 25, 1970, 6; and "Los primeros antecedentes de la UJC: Dos testimonios," *UJOTACE,* August 29, 1970, 8–9.

63. "Universitario comunista" and "La protesta estudiantil," *Marcha,* July 5, 1968, 2.

64. Walter Sanseviero, *Juventud, lucha constante* (Montevideo: UJC, 1969), 22, quoted in Landinelli, *1968: La revuelta estudiantil,* 98.

65. Universidad de la República, Facultad de Derecho y Ciencias Sociales, Instituto de Ciencias Sociales, *Registro universitario 1960: Informe general preliminar* (Montevideo, 1961), 64.

66. See, e.g., Bañales and Jara, *La rebelión estudiantil,* 88–96; Varela Petito, *El movimiento estudiantil de 1968,* 141; Copelmayer and Díaz, *Montevideo 68,* 33, 44; and the file labeled "Sucesos 18 y 20 Set./968, Universidad, Medicina y Cerro" (Folders 5093 A and B), ADNII.

67. Cores, *El 68 uruguayo,* pt. 1, chap. 4.

68. "Proyecto de manifiesto a la militancia federal," in the file labeled "Disidentes de FEUU" (Folder 3224), ADNII.

69. See "La FEUU condena la intervención," *Marcha,* September 13, 1968. See also "Del Centro de Estudiantes de Arquitectura," *Izquierda,* September 13, 1968.

70. For more information on these groups, see, e.g., Rey Tristán, *A la vuelta de la esquina,* 63–122, 185–301. As of late 1966, the Socialist Youth had its own page in *El Sol,* the official newspaper of the Socialist Party, which paid little attention to new cultural developments of the younger generation. See *El Sol,* years 1966 and 1967.

71. Manifiesto del Coordinador Juvenil Universitario Antiimperialista, published under the letters to the editor section of *Marcha,* January 20, 1967; see also *El Sol,* January 13, 1967 (where the UJC's reasons for not joining are discussed). In her detailed analysis of Argentine youth in the 1950s and 1960s, Valeria Manzano mentions similar forms of conceiving youth as a political actor, denying its condition as such in its immersion in "the people." See Valeria Manzano, *The Age of Youth in Argentina: Culture, Politics, and Sexuality from Perón to Videla* (Chapel Hill: University of North Carolina Press, 2014), chap. 6.

72. See Copelmayer and Díaz, *Montevideo 68,* 15, 41.

73. Landinelli, *1968: La revuelta estudiantil,* 94–95.

74. See the statements quoted in Bañales and Jara, *La rebelión estudiantil,* 81. On the relation between struggle as an "attitude toward life" and struggle as an "attitude toward politics," see also Copelmayer and Díaz, *Montevideo 68,* 82, 96.

75. "Declaración de los Estudiantes de Bellas Artes sobre las luchas de los estudiantes franceses," *Marcha,* May 31, 1968. On this militant

ethos among mobilized students in Europe and the United States, see Varon, *Bringing the War Home,* 75.

76. See Prieto's response to a text by the Communist historian Julio Rodríguez in "Marcuse y los estudiantes," published in Letters to the Editors, *Marcha,* December 20, 1968. Prieto, the AEBA, and other anarchists often found themselves coming up against their fellow activists in the labor movement who, in discussions regarding the Cuban experience, had a more "centralizing" view of organizational aspects and were more inclined toward revolutionary violence in strategic matters. For more information on the development and positions of the different anarchist groups of this period, see Rey Tristán, *A la vuelta de la esquina,* 198–256.

77. Hugo Cores, *Memorias de la resistencia* (Montevideo: Ediciones de la Banda Oriental, 2002), 84–85.

78. José Pedro Cardoso, "Los estudiantes," *Izquierda,* September 13, 1968.

79. Copelmayer and Díaz, *Montevideo 68,* 43.

80. Ibid., 50.

81. Ibid., 11.

82. See, e.g., Jorge Castañeda, *Utopia Unarmed: The Latin American Left after the Cold War* (New York: Vintage Books, 1994), 73–77; and Greg Grandin, *The Last Colonial Massacre: Latin America in the Cold War* (Chicago: University of Chicago Press, 2004), 12–13.

83. See, e.g., Massera, "A manera de presentación." This same line of reasoning furthered the process that culminated in the creation of the Broad Front (Frente Amplio, or FA) left-wing coalition in 1971.

84. See the speech by Ernesto Guevara published under the title "No hay revolución sin sacrificio," *Cuadernos de Marcha,* November 7, 1967, 49–57.

85. See Leibner, *Camaradas y compañeros,* 461–514.

86. Rodney Arismendi, "Anotaciones acerca de la táctica del movimiento obrero y popular," *Estudios* 30 (July–August 1964): 7; and Arismendi, "Conversación con los jóvenes," 204–14.

87. On Arismendi's role, see Silva, *Aquellos comunistas,* 113–17.

88. See Rodney Arismendi, *Lenin, la revolución y América Latina* (Montevideo: EPU, 1970), esp. 263–70, 309, 338. With respect to the

OLAS meeting, a famous anecdote has Arismendi standing up when the resolutions in favor of armed struggle in the continent and critical of the Soviet Union were acclaimed but refusing to join the other delegates in the applause. An overview of the differences of the Uruguayan delegation at that meeting can be found in Rey Tristán, *A la vuelta de la esquina,* 116–22; and Eduardo Rey Tristán, "La Organización Latinoamericana de Solidaridad (OLAS) y la polémica sobre las formas de la revolución latinoamericana: El caso uruguayo," in Antonio Gutiérrez Escudero and María Luisa Laviana Cuetos, coord., *Estudios sobre América, siglos XVI–XX* (Seville: Asociación Española de Americanistas, 2005).

89. Arismendi, *Lenin, la revolución y América Latina,* 331–38.

90. This argument was also applied to the Tupamaros. See, e.g., Arismendi's submission to the party congress of December 1970, in Rodney Arismendi, *Uruguay y América Latina en los años 70* (Mexico City: Ediciones de Cultura Popular, 1979), 22–23.

91. See, e.g., Arismendi's 1965 essay, "Conversación con los estudiantes," in Arismendi, *Insurgencia juvenil,* 124–27.

92. Arismendi, "Sobre la insurgencia juvenil."

93. Speech by Massera to the Legislative General Assembly on August 14, 1968, quoted in Clara Aldrighi, *La izquierda armada: Ideología, ética e identidad en el MLN-Tupamaros* (Montevideo: Trilce, 2001), 94.

94. See the book by the former Party leader Jaime Pérez, *El ocaso y la esperanza: Memorias políticas de medio siglo* (Montevideo: Fin de Siglo, 1996), 27–28, 32–35. For the account by a former rank-and-file member of that "armed apparatus," see the interview with Ricardo Calzada by Gabriel Bucheli and Jaime Yaffé, in *Cuadernos de la Historia Reciente, 1968–1985* 2 (2007): 65–78. For more information on this subject, see Varela Petito, *El movimiento estudiantil de 1968,* 136–37.

95. The PCU, Arismendi said in 1972, "assumed the obligations that solidarity imposes even in the case of mistaken revolutionaries" (Rodney Arismendi, "Uruguay y América Latina en los años setenta," in *Uruguay y América Latina,* 136). See also Varela Petito, *El movimiento estudiantil de 1968,* 137.

96. See "1968: La pasión por el poder (4)," *Brecha,* August 21, 1998, 8.

97. US Department of State, "Amembassy Moscow to State Department," June 15, 1970, NARA.

98. See "6000 nuevos afiliados durante 1969!!," *UJOTACE*, December 13, 1969, 3; "607.000 jóvenes uruguayos de 15 a 29 años," *UJOTACE*, August 15, 1970, 8.

99. See the speech by Arismendi reproduced in *El Popular* on October 3, 1969, and the letter sent by friends of Susana Pintos to *Marcha:* "Amigos y compañeros de Susana Pintos," *Marcha,* October 25, 1968.

100. For a more detailed examination of these paths taken by activists, see, e.g., Rey Tristán, *A la vuelta de la esquina,* 63–122, 185–301. With respect to the recent rupture of the MRO-PCU alliance over the definitions of the OLAS, see Ariel Collazo, *La OLAS: El camino revolucionario de los trabajadores* (Montevideo: L. y S., 1968), 31–43. The debates continued in 1968; see, e.g., *Marcha,* February 16 and November 22, 1968.

101. Among Guevara's writings the most relevant was *La guerra de guerrillas,* published in Cuba in 1960 (and shortly after in English as *Guerrilla Warfare*), and among Debray's works the most widely read was *¿Revolución en la revolución?,* published in 1967 in several capitals around the world, including Montevideo (and in English under the title *Revolution in the Revolution?*). *Cuadernos de Marcha* reproduced long passages from both books in 1967, thus making them more accessible to the Uruguayan Left as a whole. The preference of the Tupamaros for urban settings was explained in detail in one of their first documents, "Apuntes sobre lucha armada" (April 1968), quoted in Alfonso Lessa, *La revolución imposible: Los Tupamaros y el fracaso de la vía armada en el Uruguay del siglo XX* (Montevideo: Fin de Siglo, 2003), 208–12. On the debates surrounding the option of urban guerrilla warfare in the MLN-T and other groups in the Southern Cone, see Aldo Marchesi, "De la protesta local a la estrategia continental: debatiendo la revolución en el Cono Sur, 1964–1969" (Paper presented at the annual meeting of the Latin American Studies Association, Toronto, October 2010). For later rural incursions, see Lessa, *La revolución imposible,* 217–26.

102. See MLN-T, *Documento 3,* May 1968, quoted in INDAL, ed., *Movimiento de Liberación Nacional (Tupamaros): Documentación propia* (Caracas: INDAL, 1973), 51.

103. See MLN-T, "Los Tupamaros y el movimiento estudiantil," October 1968, in Omar Costa, *Los Tupamaros* (Mexico City: Era, 1971), 125–26. This document is apparently the same as the one that, accord-

ing to the press, was seized from Julio Marenales in October. There are some differences, however, between the fragments that were featured in the press then and the versions available later in books. See, e.g., *El País,* October 18, 1968.

104. On this experience, see, e.g., Nicolás Duffau, "El Coordinador, 1963–1965: La participación de los militantes del Partido Socialista en los inicios de la violencia revolucionaria en Uruguay," *Colección Estudiantes* 30 (Montevideo: FHCE, 2008).

105. For MLN-T references to the Pacheco government being a "dictatorship," see the Supplement to Documento 1, quoted in José Harari, *Contribución a la historia del MLN-Tupamaros* (Montevideo: Plural, 1987), 246; and an announcement made when Pereira Reverbel was kidnapped, reproduced in Costa, *Los Tupamaros,* 80. For similar conceptions within the FAU-ROE, see Cores, *El 68 uruguayo,* pt. 1, chap. 1. These definitions had points in common with the efforts by many contemporary analysts to characterize the authoritarian phenomena that had been spreading across the region since the 1964 coup in Brazil. For a good Uruguayan example of this tendency expressed in the debates on the "new authoritarianism," see Carlos Real de Azúa, "Política, poder y partidos en el Uruguay de hoy," in Luis Benvenuto et al., eds., *Uruguay hoy* (Buenos Aires: Siglo XXI, 1971).

106. For a more detailed description of all of these groups gathered under the inexact label "Revolutionary Left," see Rey Tristán, *A la vuelta de la esquina.*

107. See the file labeled "Disidentes de FEUU" (Folder 3224), ADNII. On the relations between these groups and the student mobilizations, see Rey Tristán, *A la vuelta de la esquina,* 127–31, 387–404. See also Landinelli, *1968: La revuelta estudiantil,* 95–98; and Varela Petito, *El movimiento estudiantil de 1968,* 124. According to Rey Tristán, the organic connection between students and Tupamaros dated back to late 1966 when the death of a student in a confrontation with the police revealed the existence of the organization. These first MLN-T students belonged to AREA 3. In October 1968, the press reported that at least two Tupamaros who had been arrested were active students (in the Schools of Agronomy and Veterinary Medicine, respectively). See, e.g., *El País,* October 16, 1968.

108. The reference is from the version of the document on the student movement featured in *El País*, October 18, 1968. It is not in the version published in Costa, *Los Tupamaros*, 125–26. See note 103 in this chapter.

109. See MLN-T, "Los Tupamaros y el movimiento estudiantil," October 1968, in Costa, *Los Tupamaros*, 125–26.

110. See, e.g., *Barricada*, "Un proceso, una vanguardia" and "Acerca de normas de conducta revolucionaria," undated, found in the file labeled "*Barricada*, órgano del FER" (Folder 3), ADNII.

111. Varela Petito, *El movimiento estudiantil de 1968*, 84–86, 118–25.

112. See, e.g., the information given by various authors and sources presented in Rey Tristán, *A la vuelta de la esquina*, 128–31. Varela Petito, for his part, acknowledges but puts in perspective the impact of students in the MLN-T. See Gonzalo Varela Petito, *De la república liberal al Estado militar: Uruguay 1968–1973* (Montevideo: Ediciones del Nuevo Mundo, 1988), 85–94.

113. See, e.g., Varela Petito, *El movimiento estudiantil de 1968*, 110, 141–42; Rey Tristán, *A la vuelta de la esquina*, 392, 400; and Aldrighi, *La izquierda armada*, 116, 130–31.

114. Donatella della Porta describes similar relations between social movements and armed groups in *Social Movements, Political Violence, and the State: A Comparative Analysis of Italy and Germany* (New York: Cambridge University Press, 1995).

CHAPTER THREE: CULTURAL EXPRESSIONS

1. Marisa Silva, *Aquellos comunistas, 1955–1973* (Montevideo: Taurus, 2009), 63–64.

2. Carlos Quijano, "La imagen de los desesperados," *Marcha*, May 10, 1968, 5.

3. Joven Comunista, "La imagen de los revolucionarios," *Marcha*, June 7, 1968, 2–3.

4. Ibid.

5. Rodney Arismendi, "Conversación con los jóvenes," in *Insurgencia juvenil: ¿Revuelta o revolución?* (Montevideo: EPU, 1972), 213.

6. Carlos María Gutiérrez, "Las tareas del Che," *Marcha*, October 11, 1968, 24.

7. Diana Sorensen, *A Turbulent Decade Remembered: Scenes from the Latin American Sixties* (Stanford, CA: Stanford University Press, 2007), 24.

8. Jorge Muso, "El principio de una opción," *Marcha*, October 11, 1968, 31.

9. Aldo Marchesi, "De la protesta local a la estrategia continental: Debatiendo la revolución en el Cono Sur, 1964–1969" (Paper presented at the annual meeting of the Latin American Studies Association, Toronto, October 2010). For other readings from this perspective among young Uruguayan writers, see also the statements by Cristina Peri Rossi and Julio E. Nosigilia in "El tiempo de los jóvenes," *Marcha*, December 27, 1968, 29–30.

10. Silva, *Aquellos comunistas*, 63–64.

11. One example repeatedly used by Arismendi was that of the Bulgarian Communist Georgi Dimitrov, who had been persecuted by the Nazis: "He was a professional revolutionary! He was a Party man!" See Arismendi's speech, June 23, 1972, in Rodney Arismendi, *Uruguay y América Latina en los años 70* (Mexico City: Ediciones de Cultura Popular, 1979), 87.

12. See Kenneth Cmiel, "The Politics of Civility," in David Farber, ed., *The Sixties From Memory to History* (Chapel Hill: University of North Carolina Press, 1994), 263–90.

13. This discourse was actually a remnant of the 1950s, and by 1968 it was sounding somewhat dated. On the 1950s, see Vania Markarian, "Al ritmo del reloj: Adolescentes uruguayos de los años cincuenta," in José Pedro Barrán, Gerardo Caetano, and Teresa Porzecanski, eds., *Historias de la vida privada en el Uruguay*, vol. 3, *Individuo y soledades 1920–1990* (Montevideo: Taurus, 1998). It would also be interesting to compare the conservative view of youth violence held in the 1950s, that is, its depiction as a threat posed primarily by the lower classes (in terms of "juvenile" delinquency), with the criminalization of student rebelliousness in the 1960s, which nevertheless turned the new generations (now middle-class) into a threat to society and its traditional values. See Vania Markarian, "Menores violentos: La adolescencia en el Uruguay de los cincuenta," *Brecha*, February 13, 1998.

14. See Silva, *Aquellos comunistas, 57–64.*

15. Rodney Arismendi, "Discurso en la Conferencia de Moscú de Partidos Comunistas y obreros" (1969), in *Vigencia del marxismoleninismo* (Mexico City: Grijalbo, 1984), 239.

16. Gonzalo Varela Petito, *El movimiento estudiantil de 1968: El IAVA, una recapitulación personal* (Montevideo: Trilce, 2002), 136.

17. For an account of this episode and its immediate repercussions, see Philip Agee, *Inside the Company: CIA Diary* (New York: Bantam Books, 1976), 459–60.

18. Data gathered in mid-1971 revealed that prison was already a relatively common experience among the young members of the UJC: of the 922 participants at the National Convention, 372—40 percent—reported that they had been arrested at one point. See "Los convencionales," *UJOTACE,* May 29, 1971, 3.

19. Walter Sanseviero, *El comunismo tiene la respuesta: 7° Congreso de la UJC* (Montevideo: Biblioteca de la UJC, 1969), 71.

20. In January 1969, for example, a radio station was seized by an MLN-T unit called Comando Susana Pintos. The names of Líber Arce and Hugo de los Santos were also used by the Tupamaros. See Eduardo Rey Tristán, *A la vuelta de la esquina: La izquierda revolucionaria uruguaya, 1955–1973* (Montevideo: Fin de Siglo, 2006), 179, 183; and Clara Aldrighi, *La izquierda armada: Ideología, ética e identidad en el MLN-Tupamaros* (Montevideo: Trilce, 2001), 133–34. Diego Sempol also notes something similar when he refers to the "social construction of [Líber] Arce as a revolutionary." Diego Sempol, "Los 'mártires' de ayer, los 'muertos' de hoy: El movimiento estudiantil y el 14 de agosto, 1968–2001," in Aldo Marchesi et al., eds., *El presente de la dictadura: Estudios y reflexiones a 30 años del golpe de Estado en Uruguay* (Montevideo: Trilce, 2004), 170.

21. The documentary in question is *Líber Arce, Liberarse.* Information obtained from Lucía Jacob, "*Marcha:* De un cine club a la C3M," in Mabel Moraña and Horacio Machín, eds., *Marcha y América Latina* (Pittsburgh, PA: University of Pittsburgh Press, 2003), 418.

22. José Rilla, *La actualidad del pasado: Usos de la historia en la política de partidos del Uruguay, 1942–1972* (Montevideo: Debate, 2008), 449.

23. See Gerardo Caetano and José Rilla, "Izquierda y tradición," *Brecha,* July 1, 1988. Also influential in this construction of a "leftist

Artigas" were the works from that time by academically trained historians such as José Pedro Barrán and Benjamín Nahum and the Marxist historians Lucía Sala and Julio Rodríguez, among others.

24. See Aldo Marchesi, "Imaginación política del antiimperialismo: Intelectuales y política en el Cono Sur a fines de los sesenta," *Estudios Interdisciplinarios de América Latina y el Caribe* 17, no. 1 (2006).

25. Part of this view is evident in, for example, two of the most widely read books of Uruguay's historical revisionism: Roberto Ares Pons, *Uruguay, ¿provincia o nación?* (Montevideo: Ediciones del Nuevo Mundo, 1967); and Alberto Methol Ferré, *El Uruguay como problema* (Montevideo: Diálogo, 1967).

26. José Rilla, "Prólogo," in Carlos Real de Azúa, *El impulso y su freno* (Montevideo: Colección de Clásicos Uruguayos, 2009), ix.

27. See, e.g., Varela Petito, *El movimiento estudiantil de 1968*, 82; and Hugo Cores, *El 68 uruguayo: Los antecedentes, los hechos, los debates* (Montevideo: Ediciones de la Banda Oriental, 1997), pt. 3, chap. 2. The conference was reproduced in a pamphlet: Julio Herrera Vargas, *Cómo se agrava la crisis nacional* (Montevideo: Librerías Ruben, 1968).

28. Clearly in Hebert Gatto, *El cielo por asalto: El Movimiento de Liberación Nacional (Tupamaros) y la izquierda uruguaya* (Montevideo: Taurus, 2002); and much more subtly in Rilla, *La actualidad del pasado* and "Prólogo."

29. It would otherwise be hard to explain the perception held at the time that emigration and political commitment were two sides of a single phenomenon, namely, the lack of opportunity young people saw in the country. See, e.g., U.S. Department of State, "Amembassy Montevideo to State Department: The Political Organization and Attitudes of the Democratic Youth in Uruguay," January 3, 1970, National Archives and Records Administration (NARA), College Park, MD; and Carlos Bañales and Enrique Jara, *La rebelión estudiantil* (Montevideo: Arca, 1968), 46–50.

30. This importance is illustrated, for example, by the fact that *Marcha* is mentioned by almost all the actors of that time interviewed in Clara Aldrighi, *Memorias de insurgencia: Historia de vida y militancia en el MLN-Tupamaros* (Montevideo: Ediciones de la Banda Oriental, 2009). For a paradigmatic exponent of the "new journalism" in Uruguay, see

Carlos María Gutiérrez, *En la Sierra Maestra y otros reportajes* (Montevideo: Ediciones Tauro, 1967). Aldo Marchesi stresses the role that several journalists of that generation played in the birth of the radical organizations of the Southern Cone. Marchesi, "De la protesta local a la estrategia continental."

31. See Aldrighi, *La izquierda armada*, 107–10.

32. See, e.g., Ivonne Trías, *Hugo Cores: Pasión y rebeldía en la izquierda uruguaya* (Montevideo: Trilce, 2008), 33.

33. One of the first studies on this militant culture in literature is Ángel Rama, "La generación crítica," in Luis Benvenuto et al., eds., *Uruguay hoy* (Buenos Aires: Siglo XXI, 1971). More recent analysts have examined different aspects of this same phenomenon, e.g., Gatto, *El cielo por asalto;* and Stephen Gregory, *Intellectuals and Left Politics in Uruguay, 1958–2006: Frustrated Dialogue* (Brighton: Sussex Academic Press, 2009).

34. Daniel Viglietti, "Canción del hombre nuevo," *Canciones para el hombre nuevo,* LP released in Montevideo by the record label Orfeo (1968). The sleeve of the Argentine edition of the album had another photograph with Viglietti in a similar pose and attire. See Daniel Viglietti, *Canciones para el hombre nuevo,* LP released in Buenos Aires by the record label EMI-Odeón (1970).

35. See Jacob, "*Marcha:* De un cine club a la C3M," 416–17.

36. See Mario Handler, *Me gustan los estudiantes,* 6 min., Montevideo, 1968. Available on YouTube.

37. See ad in *Marcha,* July 12, 1968. In September there was a film festival focusing exclusively on documentaries on student struggles, screened also at the Plaza movie theater, this time during late-night viewing hours, which featured Handler's film along with seven others. See *Marcha,* September 13, 1968.

38. José Wainer, quoted in Jacob, "*Marcha:* De un cine club a la C3M," 417.

39. For more on this subject, see Vania Markarian, "'Ese héroe es el joven comunista': Violencia, heroísmo y cultura juvenil entre los comunistas uruguayos de los sesenta," *Estudios Interdisciplinarios de América Latina y el Caribe* 21, no. 2 (December 2010).

40. See stills 0022–01_08–01FPEP and 0022–01_08–02FPEP, *El Popular* private collection, Centro de Fotografía de la Intendencia de Montevideo, Montevideo.

41. Alfredo Zitarrosa, "Diez décimas de autocrítica," *A los compañeros;* single released in Montevideo by the record label Cantares del Mundo (1972). More on this relationship between references to arms and youth cultural products in Markarian, "Ese héroe es el joven comunista."

42. These individual paths are difficult to document because of the small number of accounts available but also because in some cases they involved serious conflicts among the groups concerned. In addition to the young Communists who first left the UJC for the MRO and later founded the FER, Varela Petito recounts the case of Luis Latrónica, who after starting out as a member of the UJC in the IAVA high school, joined the Tupamaros and was killed in Argentina in 1974. Varela Petito, *El movimiento estudiantil de 1968,* 60, 136. Some DNII documents also refer to these shifts between the FER and the UJC in the IAVA in the file labeled "Barricada, órgano del FER" (Folder 3404) in Ministerio del Interior, Archivo de la Dirección Nacional de Información e Inteligencia (ADNII), Montevideo, Uruguay. For anecdotes, see http://generacion68.mundoforo.com.

43. Alfredo Zitarrosa, "Gatos coloquiales," *Marcha,* January 14, 1966, 9.

44. "A propósito de los Beatles opina Daniel Viglietti," *Época,* December 2, 1966, 17.

45. See, e.g., Denise Milstein, "Interacciones entre Estado y música popular bajo autoritarismo en Uruguay y Brasil" (Paper presented at the V Congresso Latinoamericano da Associação Internacional para o Estudo da Musica Popular, 2004), available at www. hist.puc.cl/iaspm /rio/Anais2004%20(PDF)/DeniseMilstein.pdf.

46. See Rama, "La generación crítica."

47. On cultural positions in the PCU during those years, see, e.g., Silva, *Aquellos comunistas,* 129–42.

48. In the 1970s, shortly after Gutiérrez was killed, his poetry was published twice: first in an edition by Gutiérrez's political group, the

Movimiento 26 de Marzo, and the other in a compilation by Mario Benedetti of the work of several young Latin American poets who had died for political reasons. In both cases, his activism was more important than his identity as a poet. See Luis Bravo, "La vida es una caída en el presente," in Ibero Gutiérrez, *Obra junta, 1966–1972* (Montevideo: Estuario, 2009).

49. See the exhibition catalog *Ibero Gutiérrez: Juventud, arte y política* (Montevideo: Biblioteca Nacional, Facultad de Artes–UDELAR and Museo de la Memoria–IMM, 2009); Gutiérrez, *Obra junta;* Fernando González Guyer, "Mi primo Ibero," *Noteolvides* o (December 2009); and Ibero Gutiérrez, *La pipa de tinta china: Cuadernos carcelarios 1970* (Montevideo: Estuario-Biblioteca Nacional, 2014).

50. Information gleaned from the articles by Silvia Visconti and Universindo Rodríguez, "Ibero Gutiérrez: Con la memoria en los tiempos de las utopías"; Elbio Ferrario, "El artista adolescente"; Alba Platero, "Ibero Gutiérrez, creador integral"; and Luis Bravo, "Ibero Gutiérrez, la voz poética del 68 uruguayo," in *Ibero Gutiérrez;* Bravo, "La vida es una caída en el presente"; and González Guyer, "Mi primo Ibero."

51. See Phillip Berryman, *Liberation Theology: The Essential Facts about the Revolutionary Movement in Latin America and Beyond* (New York: Pantheon Books, 1987). Note, however, that another five hundred Latin American bishops refrained from attending the conference in Medellín, thus revealing the weight of the conservative sectors that would soon reclaim the helm of the church in the region.

52. Paul VI, "Santa Misa a los campesinos de Colombia," accessed on the website of the Archdiocese of Bogotá, www.arquibogota.org.co.

53. See Bravo, "La vida es una caída en el presente," 12–13.

54. González Guyer, "Mi primo Ibero," 32. See also Visconti and Rodríguez, "Ibero Gutiérrez," 28; and Bravo, "La vida es una caída en el presente," 13.

55. On the "Christian wing" of the MLN-T, see Aldrighi, *La izquierda armada,* 85–87. While there are no historical accounts of the MAPU and the GAU, brief references can be found in Rey Tristán, *A la vuelta de la esquina,* 260. For a description of the JDC from the point

of view of U.S. diplomats stationed in Montevideo, see U.S. Department of State, "Amembassy Montevideo to State Department: The Political Organization and Attitudes of the Democratic Youth in Uruguay," January 3, 1970, NARA. For the transformations in Uruguay's Catholic Church at this stage, see Pablo Dabezíes Antía, *No se amolden al tiempo presente: Las relaciones Iglesia-sociedad en los documentos de la Conferencia Episcopal del Uruguay, 1965–1985* (Montevideo: OBSUR–Facultad de Teología del Uruguay Mons. Mariano Soler, 2009), 124–249.

56. Some have suggested that Ibero was involved in the group of young people linked to the priest Juan C. Zaffaroni (who had publicly declared his support for armed struggle) that in 1969 planned an attack on the presidential residence and was dubbed the "Akodike group" by the press because of the brand of gas cylinders that its members meant to use as a bomb. His cousin, González Guyer, who did participate in that experience, has emphatically denied Ibero's involvement. See González Guyer, "Mi primo Ibero," 32; Bravo, "La vida es una caída en el presente," 13–14; and Aldrighi, *Memorias de insurgencia,* 363.

57. Daniel Viglietti, "Cruz de luz," on the LP *Canciones para el hombre nuevo.*

58. Bravo, "La vida es una caída en el presente," 13.

59. Bravo, "Ibero Gutiérrez," 112.

60. His alleged involvement in the Akodike group (see note 56 above) was apparently the main reason for this persecution. In late 1969 he was charged and imprisoned for possible connections to guerrilla activities. Before that, as noted earlier, he had been arrested along with hundreds of activists for violating the Prompt Security Measures and again for the same reason in 1970 and 1971, when he was already a member of the Movimiento 26 de Marzo, a legal movement that supported the Tupamaros. In February 1972 he was kidnapped and murdered by a paramilitary group. His murder was reported by most of the media and the government's press releases as the death of a "seditious element," while unions and left-wing organizations denounced it as a murder and paid tribute to the dead activist. Nobody has ever been punished for the crime. It was not until 2009 that judicial proceedings were opened, in an action that implicates a businessman and

two former police officers. See Visconti and Rodríguez, "Ibero Gutiérrez," 28–41; and Bravo, "La vida es una caída en el presente," 8.

61. For more information on this subject, see Vania Markarian, "*Los Huevos del Plata:* Un desafío al campo intelectual uruguayo de fines de los sesenta," in Tania Medalla, Alondra Peirano, Olga Ruiz, and Regine Walch, eds., *Recordar para pensar: La elaboración del pasado reciente en el Cono Sur de América Latina* (Santiago: Ediciones Boll Cono Sur, 2010).

62. See *Los Huevos del Plata*, no. 13 (March 1969), and no. 12 (October 1968).

63. See Fernando Peláez, *De las cuevas al Solís: Cronología del rock en el Uruguay, 1960–1975*, vol. 1 (Montevideo: Perro Andaluz Ediciones, 2002–4), 146. As a lyricist, composer, and show organizer, Buscaglia contributed enormously to building this movement made up of bands that in the beginning of the 1970s shared, according to Peláez, a number of features: "the production of a repertoire of their own that was musically based on rock elements (or beat or pop elements) and with lyrics in Spanish, presented and defended in dances, festivals, joints, and concerts, and which had a following in an increasingly large sector of the population" (2:126).

64. Horacio Buscaglia, "Enciclopedia IPS," *Los Huevos del Plata*, no. 10 (December 1967); and Juan José Iturriberry, "Anti-Enciclopedia IPS," *Los Huevos del Plata*, no. 11 (March 1968).

65. Horacio Buscaglia, interview by the author, Montevideo, April 6, 2005.

66. Iturriberry, "Anti-Enciclopedia IPS."

67. Claudia Gilman, *Entre la pluma y el fusil: Debates y dilemas del escritor revolucionario en América Latina* (Buenos Aires: Siglo XXI, 2003), 158–60.

68. See *Los Huevos del Plata*, no. 12 (October 1968).

69. Another possibility is that these political issues had erupted when the magazine was already going to press. Clemente Padín, one of the leading men behind *HDP*, categorically denied this possibility in an interview conducted by the author on May 3, 2005, in Montevideo.

70. *Los Huevos del Plata*, no. 10 (December 1967).

71. *Los Huevos del Plata*, no. 7 (April 1967).

72. *La vaca sagrada, Los ex-Huevos del Plata,* no. 9 (September 1967).
73. "El tiempo de los jóvenes," *Marcha,* December 27, 1968, 29.
74. *Los Huevos del Plata,* no. 14 (November 1969).
75. Cristina Peri Rossi, *Los museos abandonados* (Montevideo: Arca, 1969), 7. In 1968, this book won the Young Authors' Prize awarded by the publishing house Arca.
76. *Los Huevos del Plata,* no. 14 (November 1969).
77. See, e.g., Cristina Peri Rossi, "A mi tía Elena," and Horacio Buscaglia, "Así nomás," *Los Huevos del Plata,* no. 14 (November 1969).
78. Interview with Clemente Padín, conducted by the author, Montevideo, May 3, 2005.
79. See "Tucumán Arde: paradigma de acción cultural revolucionaria," *OVUM 10,* no. 9 (December 1971).
80. In 1971, for example, Peri Rossi was part of a "Group of Cultural Workers" of the Movimiento 26 de Marzo. Two others mentioned here, Mario Handler and José Wainer, also participated in this group. See Aldrighi, *La izquierda armada,* 108. On cultural positions in the PCU, see Silva, *Aquellos comunistas,* 129–42.
81. Interviews conducted by the author with Padín and Buscaglia, Montevideo, May 3 and April 6, 2005. They both eventually joined the PCU (Padín in the late 1960s and Buscaglia in the early 1970s). See Vania Markarian, "To the Beat of 'The Walrus': Uruguayan Communists and Youth Culture in the Global Sixties," *The Americas* 70, no. 3 (2014).
82. María Matilde Ollier posits something along these same lines when she speaks of the "ideological radicalization" that preceded the "political radicalization" of those who joined Argentina's armed struggle movements in the 1960s and 1970s. See her book *La creencia y la pasión: Privado, público y político en la izquierda revolucionaria* (Buenos Aires: Ariel, 1998).
83. Interview quoted from Aldrighi, *Memorias de insurgencia,* 148.
84. See Raymond Williams, *Marxismo y literatura* (Barcelona: Península, 1980).
85. According to the announcements for *peñas* and other activities featured in *UJOTACE* starting in 1969, these styles coexisted without any of the resistance seen, for example, in the case of Argentina's

Communist Youth Federation just years before. See Valeria Manzano, "Ha llegado la 'nueva ola': Música, consumo y juventud en la Argentina, 1955–1966," in Isabella Cosse, Karina Felitti, and Valeria Manzano, eds., *Los 60 de otra manera: Vida cotidiana, género y sexualidades en la Argentina* (Buenos Aires: Prometeo, 2010), 33.

86. See the file labeled "Detenidos en actos no autorizados y por fijación de murales con motivo de la conferencia de Punta del Este" (Folder 2218), ADNII.

87. For a defense of this slogan by former Communist activists, see Gerardo Leibner, "Las ideologías sociales de los revolucionarios uruguayos de los 60," *Nuevo Mundo Mundos Nuevos* (2007), http://nuevomundo.revues.org//index11682.html.

88. For this view, see Alberto Altesor, *¿Cuáles son las tareas de los secretarios de organización?* (Montevideo: Ediciones de la Convención Nacional de Organización del PC, 1967); and Walter Sanseviero, "La juventud en las primeras filas," *Estudios* 42 (July–October 1967).

89. See, e.g., Rey Tristán, *A la vuelta de la esquina*, 397–404.

90. Varela Petito, *El movimiento estudiantil de 1968*, 104.

91. Ibid., 111.

92. See, e.g., the series of columns by Enrique Sobrado in *El Popular*'s Sunday supplement, *Magazine Domingo*, which began to be featured in May–June 1970, with titles such as "What Is Sexual Education?" (May 17), "Men's Sexual Education" (May 31), and "Women's Sexual Education" (July 21). Other experiences that combined left-wing activism with psychological counseling, such as that conducted by Juan Carlos Carrasco in working-class neighborhoods of Montevideo and with the sugarcane cutters of Artigas, have yet to be studied in depth.

93. See Gabriela Sapriza, "Feminismo y revolución: Sobre el 'infeliz matrimonio,' indagatoria sobre feminismos e izquierdas" (Paper presented at the Red Temática de Género conference, Universidad de la República, Montevideo, September 2006).

94. Quotes taken from Esther Ruiz and Juana Paris, "Ser militante en los sesenta," in Barrán, Caetano, and Porzecanski, *Historias de la vida privada*, 3:278.

95. On the relationship between sexual experiences, drug use, and everyday behavior of the Weather Underground and similar groups, see Jeremy Varon, *Bringing the War Home: The Weather Underground, the Red Army Faction, and Revolutionary Violence in the Sixties and Seventies* (Berkeley: University of California Press, 2004), 57–60.

96. Horacio Buscaglia, interview by the author, Montevideo, April 6, 2005; and Varela Petito, *El movimiento estudiantil de 1968,* 110.

97. See Peri Rossi, "A mi tía Elena," *Los Huevos del Plata,* no. 14 (November 1969); *Los museos abandonados;* and *El libro de mis primos* (Montevideo: Biblioteca de Marcha, 1969). This last book won first prize in 1969 in the Treinta Años de Marcha awards, in the novel category.

98. For some discussions on this climate of greater plasticity in leftist spaces see, e.g., the articles by Enrique Sobrado and Marcos Lijtenstein, "Algo más que bellas palabras," *Gaceta de la Universidad,* July–August 1968, 30; and Heleno Saña Alcón, "La sociedad sexualizada," *Izquierda,* November 1, 1968, 8–10. For opinions on these issues with respect to "university youths," see the statements by Hermógenes Álvarez, gynecologist and dean of the School of Medicine, in Bañales and Jara, *La rebelión estudiantil,* 30–40. For more general reflections, see Anonymous, *Sexo y amor en el Uruguay* (Montevideo: Editorial Alfa, 1970).

99. For the child-caring role assigned to women, see accounts by Henry Engler, Mario Teti Izquierdo, Samuel Blixen, Juan José Domínguez, Hugo Wilkins, and Luis Alemañy in Aldrighi, *Memorias de insurgencia.* This general picture does not, of course, cover all the cases, and it is a simplification that is only useful for understanding the majority of these experiences.

100. See the interviews with Celeste Cerpa and Ana Casamayou in Aldrighi, *Memorias de insurgencia;* and Y. Macchi, in Aldrighi, *La izquierda armada.* The line is from Viglietti's song "Gurisito" (Kid) from *Canciones chuecas,* LP released in Montevideo by the record label Orfeo (1971). Other lines of the song were "And even if you're born poor / I'll bring you too." Although it would require a more in-depth analysis, this emphasis on procreation can be said to have some points of contact with contemporary reports of U.S. plans to control

204 / Notes to Page 142

population growth in poor countries. See, e.g., Anonymous, *Sexo y amor en el Uruguay,* 134–35.

101. This image appears in the book by Silvia Soler, *La leyenda de Yessie Macchi* (Montevideo: Fin de Siglo, 2000), and differs from what this MLN-T leader (Macchi) herself gives, for example, in the interview published in Aldrighi, *La izquierda armada* (208–25), where she denies the "promiscuity" characterization as "pure defamation" by "the *milicos*" (police or military). The hypersexualized depictions of young guerrilla women, in connection with pop culture images that posited the political potential of feminine charms (present in movies such as the *James Bond* series and *Bonnie and Clyde*), have been associated with the specific ways in which women were targeted by repression. See, e.g., Victoria Langland, "Birth Control Pills and Molotov Cocktails: Reading Sex and Revolution in 1968 Brazil," in Gilbert M. Joseph and Daniela Spenser, eds., *In From the Cold: Latin America's New Encounter with the Cold War* (Durham, NC: Duke University Press, 2008). For references to these matters in the Uruguayan case, see Lindsey Churchill, "Gender Reorganization or Revolutionary Rhetoric? Women in the Uruguayan Tupamaros" (Paper presented at the annual meeting of the Latin American Studies Association,, Toronto, October 2010).

102. There are some accounts regarding the moral and political corrective value attributed to living side by side with the *peludos.* See, e.g., Yessie Macchi's interview in Aldrighi, *La izquierda armada,* 213. These processes of full militant incorporation into the MLN-T were alluded to in a document issued in late 1970: "The aim is for all militants to be proletarianized through a high quota of manual labor, ideological work, and preaching and practicing austerity, to avoid urban armed struggle deviations, eliminate the negative effects of individualism typical of the petite bourgeoisie and the middle class, from where many militants are recruited" (Aldrighi, *La izquierda armada,* 132). Silvina Merenson examines the effects of these conceptions in the following years in "'A mí me llaman peludo': Cultura, política y nación en los márgenes del Uruguay" (PhD diss., IDES/Universidad Nacional de General Sarmiento, 2010), 172–76.

103. Y. Macchi, in Aldrighi, *La izquierda armada*, 214. The Tupamaro leader Jorge Zabalza describes these two stages as a first stage of "puritan morality" and "idealism" followed, toward 1972, by a second stage where "there wasn't much room for idealizing." See Aldrighi, *La izquierda armada*, 195–96. Another leader, David Cámpora, also reflects on the effects of repression on sexual relations and love lives within the MLN-T (quoted in Aldrighi, *Memorias de insurgencia*, 236).

104. On the equalizing power of arms, see, e.g., the expressions that David Cámpora attributes to fellow MLN-T leader Mauricio Rosencof, in Aldrighi, *Memorias de insurgencia*, 236; on women used as "bait" and their ability to "chat up" and facilitate some operations, see the opinions of Samuel Blixen, Henry Engler, and Mario Teti Izquierdo (110, 191, 207). The lines are from Viglietti's song "Muchacha" (Girl) from the LP *Canciones chuecas*. These words were attributed to Che Guevara by his friend Ricardo Rojo in *Mi amigo el Che* (Buenos Aires: Jorge Álvarez, 1968). There are similar concepts in "El socialismo y el hombre en Cuba," text addressed to Carlos Quijano and published in *Marcha*, March 12, 1965.

105. See Rey Tristán, *A la vuelta de la esquina*, 298.

106. For this same "notion of couples in the intersection between political and personal lives" based on the meanings associated with the words *compañero* and *compañera* in Argentina's case, see Isabella Cosse, *Pareja, sexualidad y familia en los años sesenta* (Buenos Aires: Siglo XXI, 2010).

107. See, e.g., Varela Petito, *El movimiento estudiantil de 1968*, 110–11; and Sobrado and Lijtenstein, "Algo más que bellas palabras," 30.

108. For an initial approach to these issues based on personal impressions, see Ruiz and Paris, "Ser militante en los sesenta."

109. Quoted in Trías, *Hugo Cores*, 89–90.

110. Quoted in Ruiz and Paris, "Ser militante en los sesenta," 294. See also the accounts by Hugo Wilkins, in Aldrighi, *Memorias de insurgencia*, 259–60; and by Jorge Zabalza and Yessie Macchi, in Aldrighi, *La izquierda armada*, 197, 214. On homophobia among Communists, see Leibner, "Las ideologías sociales de los revolucionarios uruguayos de los 60." The criteria applied in cultural circles may have been

different, at least in the case of the Communists, as in those circles the idea of integration was more important than the idea of censorship. This is hinted at in the accounts by Alberto Restuccia regarding the activities of the theater company Teatro Uno, which featured nude performances and cross-dressing acts and included PCU members among its ranks and as contributors. See Nelson Barceló and Gustavo Rey, *Uno diferente: La vida de Alberto Restuccia* (Montevideo: Estuario, 2009).

111. Similar processes have been analyzed for Argentina in Valeria Manzano, *The Age of Youth in Argentina: Culture, Politics, and Sexuality from Perón to Videla* (Chapel Hill: University of North Carolina Press, 2014), 193 ff.; and Vera Carnovale, "Moral y disciplinamiento interno en el PRT-ERP," *Nuevo Mundo Mundos Nuevos* (2008), http://nuevomundo .revues.org/38782.

112. Varela Petito, *El movimiento estudiantil de 1968,* 108–11.

113. According to Leibner, this attitude can be traced to the late 1930s, when the "popular front" policy and solidarity with the Spanish Republic turned the PCU into a meeting ground for people from various urban social classes. In that context, this author associates the multiclass makeup of the PCU with its receptiveness to the various manifestations of "plebeian culture," as he calls it. See Gerardo Leibner, "Nosotras (Uruguay, 1945–1953): Las contradicciones de una revista femenina comunista y sus significados sociales," in Roland Forgues and Jean-Marie Flores, eds., *Escritura femenina y reivindicación de género en América Latina* (Paris: Mare & Martin, 2005).

114. See Leibner, "Las ideologías sociales de los revolucionarios."

115. See the chapter "Afíliate y baila," in Gerardo Leibner, *Camaradas y compañeros: Una historia política y social de los comunistas del Uruguay* (Montevideo: Trilce, 2011), 300–327.

116. "En el Uruguay actual nada, simplemente tratar de cambiarlo," *UJOTACE,* May 30, 1970, 12.

117. See "¡¡6000 nuevos afiliados durante 1969!!," *UJOTACE,* December 13, 1969, 3; and "Los convencionales," *UJOTACE,* May 29, 1971, 3.

118. A more difficult task is making sense of the percentage of unemployed. Were they young people from poor households who

were looking for work, or were they from well-off families and therefore did not need to work because their parents supported them? Although there were certainly some members who were paid by the organization, the low percentage of this category among convention delegates suggests that that was not the main reason for such a high number of unemployed. Neither does it seem very likely that the organization's cadres would describe themselves as unemployed.

119. The sources available, summarized by Rey Tristán, indicate that students made up 33 to 39 percent of the total membership of the MLN-T and were always the largest group, followed by professionals, white-collar workers, and manual workers. Most of the data are obtained from detention records, both official and from humanitarian organizations. See Rey Tristán, *A la vuelta de la esquina,* 128–31.

120. For Argentina's case, see Ezequiel Adamovsky, *Historia de la clase media argentina: Apogeo y decadencia de una ilusión, 1919–2003* (Buenos Aires: Planeta, 2009), 381–403.

121. In the Senate session held on October 8 and 9, 1968, quoted in Información Documental de América Latina (INDAL), ed., *Las Medidas Prontas de Seguridad: Actas de la Cámara de Senadores del Uruguay* (Caracas: INDAL, 1973), 89.

122. See, e.g., Arismendi's 1965 essay: Rodney Arismendi, "Conversación con los estudiantes," in *Insurgencia juvenil,* 124–27. On this issue, see also Leibner, "Las ideologías sociales de los revolucionarios."

123. See A. O., "¿Marxistas libertarios?," *Marcha,* July 26, 1968, 2; and José Pedro Massera, "Al señor A. O.," *Marcha,* August 2, 1968, 2–3. This exchange was played out in the Letters to the Editor section of *Marcha.* "A. O." accused "a young man from a well-to-do family" of being "irresponsible" in his appreciation of Uruguayan anarchists. The UJC student leader, José Pedro Massera, son of José Luis Massera and another important member of the PCU, responded, "My family is a family of Communist activists. Period."

124. With respect to the sugarcane cutters, Merenson has accurately described this "miserabilist and epic representation" and its impact on the radicalization, nationalization, and Latin Americanization of sectors of Uruguay's Left in the 1960s (see Merenson, "A mi me

llaman peludo," 111 ff.). See also Rey Tristán, *A la vuelta de la esquina,* 400; and Aldrighi, *La izquierda armada,* 132–34.

125. Leibner, "Las ideologías sociales de los revolucionarios."

CONCLUSION

1. For a more in-depth analysis on these issues, see Aldo Marchesi and Vania Markarian, "Cinco décadas de estudios sobre la crisis, la democracia y el autoritarismo en Uruguay," *Contemporánea* 3 (2012).

2. See Aldo Marchesi and Jaime Yaffé, "La violencia bajo la lupa: Una revisión de la literatura sobre violencia y política en los sesenta," *Revista Uruguaya de Ciencia Política* 19 (2010).

3. See Donatella della Porta, *Social Movements, Political Violence, and the State: A Comparative Analysis of Italy and Germany* (New York: Cambridge University Press, 1995).

4. Greg Grandin, *The Last Colonial Massacre: Latin America in the Cold War* (Chicago: University of Chicago Press, 2004), 15.

5. Eric Zolov, "Expanding our Conceptual Horizons: The Shift from an Old to a New Left in Latin America," *A Contracorriente* 5, no. 2 (Winter 2008): 73.

6. See Jeremy Varon, *Bringing the War Home: The Weather Underground, the Red Army Faction, and Revolutionary Violence in the Sixties and Seventies* (Berkeley: University of California Press, 2004).

7. See Jeremi Suri, *Power and Protest: Global Revolution and the Rise of Détente* (Cambridge, MA: Harvard University Press, 2003), esp. 81–130.

8. Ibid., 164–212.

9. Ibid., 88–94. Norbert Elias also notes the frustration caused by the difficulty of social integration faced by German youths who in the 1960s were accessing high levels of education for the first time and who saw violent protest as an attractive option. See Norbert Elias, "El terrorismo en la República Federal Alemana: Expresión de un conflicto social intergeneracional," in Norbert Elias, *Los alemanes* (Mexico City: Instituto Mora, 1999).

10. Jeffrey L. Gould, "Solidarity under Siege: The Latin American Left, 1968," *American Historical Review* 114, no. 2 (April 2009): 374.

11. See Suri, *Power and Protest,* 212.

Bibliography

ARCHIVES AND COLLECTIONS

Archivo General de la Universidad de la República (AGU), Montevideo, Uruguay:
Asamblea General del Claustro Universitario, *Actas,* 1968
Archivo Maggiolo
Consejo Central Universitario, *Actas,* 1967–68
Consejo Central Universitario, *Distribuidos,* 1967
Colección Trayectorias Universitarias
Fondo ICUR/DMTC
    Centro de Fotografía de Montevideo (CdF), Montevideo, Uruguay:
El Popular Private Collection (EP-CdF)
    Dirección Nacional de Información e Inteligencia (ADNII), Ministerio del Interior, Montevideo, Uruguay: Files made available by archive staff (approximately 1,270 photographic records).
    National Archives and Records Administration (NARA), College Park, MD, United States

INTERVIEWS

Buscaglia, Horacio. April 6, 2005. Montevideo, Uruguay
Padin, Clemente. May 3, 2005. Montevideo, Uruguay

PERIODICALS

Acción, 1968
Chasque, 1968
Cuadernos de Marcha, 1967
El País, 1968
El Popular, 1969
El Sol, 1966–67
Época, 1966
Estudios, 1964–68
Extra, 1968
Gaceta Universitaria, 1968
Izquierda, 1968
Jornada, 1968
La Morsa (El Popular supplement), 1970–71
Los Huevos del Plata, 1965–69
Magazine Domingo (El Popular supplement), 1970–73
Marcha, 1966–73
OVUM 10, 1969–72
UJOTACE (El Popular supplement), 1969–71
Vanguardia, 1968

FILMS AND RECORDS

Handler, Mario. *El "entierro" de la Universidad.* Black-and-white film; 2 min.; 16mm. Montevideo: Instituto de Cinematografía de la Universidad de la República, 1967 (in Fondo ICUR/DMTC, AGU).
———. *Me gustan los estudiantes.* Black-and-white film; 6 min.; 16mm. Montevideo, 1968 (available on YouTube).
Viglietti, Daniel. *Canciones chuecas.* Long play. Montevideo: Orfeo, 1971.
———. *Canciones para el hombre nuevo.* Long play. Montevideo: Orfeo, 1968.
———. *Canciones para el hombre nuevo.* Long play. Buenos Aires: EMI-Odeón, 1970.
Zitarrosa, Alfredo. *A los compañeros.* Single. Montevideo: Cantares del Mundo, 1972.

BOOKS, ARTICLES, AND PUBLISHED DOCUMENTS

Adamovsky, Ezequiel. *Historia de la clase media argentina: Apogeo y decadencia de una ilusión, 1919–2003.* Buenos Aires: Planeta, 2009.

Agee, Philip. *Inside the Company: CIA Diary.* New York: Bantam Books, 1976.

Aldrighi, Clara. *La izquierda armada: Ideología, ética e identidad en el MLN-Tupamaros.* Montevideo: Trilce, 2001.

———. *El caso Mitrione: La intervención de los Estados Unidos en Uruguay, 1965–1973.* Montevideo: Trilce, 2007.

———. *Memorias de insurgencia: Historias de vida y militancia en el MLN-Tupamaros.* Montevideo: Banda Oriental, 2009.

Altesor, Alberto. *¿Cuáles son las tareas de los secretarios de organización?* Montevideo: Ediciones de la Convención Nacional de Organización del PC, 1967.

Anguita, Eduardo, and Martín Caparrós. *La voluntad: Una historia de la militancia revolucionaria en la Argentina, 1966–1973.* Buenos Aires: Grupo Editor Norma, 1997.

Araújo, Ana María, and Horacio Tejera. *La imaginación al poder, 1968–1988: ¿Un sueño postergado? Entrevistas a protagonistas de la insurrección juvenil de 1968.* Montevideo: Fundación de Cultura Universitaria, 1988.

Ares Pons, Roberto. *Uruguay, ¿provincia o nación?* Montevideo: Ediciones del Nuevo Mundo, 1967.

Aries, Philippe. "Las edades de la vida." In *Ensayos de la memoria,* by Philippe Aries. Bogotá: Norma, 1996.

Arismendi, Rodney. *Lenin, la revolución y América Latina.* Montevideo: EPU, 1970.

———. "Conversación con los jóvenes." In *Insurgencia juvenil: ¿Revuelta o revolución?* Montevideo: EPU, 1972.

———. *Insurgencia juvenil: ¿Revuelta o revolución?* Montevideo: EPU, 1972.

———. *Uruguay y América Latina en los años 70.* Mexico City: Ediciones de Cultura Popular, 1979.

———. "Discurso en la Conferencia de Moscú de Partidos Comunistas y obreros" (1969). In *Vigencia del marxismo-leninismo.* Mexico City: Grijalbo, 1984.

———. *Vigencia del marxismo-leninismo.* Mexico City: Grijalbo, 1984.

———. "Sobre la insurgencia juvenil." *Estudios* 47 (October 1968).

————."Anotaciones acerca de la táctica del movimiento obrero y popular." *Estudios* 30 (July–August 1964): 7.

Badiou, Alain. *Being and Event*. New York: Continuum, 2005.

Bañales, Carlos, and Enrique Jara. *La rebelión estudiantil*. Montevideo: Arca, 1968.

Barceló, Nelson, and Gustavo Rey. *Uno diferente: La vida de Alberto Restuccia*. Montevideo: Estuario, 2009.

Barr-Melej, Patrick. "Siloísmo and the Self in Allende's Chile: Youth, 'Total Revolution,' and the Roots of the Humanist Movement." *Hispanic American Historical Review* 86, no. 4 (November 2006).

Barrán, José Pedro, Gerardo Caetano, and Teresa Porzecanski, eds. *Historias de la vida privada en el Uruguay III: Individuo y soledades, 1920–1990*. Montevideo: Taurus, 1998.

Berryman, Phillip. *Liberation Theology: The Essential Facts about the Revolutionary Movement in Latin America and Beyond*. New York: Pantheon Books, 1987.

Blixen, Samuel. *Seregni: La mañana siguiente*. Montevideo: Ediciones de Brecha, 1997.

Bourdieu, Pierre. "Algunas propiedades de los campos." In *Campo de poder, campo intelectual: Itinerario de un concepto*, by Pierre Bourdieu. Buenos Aires: Quadrata, 2003.

Braunstein, Peter, and Michael William Doyle. "Introduction: Historicizing the American Counterculture of the 1960s and '70s." In *Imagine Nation: The American Counterculture of the 1960s and 1970s*, edited by Peter Braunstein and Michael William Doyle. New York: Routledge, 2001.

————, eds. *The American Counterculture of the 1960s and 1970s*. New York: Routledge, 2001.

Bravo, Luis. "La vida es una caída en el presente." In *Obra junta, 1966–1972: Ibero Gutiérrez*, compiled by Luis Bravo and Laura Oreggioni de Infantozzi. Montevideo: Estuario, 2009.

————. "Ibero Gutiérrez, la voz poética del 68 uruguayo." In *Obra junta, 1966–1972: Ibero Gutiérrez*, compiled by Luis Bravo and Laura Oreggioni de Infantozzi. Montevideo: Estuario, 2009.

————. "La contracultura sicodélica en los cuadernos carcelarios de Ibero Gutiérrez." Prologue to *Ibero Gutiérrez, la pipa de tinta china: Cuadernos carcelarios 1970*. Montevideo: Estuario-Biblioteca Nacional, 2014.

Bravo, Luis, and Laura Oreggioni de Infantozzi, comps. *Obra junta, 1966–1972: Ibero Gutiérrez.* Montevideo: Estuario, 2009.

Bucheli, Gabriel, and Jaime Yaffé. "Entrevista a Ricardo Calzada." *Cuadernos de la Historia Reciente, 1968–1985* 2 (2007).

Caetano, Gerardo, Javier Gallardo, and José Rilla. *La izquierda uruguaya: Tradición, innovación y política.* Montevideo: Trilce, 1995.

Caetano, Gerardo, and Raúl Jacob. *El nacimiento del terrismo, 1930–1933.* 3 vols. Montevideo: Ediciones de la Banda Oriental, 1989–91.

Caetano, Gerardo, and José Rilla. "Izquierda y tradición." *Brecha,* July 1, 1988.

———. *Historia contemporánea del Uruguay: De la colonia al MERCOSUR.* Montevideo: CLAEH/Fin de Siglo, 1994.

Cancela, Walter, and Alicia Melgar. *El desarrollo frustrado: 30 años de economía uruguaya, 1955–1985.* Montevideo: CLAEH/EBO, 1985.

Carassai, Sebastián. *The Argentine Silent Majority: Middle Classes, Politics, Violence, and Memory in the Seventies.* Durham, NC: Duke University Press, 2014.

Carnovale, Vera. "Moral y disciplinamiento interno en el PRT-ERP." *Nuevo Mundo Mundos Nuevos* 2008. http://nuevomundo.revues.org/38782.

Castañeda, Jorge. *Utopia Unarmed: The Latin American Left after the Cold War.* New York: Vintage Books, 1994.

———. *La vida en rojo: Una biografía del Che Guevara.* Madrid: Alfaguara, 1997.

Churchill, Lindsey. "Gender Reorganization or Revolutionary Rhetoric? Women in the Uruguayan Tupamaros." Paper presented at LASA 2010, Toronto, October 2010.

Cmiel, Kenneth. "The Politics of Civility." In *The Sixties: From Memory to History,* edited by David Farber, 263–90. Chapel Hill: University of North Carolina Press, 1994.

Collazo, Ariel. *La OLAS: El camino revolucionario de los trabajadores.* Montevideo: L. y S., 1968.

Copelmayer, Roberto, and Diego Díaz. *Montevideo 68: La lucha estudiantil.* Montevideo: Diaco, 1969.

Cores, Hugo. *El 68 uruguayo: Los antecedentes, los hechos, los debates.* Montevideo: Ediciones de la Banda Oriental, 1997.

———. *Memorias de la resistencia*. Montevideo: Ediciones de la Banda Oriental, 2002.

Cosse, Isabella. *Pareja, sexualidad y familia en los años sesenta*. Buenos Aires: Siglo XXI, 2010.

———, coord. "Clases medias, sociedad y política en la América Latina contemporánea." *Contemporánea*, year 5, vol. 5 (2014).

Cosse, Isabella, Karina Felitti, and Valeria Manzano, eds. *Los 60 de otra manera: Vida cotidiana, género y sexualidades en la Argentina*. Buenos Aires: Prometeo, 2010.

Costa, Omar. *Los Tupamaros*. Mexico City: Era, 1971.

Dabezíes Antía, Pablo. *No se amolden al tiempo presente: Las relaciones Iglesia-sociedad en los documentos de la Conferencia Episcopal del Uruguay, 1965–1985*. Montevideo: OBSUR-Facultad de Teología del Uruguay Mons. Mariano Soler, 2009.

de Alencar Pinto, Guilherme. *Razones locas: El paso de Eduardo Mateo por la música uruguaya*. Montevideo: Ediciones del TUMP, 1995.

de Giorgi, Ana Laura. *Las tribus de la izquierda en los sesenta: Tupas, latas y bolches*. Montevideo: Fin de Siglo, 2011.

Della Porta, Donatella. *Social Movements, Political Violence, and the State: A Comparative Analysis of Italy and Germany*. New York: Cambridge University Press, 1995.

Demasi, Carlos, ed. *La caída de la democracia: Cronología comparada de la historia del Uruguay, 1967–1973*. Montevideo: Fondo de Cultura Universitaria/ CEIU/FHUCE, 2001.

Di Candia, César. *El camino de la violencia uruguaya, 1940–1973*. Montevideo: Ediciones El País, 2006.

Donas, Ernesto, and Denise Milstein. *Cantando la ciudad: Lugares, imaginarios y mediación en la canción popular montevideana*. Montevideo: Nordan, 2003.

Duffau, Nicolás. "El Coordinador, 1963–1965: La participación de los militantes del Partido Socialista en los inicios de la violencia revolucionaria en Uruguay." *Colección Estudiantes* 30. Montevideo: FHCE, 2008.

Dunn, Christopher. *Brutality Garden: Tropicalia and the Emergence of a Brazilian Counterculture*. Chapel Hill: University of North Carolina Press, 2001.

Elias, Norbert. "El terrorismo en la República Federal Alemana: Expresión de un conflicto social intergeneracional." In *Los alemanes*, by Norbert Elias. Mexico City: Instituto Mora, 1999.

Errandonea, Alfredo. *Las clases sociales en el Uruguay*. Montevideo: CLAEH/ EBO, 1989.

Evans, Sara. *Personal Politics: The Roots of Women's Liberation in the Civil Rights Movement and the New Left*. New York: Vintage Books, 1980.

Farber, David, ed. *The Sixties: From Memory to History*. Chapel Hill: University of North Carolina Press, 1994.

Ferrario, Elbio. "El artista adolescente." In *Obra junta, 1966–1972: Ibero Gutiérrez*, compiled by Luis Bravo and Laura Oreggioni de Infantozzi. Montevideo: Estuario, 2009.

Finch, Henry. *A Political Economy of Uruguay since 1870*. New York: St. Martin's Press, 1981.

Flo, Juan. "La universidad agredida responde junto con todo el pueblo." *Estudios* 48 (December 1968).

Frank, Thomas. *The Conquest of Cool: Business Culture, Counterculture, and the Rise of Hip Consumerism*. Chicago: University of Chicago Press, 1997.

Frega, Ana, Mónica Maronna, and Ivette Trochón. *Baldomir y la restauración democrática*. Montevideo: Ediciones de la Banda Oriental, 1987.

Gair, Christopher. *The American Counterculture*. Edinburgh: Edinburgh University Press, 2007.

Ganón, Isaac. *Estructura social del Uruguay*. Montevideo: Editorial As, 1966.

Garcé, Adolfo. *Ideas y competencia política en Uruguay, 1960–1973: Revisando el "fracaso" de la CIDE*. Montevideo: Trilce, 2002.

Gascue, Álvaro. "Apuntes para una historia del Frente Estudiantil Revolucionario (FER)." *Cuadernos de la Historia Reciente* 6 (2010).

Gatto, Hebert. *El cielo por asalto: El Movimiento de Liberación Nacional (Tupamaros) y la izquierda uruguaya*. Montevideo: Taurus, 2004.

Gillis, John R. "Youth and History: Progress and Prospects." *Journal of Social History* 7, no. 2 (1974).

Gilman, Claudia. *Entre la pluma y el fusil: Debates y dilemas del escritor revolucionario en América Latina*. Buenos Aires: Siglo XXI, 2003.

Gitlin, Todd. *The Sixties: Years of Hope, Days of Rage*. New York: Bantam Books, 1993.

Giunta, Andrea. *Vanguardia, internacionalismo y política: Arte argentino en los años sesenta*. Buenos Aires: Paidós, 2001.

González, Yamandú. *Continuidad y cambio en el movimiento sindical uruguayo: Una perspectiva histórica de su problemática actual*. Montevideo: CIEDUR/DATES, 1993.

González Guyer, Fernando. "Mi primo Ibero." *Noteolvides* o (December 2009).

Gould, Jeffrey L. "Solidarity under Siege: The Latin American Left, 1968." *American Historical Review* 114, no. 2 (April 2009).

Grandin, Greg. *The Last Colonial Massacre: Latin America in the Cold War*. Chicago: University of Chicago Press, 2004.

Gregory, Stephen. *Intellectuals and Left Politics in Uruguay, 1958–2006: Frustrated Dialogue*. Brighton: Sussex Academic Press, 2009.

Guevara, Ernesto. "No hay revolución sin sacrificio." *Cuadernos de Marcha* 7 (November 1967).

Gutiérrez, Carlos María. *En la Sierra Maestra y otros reportajes*. Montevideo: Ediciones Tauro, 1967.

Gutiérrez, Ibero. *La pipa de tinta china: Cuadernos carcelarios 1970*. Montevideo: Estuario–Biblioteca Nacional, 2014.

Harnecker, Martha. *Haciendo posible lo imposible: La izquierda en el umbral del siglo XXI*. Mexico City: Siglo XXI, 1999

Harari, José. *Contribución a la historia del MLN-Tupamaros*. Montevideo: Plural, 1987.

Herrera Vargas, Julio. *Cómo se agrava la crisis nacional*. Montevideo: Librerías Ruben 1968.

Hobsbawm, Eric. *The Age of Extremes: The Short Twentieth Century, 1914–1991*. London: Michael Joseph, 1994.

———. "May 68." In *Uncommon People: Resistance, Rebellion and Jazz*, by Eric Hobsbawm. New York: New Press, 1998.

Ibero Gutiérrez: Juventud, arte y política. Edited by MUMA. Exhibition catalog. Montevideo: Biblioteca Nacional, Facultad de Artes-Udelar, and Museo de la Memoria–IMM, 2009.

Información Documental de América Latina (INDAL), ed. *Las medidas prontas de seguridad: Actas de la Cámara de Senadores del Uruguay*. Caracas: INDAL, 1973.

————. *Movimiento de Liberación Nacional (Tupamaros): Documentación propia.* Caracas: INDAL, 1973.

Jacob, Lucía. "*Marcha:* De un cine club a la C3M." In *Marcha y América Latina,* edited by Mabel Moraña and Horacio Machín. Pittsburgh: University of Pittsburgh Press, 2003.

Jarausch, Konrad H. "Essay Review: Restoring Youth to Its Own History." *History of Education Quarterly 15,* no. 4 (1975).

Landinelli, Jorge. *1968: La revuelta estudiantil.* Montevideo: Facultad de Humanidades y Ciencias and Ediciones de la Banda Oriental, 1989.

Lange, Peter, Cynthia Irvin, and Sidney Tarrow. "Mobilization, Social Movements and Party Recruitment: The Italian Communist Party since the 1960s." *British Journal of Political Science 20,* no. 1 (January 1990).

Langland, Victoria. "Birth Control Pills and Molotov Cocktails: Reading Sex and Revolution in 1968 Brazil." In *In from the Cold: Latin America's New Encounter with the Cold War,* edited by Gilbert M. Joseph and Daniela Spenser. Durham, NC: Duke University Press, 2008.

————. *Speaking of Flowers: Student Movements and the Making and Remembering of 1968 in Military Brazil.* Durham, NC: Duke University Press, 2013.

Leibner, Gerardo. "*Nosotras* (Uruguay, 1945–1953): Las contradicciones de una revista femenina comunista y sus significados sociales." In *Escritura femenina y reivindicación de género en América Latina,* edited by Roland Forgues and Jean-Marie Flores. Paris: Mare & Martin, 2005.

————. "Las ideologías sociales de los revolucionarios uruguayos de los 60." *Nuevo Mundo Mundos Nuevos* 2007. www.nuevomundo.revues.org//index11682.html.

————. *Camaradas y compañeros: Una historia política y social de los comunistas del Uruguay.* Montevideo: Trilce, 2011.

Lessa, Alfonso. *La revolución imposible: Los Tupamaros y el fracaso de la vía armada en el Uruguay del siglo XX.* Montevideo: Fin de Siglo, 2003.

Lichtensztejn, Samuel. *Comercio internacional y problemas monetarios.* Montevideo: Nuestra Tierra, 1969.

Lipsitz, George. "Who'll Stop the Rain? Youth Culture, Rock 'n' Roll, and Social Crisis." In *The Sixties: From Memory to History,* edited by David Farber. Chapel Hill: University of North Carolina Press, 1994.

Longoni, Ana. "Tucumán Arde: Encuentros y desencuentros entre vanguardia artística y política." In *Cultura y política en los años 60*, edited by
Enrique Oteiza. Buenos Aires: Facultad de Ciencias Sociales, 1997.

Longoni, Ana, and Mariano Mestman. *Del Di Tella a Tucumán Arde: Vanguardia artística y política en el 68 argentino*. Buenos Aires: El Cielo por Asalto,
2000.

López, Sara. "La cultura toma partido." *Revista Encuentros* 7 (July 2001).

Manzano, Valeria. *The Age of Youth in Argentina: Culture, Politics, and Sexuality
from Perón to Videla*. Chapel Hill: University of North Carolina Press, 2014.

————. "Ha llegado la 'nueva ola': Música, consumo y juventud en la
Argentina, 1955–1966." In *Los 60 de otra manera: Vida cotidiana, género y sexualidades en la Argentina*, edited by Isabella Cosse, Karina Felitti, and Valeria Manzano. Buenos Aires: Prometeo, 2010.

Marchesi, Aldo. "Imaginación política del antiimperialismo: Intelectuales y
política en el Cono Sur a fines de los sesenta." *Estudios Interdisciplinarios de
América Latina y el Caribe* 17, no. 1 (2006).

————. "De la protesta local a la estrategia continental: Debatiendo la revolución en el Cono Sur, 1964–1969." Paper presented at annual meeting
of the Latin American Studies Association (LASA2010), Toronto, October 2010.

Marchesi, Aldo, and Jaime Yaffé. "La violencia bajo la lupa: Una revisión de
la literatura sobre violencia y política en los sesenta." *Revista Uruguaya de
Ciencia Política* 19 (2010).

Markarian, Vania. "Al ritmo del reloj. Adolescentes uruguayos de los años
cincuenta." In *Historias de la vida privada en el Uruguay III: Individuo y
soledades, 1920–1990*, edited by José Pedro Barrán, Gerardo Caetano, and
Teresa Porzecanski. Montevideo: Taurus, 1998.

————. "Menores violentos. La adolescencia en el Uruguay de los cincuenta." *Brecha*, February 13, 1998.

————. "Treinta años de debates públicos sobre el movimiento estudiantil
de 1968." *Anuario de Espacios Urbanos*, 2001.

————. *Left in Transformation: Uruguayan Exiles and the Latin American Human
Rights Networks, 1967–1984*. New York: Routledge, 2005.

————. *Idos y recién llegados: La izquierda uruguaya en el exilio y las redes transnacionales de derechos humanos, 1967–1984*. Mexico City: Ediciones La Vasija
/Correo del Maestro-CEIU, 2006.

————. "'Ese héroe es el joven comunista': Violencia, heroísmo y cultura juvenil entre los comunistas uruguayos de los sesenta." *Estudios Interdisciplinarios de América Latina y el Caribe* 21, no. 2 (2010).

————. "*Los Huevos del Plata:* Un desafío al campo intelectual uruguayo de fines de los sesenta." In *Recordar para pensar: La elaboración del pasado reciente en el Cono Sur de América Latina,* edited by Tania Medalla, Alondra Peirano, Olga Ruiz, and Regine Walch. Santiago de Chile: Ediciones Böll Cono Sur, 2010.

————. "To the Beat of 'The Walrus': Uruguayan Communists and Youth Culture in the Global Sixties." *The Americas* 70, no. 3 (January 2014).

Markarian, Vania, María Eugenia Jung, and Isabel Wschebor. *1958: El cogobierno autonómico.* Montevideo: Archivo General de la Universidad de la República, 2008.

————. *1968: La insurgencia estudiantil.* Montevideo: Archivo General de la Universidad de la República, 2008.

Melgar, Alicia. *Distribución del ingreso en el Uruguay.* Montevideo: CLAEH, 1981.

Merenson, Silvina. "'A mi me llaman peludo': Cultura, política y nación en los márgenes del Uruguay." PhD dissertation, Social Sciences, IDES/Universidad Nacional de General Sarmiento, 2010.

Massera, José Luis. "A manera de presentación." In *Insurgencia juvenil: ¿Revuelta o revolución?,* by Rodney Arismendi. Montevideo: EPU, 1972.

Methol Ferré, Alberto. *El Uruguay como problema.* Montevideo: Diálogo, 1967.

Milstein, Denise. "Interacciones entre estado y música popular bajo autoritarismo en Uruguay y Brasil." Paper presented at V Congresso da Seção Latino-Americana da Associação Internacional para o Estudo da Música Popular, Rio de Janeiro, Brazil, 2004. www.iaspmal.net/wp-content/uploads/2011/12/DeniseMilstein.pdf.

————. "The Interactions of Musicians, Mass Media, and the State in the Context of Brazilian and Uruguayan Authoritarianism." *Estudios Interdisciplinarios de América Latina y el Caribe* 17, no. 1 (2006).

Nahum, Benjamín. *Manual de historia del Uruguay.* 2 vols. Montevideo: Ediciones de la Banda Oriental, 1995.

Nahum, Benjamín, Ana Frega, Mónica Maronna, and Ivette Trochón. *Historia uruguaya.* Vol. 8, *El fin del Uruguay liberal, 1959–1973.* Montevideo: Ediciones de la Banda Oriental, 1990.

Nora, Pierre. "La génération." In *Les lieux de mémoire*, edited by Pierre Nora. Sèvres: Gallimard, 1992.

O'Brien, Thomas. *The Century of U.S. Capitalism in Latin America*. Albuquerque: University of New Mexico Press, 1999.

Oddone, Juan. *Uruguay en los años 30*. Montevideo: CID/FCU, 1989.

——. *Uruguay entre la depresión y la guerra, 1929–1945*. Montevideo: FCU, 1990.

Ollier, María Matilde. *La creencia y la pasión: Privado, público y político en la izquierda revolucionaria*. Buenos Aires; Ariel, 1998.

Oteiza, Enrique, ed. *Cultura y política en los años 60*. Buenos Aires: Facultad de Ciencias Sociales, 1997.

Pacine Hernández, Deborah, Héctor Fernández L'Hoeste, and Eric Zolov. "Mapping Rock Music Cultures across the Americas." In *Rockin' las Américas: The Global Politics of Rock in Latin/o America*. Pittsburgh, PA: University of Pittsburgh Press, 2004.

Padín, Clemente. "Denunciamos los vicios decadentes." *La Hora Cultural* 2, no. 98.

Panizza, Francisco. *Uruguay, Batllismo y después: Pacheco, militares y Tupamaros en la crisis del Uruguay batllista*. Montevideo: Ediciones de la Banda Oriental, 1990.

París de Oddone, M. Blanca. *La Universidad de la República de la crisis a la intervención, 1958–1973*. Montevideo: Universidad de la República, 2011.

Paul VI. "Santa Misa a los campesinos de Colombia." Archdiocese of Bogotá, www.arquibogota.org.co.

Peláez, Fernando. *De las cuevas al Solís: Cronología del rock en el Uruguay, 1960–1975*. 2 vols. Montevideo: Perro Andaluz Ediciones, 2002–4.

Peluffo, Gabriel. "Instituto General Electric de Montevideo: Medios masivos, poder transnacional y arte contemporáneo." In *Cultura y política en los años 60*, edited by Enrique Oteiza. Buenos Aires: Facultad de Ciencias Sociales, 1997.

Pensado, Jaime M. *Rebel Mexico: Student Unrest and Authoritarian Political Culture during the Long Sixties*. Stanford, CA: Stanford University Press, 2013.

Perelli, Carina, and Juan Rial, eds. *De mitos y memorias políticas: La represión, el miedo y después . . .* Montevideo: Ediciones de la Banda Oriental, 1986.

Pérez, Jaime. *El ocaso y la esperanza: Memorias políticas de medio siglo*. Montevideo: Fin de Siglo, 1996.

Peri Rossi, Cristina. *El libro de mis primos*. Montevideo: Biblioteca de Marcha, 1969.

———. *Los museos abandonados*. Montevideo: Arca, 1969.

Platero, Alba. "Ibero Gutiérrez, creador integral." In *Obra junta, 1966–1972: Ibero Gutiérrez*, compiled by Luis Bravo and Laura Oreggioni de Infantozzi. Montevideo: Estuario, 2009.

Pujol, Sergio. *La década rebelde: Los años 60 en la Argentina*. Buenos Aires: Emecé, 2002.

———. "Rebeldes y modernos: Una cultura de los jóvenes." In *Nueva historia argentina*. Vol. 9, *Violencia, proscripción y autoritarismo, 1955–1976*, edited by Daniel James. Buenos Aires: Sudamericana, 2003.

Rama, Angel. "La generación crítica." In *Uruguay hoy*, edited by Luis Benvenuto et al. Buenos Aires: Siglo XXI, 1971.

Rama, Germán. *Grupos sociales y enseñanza secundaria*. Montevideo: Arca, 1963.

———. *La democracia en Uruguay: Una perspectiva de interpretación*. Buenos Aires: GEL, 1987.

Real de Azúa, Carlos. "Política, poder y partidos en el Uruguay de hoy." In *Uruguay hoy*, edited by Luis Benvenuto et al. Buenos Aires: Siglo XXI, 1971.

Rey Tristán, Eduardo. "Movilización estudiantil e izquierda revolucionaria en el Uruguay (1968–1973)." *Revista Complutense de Historia de América* 28 (2002).

———. "La Organización Latinoamericana de Solidaridad (OLAS) y la polémica sobre las formas de la revolución latinoamericana: El caso uruguayo." In *Estudios sobre América siglo XVI–XX*, coordinated by Antonio Gutiérrez Escudero and María Luisa Laviana Cuetos. Seville: Asociación Española de Americanistas, 2005.

———. *A la vuelta de la esquina: La izquierda revolucionaria uruguaya, 1955–1973*. Montevideo: Fin de Siglo, 2006.

Rial, Juan. "El 'imaginario social' uruguayo y la dictadura: Los mitos políticos de [re]construcción." In *De mitos y memorias políticas: La represión, el miedo y después ...*, edited by Carina Perelli and Juan Rial. Montevideo: Ediciones de la Banda Oriental, 1986.

Ribeiro, Darcy. *La universidad latinoamericana*. Montevideo: Departamento de Publicaciones de la Universidad de la República, 1968.

Rico, Álvaro. *1968: El liberalismo conservador.* Montevideo: FHC/Udelar y Ediciones de la Banda Oriental, 1989.

Ridenti, Marcelo. *Em busca do povo brasileiro: Artistas da revolução do CPC a era da tv.* Rio de Janeiro: Editora Record, 2000.

Rilla, José. *La actualidad del pasado: Usos de la historia en la política de partidos del Uruguay, 1942–1972.* Montevideo: Debate, 2008.

———. "Prólogo." In *El impulso y su freno,* by Carlos Real de Azúa. Montevideo: Colección de Clásicos Uruguayos, 2009.

Rodríguez, Héctor. "El arraigo de los sindicatos." *Enciclopedia Uruguaya 51* (1969).

Romano, Antonio. *De la reforma al proceso: Una historia de la Enseñanza Secundaria, 1955–1977.* Montevideo: Trilce/CSIC/Udelar, 2010.

Ross, Kristin. *May 68 and Its Afterlives.* Chicago: University of Chicago Press, 2002.

Rossinow, Douglas C. *The Politics of Authenticity: Liberalism, Christianity, and the New Left in America.* New York: Columbia University Press, 1998.

———. "'The Revolution Is about Our Lives': The New Left's Counterculture." In *Imagine Nation: The American Counterculture of the 1960s and 1970s,* edited by Peter Braunstein and Michael William Doyle. New York: Routledge, 2001.

Roszak, Theodore. *The Making of a Counter Culture: Reflections on the Technocratic Society and Its Youthful Opposition.* Garden City, NY: Doubleday, 1969.

Ruiz, Esther, and Juana Paris. "Ser militante en los sesenta." In *Historias de la vida privada en el Uruguay III: Individuo y soledades, 1920–1990,* edited by José Pedro Barrán, Gerardo Caetano, and Teresa Porzecanski. Montevideo: Taurus, 1998.

Sanseviero, Walter. *El comunismo tiene la respuesta: 7° Congreso de la UJC.* Montevideo: Biblioteca de la UJC, 1969.

Sapriza, Graciela. "Feminismo y revolución: Sobre el 'infeliz matrimonio,' indagatoria sobre feminismos e izquierdas." Paper presented at the Red Temática de Género convention, Universidad de la República, Montevideo, September 2006.

Seidman, Michael. *The Imaginary Revolution: Parisian Students and Workers in 1968.* New York: Berghahn Books, 2004.

Sempol, Diego. "Los 'mártires' de ayer, los 'muertos' de hoy: El movimiento estudiantil y el 14 de agosto, 1968–2001." In *El presente de la dictadura: Estu-*

dios y reflexiones a 30 años del golpe de Estado en Uruguay, edited by Aldo Marchesi, Vania Markarian, Álvaro Rico, and Jaime Yaffé. Montevideo: Trilce, 2004.

Sexo y amor en el Uruguay. Montevideo: Editorial Alfa, 1970.

Sigal, Silvia. *Intelectuales y política en Argentina: La década del sesenta*. Buenos Aires: Siglo XXI, 2002.

Silva, Marisa. *Aquellos comunistas, 1955–1973*. Montevideo: Taurus, 2009.

Smith, Peter H. *Talons of the Eagle: Dynamics of U.S.–Latin American Relations*. New York: Oxford University Press, 2000.

Solari, Aldo E. "La universidad en transición en una sociedad estancada: El caso de Uruguay." In *Estudiantes y política en América Latina*, edited by Aldo E. Solari. Caracas: Monte Ávila Editores, 1968.

Soler, Silvia. *La leyenda de Yessie Macchi*. Montevideo: Fin de Siglo, 2000.

Sorensen, Diana. *A Turbulent Decade Remembered: Scenes from the Latin American Sixties*. Stanford, CA: Stanford University Press, 2007.

Suri, Jeremi. *Power and Protest: Global Revolution and the Rise of Détente*. Cambridge, MA: Harvard University Press, 2003.

Terán, Óscar. *Nuestros años sesentas*. Buenos Aires: Puntosur, 1991.

Tomlinson, John. *Cultural Imperialism: A Critical Introduction*. Baltimore, MD: Johns Hopkins University Press, 1993.

Trías, Ivonne. *Hugo Cores: Pasión y rebeldía en la izquierda uruguaya*. Montevideo: Trilce, 2008.

Universidad de la República, Facultad de Derecho y Ciencias Sociales, Instituto de Ciencias Sociales. *Registro universitario 1960: Informe general preliminar*. Montevideo, 1961.

Uruguay, Poder Ejecutivo. *Registro Nacional de Leyes y Decretos*. 1968.

Van Aken, Mark. *Los militantes: Una historia del movimiento estudiantil universitario uruguayo desde sus orígenes hasta 1966*. Montevideo: Fundación de Cultura Universitaria, 1990.

Varela Petito, Gonzalo. *De la república liberal al Estado militar: Crisis política en Uruguay, 1968–1973*. Montevideo: Nuevo Mundo, 1988.

———. *El movimiento estudiantil de 1968: El IAVA, una recapitulación personal*. Montevideo: Trilce, 2002.

Varon, Jeremy. *Bringing the War Home: The Weather Underground, the Red Army Faction, and Revolutionary Violence in the Sixties and Seventies*. Berkeley: University of California Press, 2004.

Visconti, Silvia, and Universindo Rodríguez. "Ibero Gutiérrez: Con la memoria en los tiempos de las utopías." In *Obra junta, 1966–1972: Ibero Gutiérrez,* compiled by Luis Bravo and Laura Oreggioni de Infantozzi. Montevideo: Estuario, 2009.

Williams, Raymond. *Marxismo y literatura.* Barcelona: Península, 1980.

———. *Keywords: A Vocabulary of Culture and Society.* Rev. ed. New York: Oxford University Press, 1985.

Wonsewer, Israel, and Ana Maria Teja. *La emigración uruguaya, 1963–1975: Sus condicionantes económicas.* Montevideo: CINVE/EBO, 1985.

Younger, Michael. *Counterculture.* New York: Free Press, 1982.

Zolov, Eric. *Refried Elvis: The Rise of the Mexican Counterculture.* Berkeley: University of California Press, 1999.

———. "Expanding our Conceptual Horizons: The Shift from an Old to a New Left in Latin America." *A contracorriente 5,* no. 2 (Winter 2008).

———. "Introduction: Latin America in the Global Sixties." *The Americas* 70, no. 3 (January 2014).

Zubillaga, Carlos. "Los partidos políticos ante la crisis (1958–1983)." In *De la tradición a la crisis: Pasado y presente de nuestro sistema de partidos,* complied by Gerardo Caetano, José Rilla, Pablo Mieres, and Carlos Zubillaga. Montevideo: CLAEH/EBO, 1991.

Index